THE ART OF
THOMAS MIDDLETON

From a woodcut inserted in Bodleian Malone 245(1)
(*Your Five Gallants*)

THE ART OF
Thomas Middleton

A Critical Study

BY

DAVID M. HOLMES

CLARENDON PRESS · OXFORD

1970

Oxford University Press, Ely House, London W. 1

GLASGOW NEW YORK TORONTO MELBOURNE WELLINGTON
CAPE TOWN SALISBURY IBADAN NAIROBI DAR ES SALAAM LUSAKA ADDIS ABABA
BOMBAY CALCUTTA MADRAS KARACHI LAHORE DACCA
KUALA LUMPUR SINGAPORE HONG KONG TOKYO

© DAVID M. HOLMES 1970

PRINTED IN GREAT BRITAIN
BY SPOTTISWOODE, BALLANTYNE AND CO. LTD
LONDON AND COLCHESTER

To

NORMAN DAVIS,
M.A., M.B.E.

in gratitude and esteem

In Tragaedium
Ut Lux ex Tenebris ictu percussa Tonantis;
Illa, Ruina Malis, claris fit Vita Poetis.
> *Thomas Middletonus,*
> *Poeta & Chron:*
> *Londinensis.*

PREFACE

UNLESS otherwise noted, quotations from Middleton's nondramatic writings have been taken from A. H. Bullen's edition of Middleton's works (1885).

Except in the case of *The Witch*, where the Ralph Crane MS. has been used, quotations from the plays have been taken from copies of the earliest known printed editions (the only thoroughly trustworthy modern texts of Middleton plays that are generally available at present are J. S. Farmer's reprint of *The Roaring Girl* quarto [Tudor Facsimile Texts, 1914], F. P. Wilson's and W. W. Greg's edition of *The Witch* MS., and R. C. Bald's edition of the *A Game at Chess* holograph). Quotations preserve the spelling of the early texts except where noted. The Elizabethan use of 'i' and 'j', and 'u' and 'v', and typographical errors, have been silently regularized or eliminated; and proper nouns italicized in the original have not been so indicated. Where punctuation in the original appears questionable, for example a colon or comma entered where a full stop or question mark would normally be used, I have silently altered it to suit the sense and syntax. Footnote or other reference to the early texts is made by page number or signature; and since some of them contain no act divisions, I have made it a practice to indicate those used by Alexander Dyce in his edition of 1840 and followed by Bullen. Also, for the convenience of the reader, I have included in parentheses the volume and page reference for the corresponding passage in the Bullen edition. For a quotation from Act IV of *The Phoenix*, for example, which is found on signature H[1]ᵛ of Mal. 225 (5),[1] and for which the corresponding passage in the Bullen edition is on page 183 of the first volume, the reference would appear as follows: IV. sig. H[1]ᵛ (Bullen: I, 183).

In my discussion of Middleton's drama I have tried to spare the reader as much as possible from tedious refutations. That 'Middleton . . . does not seem to have reflected much on matters spiritual', that 'human dignity . . . is not a quality that Middleton seems to be much aware of', and that Middleton is without personality—that he has 'no point of view . . . no message'—

[1] For the Bodleian Library shelf-marks of the early texts used, see Appendix A.

are among the erroneous generalizations that have been made. They are generalizations that overlook the character of the writing that Middleton did before he became a playwright, the intimative modes of his dramatic technique, and the strong thematic threads that extend throughout his work from his early poetry to his last play. The incomplete appreciation of Middleton's work that stems from the view of him as a man without a personality or distinctive point of view is reflected in a work of criticism which, while acknowledging that he is a realist, attempts to give his drama romantic interpretation, or in another piece which tries to draw a facile and misconceived parallel between the nature of the tragedies of Faustus and Macbeth on the one hand, and Beatrice-Joanna in *The Changeling* on the other; it is likewise reflected in uncertainty about such matters as the authorship of *Blurt Master-Constable,* Middleton's intentions in regard to *The Mayor of Queenborough,* and the nature of Middleton's relationship with William Rowley. Students of Middleton must always be indebted to William Empson, whose remarks on *The Changeling* in *Some Versions of Pastoral* shed a ray of light throughout the entire canon.

Oxford,
February 1968

ACKNOWLEDGEMENTS

I WISH to express my gratitude to the Keeper of Printed Books for permission to quote from copies of early texts in the Bodleian Library, and to the following for permission to make use of copyright and other material: Basil Blackwell, Publisher; Methuen & Co. Ltd.; Chatto & Windus Ltd.; Longmans Group Limited; Charles Scribner's Sons; Cambridge U.P.; Melbourne U.P.; New York U.P.; Columbia U.P.; the executors of the estate of the late H. D. Sykes; and the publishers of *Modern Language Review*, *Notes and Queries*, *The Library*, *English Studies*, *Studies in Philology*, and *PMLA*. I am indebted to Marian I. Holmes, Samuel S. Stollman, and Eugene D. LeMire for assistance with proofreading.

D. M. H.

CONTENTS

LIST OF PLATES	xiii
INTRODUCTION	xv

PART ONE—AN INTEREST IN SIN

I.	Middleton's Early Poetry	3
II.	*Blurt Master-Constable* or *The Spaniard's Night-Walk*	10
III.	Other Early Plays	24
IV.	Characteristics of Middleton's Early Drama	38

PART TWO—AN INTEREST IN CHARACTER

V.	*More Dissemblers Besides Women*	59
VI.	Other Studies in Conscience and Character	78
VII.	*The Roaring Girl* or *Moll Cut-Purse*	100

PART THREE—VARIATIONS ON THEMES

VIII.	*A Fair Quarrel* and *The Old Law*	113
IX.	*The Mayor of Queenborough*, *The Widow*, and *The Witch*	130

PART FOUR—MIDDLETON'S LAST PLAYS

X.	*Anything for a Quiet Life*	153
XI.	*Women Beware Women* and *The Changeling*	161
XII.	*A Game at Chess*	185
	CONCLUSION	194
	APPENDICES	
	A. The Canon and Chronology of Middleton's Plays	201
	B. An excerpt from the Epistle to the Reader in *The Black Book*	204
	The soliloquy on 'impudence' in *Your Five Gallants*	204
	The Letter to the Reader in *The World Tost at Tennis*	205
	C. (a) Thomas Middleton and William Rowley	207
	(b) *The Spanish Gipsy*	219

D. Some readings from Alexander Dyce's edition of *A Fair Quarrel* compared with the editions of 1622 and 1617 222

E. *A Fair Quarrel*, *The Peace-Maker*, and *The Charge of Sir Francis Bacon Knight* 224

BIBLIOGRAPHY

Books 227

Essays and Articles 230

INDEX 233

LIST OF PLATES

Thomas Middleton, from a woodcut inserted in Bodleian Malone 245 (1) (*Your Five Gallants*) *Frontispiece*

Two pages from Bodleian Malone 187 (2), pp. 2, 3 (William Rowley's *A New Wonder, a Woman Never Vext*) PLATES I & II: *Between pp.* 218 and 219

INTRODUCTION

IN his edition of Una Ellis-Fermor's essay, 'Shakespeare the Dramatist', Professor Kenneth Muir included the following authorial addition to a note that mentions Thomas Middleton's appearance of detachment from his characters:

[Nor should we perhaps accept the appearance without inspection. Middleton's pictures of the travelling mind lost upon a strange and sinister road of experience convey into the imagination of the reader the terror and the pity which do not come by chance but only from the operation of deep, if hidden, emotion. Middleton, like Swift, appears not to feel; but inasmuch as each stirs in reader or audience a powerful and painful response, the sympathy of the writer cannot be doubted.][1]

My discussion of Middleton's drama is an attempt to provide an appreciation of his art and of the point of view and feeling that underlie it.

Many existing commentaries on Middleton and the nature of his work attempt to generalize on the basis of a few plays, and without due regard to his non-dramatic writing. By studying the devices—'soliloquies, asides, the use of the balcony for asides, documents read aloud, masques and plays within the plays, songs, and disguises'—in six plays, W. D. Dunkel was led to the important discovery of Middleton's 'habit of repeating characters, incidents, and devices'. But finding no lines in these plays to compare with Jonson's 'Ile strip the ragged follies of the time' and 'I will scourge those apes; and to these courteous eyes oppose a mirrour' in *Every Man out of his Humour*, he assumed that Middleton had no 'motive of reform'.[2]

It is incorrect to say that Middleton made 'no pronouncements' about a motive of reform. His early poems contain several; and these were followed, after he had begun his career as a playwright, by his statement of moral purpose in *The Black Book*, where he dedicates himself to the task of representing the ugliness of vice in order that the uncorrupted may be 'confirmed the more

[1] *Shakespeare the Dramatist* (London, 1961), p. 9, n. 1.
[2] See *The Dramatic Technique of Thomas Middleton in his Comedies of London Life* (Chicago, 1925), p. 87.

in their honest estates and the uprightness of their virtues'.³ As regards Middleton's plays, it is difficult to know him from only a few. In his dramatic writing Middleton contrives to mask himself in various ways, and his appearance 'not to feel' is, as Professor Ellis-Fermor suggests, an illusion.

This study begins with a short consideration of Middleton's early poetry, which contains several important foreshadowings of the matter of his drama. It then goes on to consider the plays that comprise the Middleton canon as represented in A. H. Bullen's edition of Middleton's works, with one exception. I have omitted from my discussion *The Spanish Gipsy*, for although this play contains indications of Middleton's influence, there is reason to doubt that he had a hand in the actual writing of it.⁴ I have also omitted questionable attributions to Middleton. The four parts of my study correspond to the periods 1601–5, 1606–15, 1616–20, and 1621–4, according to dates of composition assigned by Professor R. C. Bald,⁵ but in the first three parts some of the plays are not treated in individual chronological order. Some of the plays present more claims to a fuller treatment than others, and I have varied the extent of my discussion accordingly.

A SKETCH OF MIDDLETON'S LIFE

Middleton was baptized on 18 April 1580, at the church of St. Lawrence in the Old Jewry.⁶ His father, a prosperous brickmason and landlord, died while Middleton and his younger sister were infants. Within a year their mother made a second marriage to a broken grocer named Harvey, who had gambled and lost everything as a member of Raleigh's and Grenville's abortive expedition to Roanoke Island.⁷ Mr. and Mrs. Harvey were soon in conflict over William Middleton's estate,⁸ and the strife continued throughout Middleton's boyhood. In due course, his

---

³ See Appendix B.
⁴ See Appendix C (b).
⁵ 'The Chronology of Middleton's Plays', *Modern Language Review*, XXXII (Jan. 1937), 43.
⁶ See M. Eccles's 'Middleton's Birth and Education', *Review of English Studies*, VII (Oct. 1931), 431.
⁷ See M. G. Christian's 'A Side-light on the Family History of Thomas Middleton', *Studies in Philology*, XLIV (Feb. 1947), 490–6.
⁸ For the details of William Middleton's will, see J. Q. Adams's edition of Middleton's *The Ghost of Lucrece* (New York, 1937), p. xxiv f., n. 5.

INTRODUCTION

sister's husband moved in with the family and contributed to the discord.[9]

At the age of eighteen Middleton subscribed at Queen's College, Oxford, *plebei filius*,[10] and he eventually sold his share of his father's estate for the specific purpose of obtaining money to support himself at the University.[11] Middleton's university experience is evident in a number of ways in his works.[12] The passage between Tim Yellowhammer and his tutor at the beginning of Act IV of *A Chaste Maid in Cheapside* is a humorous indication of his familiarity with academic disputation for example, and the short history of the scholar in *The Ant and the Nightingale*[13] shows his acquaintance with university life.

Middleton's interest in writing had begun before his subscription at Queen's College. His *The Wisdom of Solomon Paraphrased* was published when he was seventeen. It is no such poetry as the scholar in *The Ant and the Nightingale* 'was unfruitfully led to', 'that sweet honey-poison that swells a supple scholar with unprofitable sweetness and delicious false conceits', but a serious work of 706 sextets in nineteen chapters. *Micro-cynicon*, comprising six short 'Snarling Satyres' in verse, and a complaint, *The Ghost of Lucrece*, were presumably written while Middleton was an undergraduate; they were published in 1599 and 1600 respectively.

Middleton was in London, 'daylie accompaninge the players', early in 1601.[14] He married a sister of one of the Admiral's Men, and had one son, Edward, who was to answer a summons in his father's stead in connection with the trouble over *A Game at Chess* more than twenty years later.

---

[9] For details of the embroilments of the Harveys and their son-in-law see P. G. Phialas's 'Middleton's Early Contact with the Law', *Studies in Philology*, LII (Apr. 1955), 186–94, and M. Eccles's '"Thomas Middleton a Poett"', ibid., LIV (Oct. 1957), 516–36.

[10] Eccles, 'Middleton's Birth and Education', 437.

[11] See M. G. Christian's 'Middleton's Residence at Oxford', *Modern Language Notes*, LXI (Feb. 1946), 90–1.

[12] *The Triumphs of Love and Antiquity* contains the following statement: 'queen Philip[pa] his [Edward III's] wife . . . both founded and endowed Queen's College in Oxford, to the continuing estate of which I myself wish all happiness.' M. G. Christian was the first to point out this verification of Eccles's evidence (see 'An Autobiographical Note by Thomas Middleton', *Notes and Queries*, CLXXV [Oct. 1938], 259–60).

[13] *The Works of Thomas Middleton*, ed. A. H. Bullen (London, 1885), VIII, 101–8.

[14] Phialas, 'Middleton's Early Contact with the Law', 192.

Middleton's name first appears in Henslowe's diary in entries for the 22nd and 29th of May 1602. He is mentioned with Munday, Drayton, Dekker, and Webster in connection with payments for *sesers ffalle* and *too shapes*. In other entries of that year his name appears alone: in October he was paid for an unnamed play, in October and November for the *Chester tragedie* or *Randowlle earlle of chester*, and in December for 'a prologe & A epeloge for the play of bacon for the corte'. Henslowe recorded Middleton's name only once again—with Dekker's, in 1604, in regard to *The Honest Whore*. Except for *The Honest Whore*, none of the work mentioned immediately above has survived. *The Viper and her Brood*, written in 1606,[15] has also been lost.

Middleton's earliest extant plays were written for the Children of Paul's. At various other times during the rest of his career he wrote for the Children of the Revels, and the Lady Elizabeth's and Prince Charles's companies, but from 1615 onward most of his work was done for the King's Men. Beginning in 1613, he also became a writer of masques, pageants, and civic entertainments. His prose pamphlet, *The Black Book*, and *The Ant and the Nightingale or Father Hubburd's Tales*, both of which were published in 1604, were probably written while the theatres were closed during 1603 and 1604. In 1607–8 Middleton obtained Dekker's assistance for a special scene in *The Roaring Girl*, and in 1617, or shortly before, he began an association with William Rowley, in which it appears that the latter was allowed either to undertake the revision of a few plays by Middleton, or to write, under Middleton's close supervision, some parts of them in the capacity of pupil-assistant.[16]

Middleton was appointed City Chronologer in 1620,[17] and held that post until his death, when he was succeeded by Jonson. His last play, *A Game at Chess*, seems to have been the greatest 'hit' in the history of the English theatre to 1624. King James, acting on official protests from the Spanish ambassador pertaining to its topical subject-matter, eventually decided to terminate its performance; but it ran for nine days beforehand, and the crowds that

---

[15] See H. N. Hillebrand's 'Thomas Middleton's *The Viper's Brood*', *Modern Language Notes*, XLII (Jan. 1927), 35–8.

[16] See Appendix C (a).

[17] See R. C. Bald's 'Middleton's Civic Employments', *Modern Philology*, XXXI (Aug. 1933), 66–7.

formed its audience and the profits realized from its production were unusually large.

Middleton died in 1627. He had been a resident of Newington Butts for many years, and his burial on 4th July is recorded in the parish church register.[18]

[18] Eccles, ' "Thomas Middleton a Poett" ', 536.

PART ONE

AN INTEREST IN SIN

Early Poetry
Blurt Master-Constable
The Phoenix
The Family of Love
Michaelmas Term
A Mad World, My Masters
Your Five Gallants

I
MIDDLETON'S EARLY POETRY

THOMAS Middleton provided an implicit introduction and an explicit credo for his literary career in three poems published before his final return to London from Oxford, and in two pamphlets, one almost all in prose and the other in alternate sections of prose and verse, that were probably written when his early career in the theatre was interrupted by the outbreak of plague in 1603.

Critics who have looked at Middleton's earliest work have commented upon its prosodic deficiencies and heaviness. A. H. Bullen, for example, in writing the Introduction to his edition of Middleton's works, expressed himself as follows in regard to Middleton's first literary effort, *The Wisdom of Solomon Paraphrased*:

As we know of no other writer of the same name, I fear we must hold the dramatist responsible for this intolerable and interminable performance. The fluency of the versification is aggravating to the last degree. Through stanza after stanza . . . we plod, vainly hoping to find something to reward us, some flash of inspiration; and when we reach the end, we are too dejected to congratulate ourselves on our release. It is extraordinary that a man of Middleton's brilliant ability should have perpetrated so insipid a piece of work.[1]

After having penetrated to sextet 706, he had been able to make the following acknowledgement in a note at the end of the text: 'I have read at various times much indifferent verse and much execrable verse, but I can conscientiously state that *The Wisdom of Solomon Paraphrased* is the most damnable piece of flatness that has ever fallen in my way. *Silius Italicus* is bracing after it.'[2]

Bullen can be partly excused for these outbursts because of two facts. First, the date of Middleton's baptism was not

---
[1] *Works*, I, xiii.
[2] Ibid., VIII, 297, n. 1.

discovered until 1931,[3] and a conjectural birth year of 1570, suggested by Dyce, was used before that time. Had he realized that the poem was the earnest work of a precocious youth of seventeen, and not the production of a middle-aged Elizabethan of twenty-seven, he might not have so indulged himself. Second, while he failed to see the relationship which the poem bears to Middleton's later work, he was able at least to remark upon its relative naiveté.

It is true that Middleton's adolescent writing smacks thoroughly of adolescence. The verse of *The Wisdom of Solomon Paraphrased* is often painfully contrived, the expression is immature and self-conscious, and the themes are attenuated. All of these things are quite obvious, quite natural, and quite unimportant. What is significant about this poem is the fact that a young man should have thought that anything so ponderous as the wisdom of Solomon was worth paraphrasing.

Sufficient biographical information is available to make it clear that Middleton had seen enough of greed and contentiousness during his childhood to be under few delusions about the human condition, even before his days at Oxford. The mood of *The Wisdom of Solomon Paraphrased*, and the response to man's baser propensities which the poem conveys, prefigure the attitude which came to underlie all Middleton's writing for the stage:

> The sun of righteousness, which should have
>   shin'd,
> And made our hearts the cabins of his east,
> Is now made cloudy night through vice's wind,
> And lodgeth with his downfall in the west;
> That summer's day, which should have been
>   night's bar,
> Is now made winter in her icy car.
>
> Too much our feet have gone, but never right;
> Much labour have we took, but none in good;
> We wearièd ourselves with our delight,
> Endangering ourselves to please our mood;
> Our feet did labour much, 'twas for our
>   pleasure;
> We wearièd ourselves, 'twas for our leisure.

[3] See above, p. xvi, n. 6.

> In sin's perfection was our labour spent,
> In wickedness' preferment we did haste;
> To suffer perils we were all content
> For the advancement of our vices past:
> Through many dangerous ways our feet have
>   gone,
> But yet the way of God we have not known.[4]

These three stanzas typify the whole work. They show an awareness of, and concern with, the conflict of good and evil, and they suggest that Middleton was persuaded, even at this earliest stage, that the uses of literature are serious. Beneath their puerile sententiousness subsists the rudiment of a civilizing instinct.

Micro-cynicon, published two years later, reveals both a change of focus from general viciousness to particular sins, and a significant progression in artistic stance: sententiousness gives way to didacticism. In the Author's Prologue the poet speaks of himself as having descended from 'the high-aspiring hills'—

> . . . and now, at last,
> Am veilèd with a stony sanctuary,
> To save my ire-stuft soul, lest it miscarry,
> From threatening storms, o'erturning verity,
> That shames to see truth's refin'd purity.[5]

He continues in defiance of the enemies of virtue, those 'threatening storms' with their 'stormy-raging power', calling them to 'Witness this black-defying embassy . . . Undaunted of their bugbear threatening words', and promising to 'drink . . . up' their 'devilish venom' and 'belch it into [their] throats'. Again the signs of adolescent posturing are obvious, but Middleton's period of puerility was a short one. The art of his earliest extant dramatic writing is that of a man and not a boy, but the determination, which he expresses here, to use literature to defy the forces of evil, remains, quite unabated.

The subjects of the six parts of *Micro-cynicon* are uncomplicated. Insatiate Cron ('greedy Gain') and his son, Prodigal Zodon, are types of viciousness to which Middleton was to give dramatic form time and again. Sexual depravity is generalized in

---

[4] *Works*, VIII, 177.   [5] *Works*, VIII, [115].

Insolent Superbia. For Middleton it was always the ugliest manifestation of spiritual dereliction, and the following lines are especially noteworthy because they indicate an interest in appearance versus reality which was soon to become part of the fabric of his plays:

> And sin, though it be foul, yet fair in this,
> In being painted with a show of bliss;
> For what more happy creature to the eye
> Than is Superbia in her bravery?
> Yet who more foul, disrobèd of attire?
> Pearl'd with the botch as children burnt with fire;
> That for their outward cloak upon the skin,
> Worser enormities abound within. . . .[6]

The fourth and fifth subjects, Cheating Droone and Ingling Pyander, are self-explanatory. The sixth, however, deserves special attention: Wise Innocent is Middleton himself. In the duologue of which this final part consists the words of the other speaker may be only generalized opposition, but I suspect that they represent those of some real person who questioned the young man's qualifications for setting himself up as a social critic. In any case, the passage provides him with an opportunity to re-express his purpose and determination:

> . . . streams that are barr'd their course
> Swell with more rage and far more greater force,
> Until their full-stuft gorge a passage makes
> Into the wide maws of more scopious lakes.
> Spite me! not spite itself can discontent
> My steelèd thoughts, or breed disparagement:
> Had pale-fac'd coward fear been resident
> Within the bosom of me, innocent,[7]
> I would have hous'd me from the eyes of ire,
> Whose bitter spleen vomits forth flames of fire.[8]

---

[6] *Works*, VIII, 123–4.

[7] Middleton shared Shakespeare's fondness for puns. The word 'innocent' (also 'ass' and 'fool') is used by both parties to the conversation and may be variously understood to mean virtuous, naïve, and half-wit. Here Middleton applies the term to his antagonist in the last sense, but the context makes it susceptible of the two other interpretations as well.

[8] *Works*, VIII, 134–5.

What is more important about 'Wise Innocent' is its foreshadowing of the authorial point of view which characterizes Middleton's drama. His not being inclined to suppress criticism of himself, but rather to anticipate and answer it, looks forward to the objective attitude of mind which refuses to suppress, or peremptorily dismiss, arguments which would seem to justify evil and run counter to his criticisms of society. His readiness to make himself an object of his own satire is not only significant of his intellectual courage and honesty, but indicates a decisive movement away from the overearnestness of *The Wisdom of Solomon Paraphrased*.

One other point is worth noticing. Early in the duologue his tormentor says, 'Twenty to one this fool's some satirist', and the poet replies, 'Still doth the fool haunt me; fond fool, begone!' Evidently the term 'satirist' had a contemptuous flavour for Middleton, and it can only be applied to him with qualification. His method in *Micro-cynicon*, and later on in *The Ant and the Nightingale* and *The Black Book*, is essentially straightforward description and narration. In his drama he sometimes makes effective use of burlesque, but his personality, in so far as it is revealed in his works, lacked bitterness, and he could not be satisfied with the kind of satire that exaggerates one feature of a character to the neglect or complete oversight of others. Middleton's satire is usually accomplished by subtle means, in his use of words and dramatic technique. Exaggeration is not part of the usual equipment of a realist, and very early the various manifestations of human depravity came to appear quite spectacular enough to Middleton in their natural state to free him from the necessity of resorting to that method. The half-whimsical, half-serious tone of 'Wise Innocent', the last of the 'Snarling Satyres' of *Micro-cynicon*, is the first indication of the all-inclusive balance which is among the most remarkable features of Middleton's writing for the stage.

A third poem of Middleton's was published when he was twenty, but its intensity of tone suggests that it was written some time before *Micro-cynicon*. In *The Ghost of Lucrece* Middleton employed the stanzaic form used by Shakespeare in *The Rape of Lucrece*. It was clearly inspired by the latter, and it provides an interesting comment upon what has been called Shakespeare's 'beautiful celebration of chastity'. Throughout the eighty-nine verses of Lucrece's monologue there is never the slightest suggestion of salacious intent:

> Then shall I stamp the figure of the night
> On Tarquins brow, and marke him for her sonne,
> The heire of darknesse, bastard of the light,
> The clowde of heaven, th'eclipser of the sunne,
> The staine in Vestaes cheekes, which first begunne
> In Tarquins flesh, begot of fiery dust.
> 'O thou the hell of love, untutred lust.

> 'It bribes the flesh to warre against the spirit,
> 'With tickling bloud mustring in everie vaine,
> 'It weanes the conscience from her heavenly merit,
> 'Depraving all chaste thoughts, her maiden traine,
> 'It makes the heart thinke, and unthinke againe:
> 'It taints the breath with fire, the braine with bloud,
> 'And sets a divel where a God had stood.

The entire poem is an unremitting condemnation of sexual animalism, and the young writer pointed to his intended audience in the Prologue:

> Black spirits, hard harts, thick thoghts, souls boild in lust,
> Drie fierie eyes, dull eares, high bloudy lookes
> Made of hot earth, moulded in fire and dust,
> Desires true Graduates, reade in Tarquins bookes:
> Be ye our stages Actors; play the Cookes:
> Carve out the daintiest morsel, thats your part,
> With lust-keene Faulchon even in Lucrece heart.[9]

Overwrought and self-consciously formal as they are, these three poems contain the main ingredients which are to be found—in proportions, groupings, and perspectives which vary with his maturity—in Middleton's subsequent writing. However inconsiderable they may be as literature, they are diacritically significant of the man who wrote them, and are valuable guides to many of the thematic patterns of his drama.

In the tone and choice of subject in *The Wisdom of Solomon Paraphrased* is revealed the acceptance of literature as an instrument of human edification, and while Middleton was able to

---

[9] *The Ghost of Lucrece* was not discovered until 1920. The unique copy of the edition printed by Valentine Simmes in 1600 is in the Folger Shakespeare Library. This quotation and the preceding one are taken from a facsimile edition produced by J. Q. Adams (noted above, p. xvi, n. 8), sigs. C[1] and [B8]ᵛ respectively.

MIDDLETON'S EARLY POETRY

assimilate some of the outward appearances of more conventional Elizabethan drama, what Una Ellis-Fermor called the 'pitiless abstemiousness' of his latest work,[10] is the sign that he ever did so without abandoning or compromising that earliest philosophical-artistic principle. His choice of materials and his method were always strictly limited by it. He never exploited fortuitous Senecan spectacle, for example; and although his sense of purpose did not blind him to the fact that life has comic as well as tragic aspects, the remarkable balance of his nature enabled him to blend the comic and tragic realistically, and make them comment on each other.

Yet these poems have a more direct relevance to Middleton's early drama than to his late.[11] Their chief characteristic in common is preoccupation with sins in the abstract, sins somehow disembodied or dissociated from the complex human beings who perpetrate them. The central event of the Lucrece story, for example, has shocked his youthful susceptibilities. His whole response is one of outrage. The experience of the world which enabled the thirty-year-old Shakespeare to deal with the same materials with more understanding of human nature had yet to be acquired by his adolescent contemporary: a quarter of a century lies between Middleton's marble Tarquin and his breathing Deflores. So, like *The Wisdom of Solomon Paraphrased*, the earliest plays tell us, among other things, that men sin, and, like *The Ghost of Lucrece* and *Micro-cynicon*, they tell us how men sin, but they lack the more sensitive insights which came to characterize the works of his early maturity.

[10] *The Jacobean Drama* (London, 1958), p. 152.
[11] *The Ant and the Nightingale* and *The Black Book* are non-dramatic works which belong to Middleton's third year in the theatre. Both bear relationships to his dramatic writing which I shall mention later in connection with the plays themselves. In Appendix B, for the convenience of the reader, I quote in part the Epistle to the Reader in *The Black Book*, which attests to the continuing intensity of Middleton's didactic motive.

II
BLURT MASTER-CONSTABLE OR *THE SPANIARD'S NIGHT-WALK*

OF Middleton's extant plays, *Blurt Master-Constable* was the earliest printed (1602). Exactly how much experience he had had when he wrote it is not known, but as we first hear of him in London 'daylie accompaninge the players' in 1601, it could not have been great. Henslowe's diary entries for 1602 prove that his apprenticeship was short: in May he is mentioned in connection with two collaborative plays; by October his name begins appearing alone.[1] Middleton had small tendency to be dependent upon others, and by the time he came to write *Blurt Master-Constable*, he had already thought of one way of achieving a purpose for his drama that went beyond mere entertainment. Since there has been a history of confusion about the technique and theme of *Blurt Master-Constable*, both of which continued to be important parts of his dramatic idiom, the play requires independent and extensive treatment.

Each of the titles has connections, which I shall refer to later, with the goings-on in both plots, a fact which points to the most essential characteristic of the play's structure: the deliberate juxtaposition of plots. Plot and character *montage* is a frequently recurring feature of Middleton's dramatic technique, and it is in the reciprocal comments generated by the concurrent actions of seemingly unrelated characters, in ostensibly independent plots, that the themes of his art are often to be found.

Middleton was not only early to apply the structural principle of complementary plots, but, in fulfilment of the promise of his first literary efforts, he was early to dedicate himself to disenchanting realism. Quite simply put, the main idea conveyed by *Blurt Master-Constable* is that love between the sexes, despite the romantic fuss so often made about it, is often no more than a tawdry, glandular business. Quite distinctly, the play is a travesty of the poetic treatment given to love in conventional

[1] See above, p. xviii.

romantic drama; and there is reason to believe that Middleton had *Romeo and Juliet* especially in mind for a target, both here and in one other early play. The principals of the main plot are two young Venetian gentlemen, Hippolito and Camillo, who have just returned from fighting in France, a French gallant, Fontinell, whom Camillo has vanquished in battle and brought home as a curiosity like a pet monkey, and Hippolito's sister, Violetta. In the first scene, Camillo, intent on humiliating the Frenchman, gives him to his beloved Violetta to be her 'prisoner'. At the end of the scene we learn from asides that Fontinell (although he fears that within her 'Angels bodie . . . there lyes a heart of flint') and Violetta are mutually smitten. Fontinell reassures himself and goes on to say,

> Such beautie be my Jaylor? a heavenly hell!
> The darkest dungeon, which spite can devise,
> To throw this carkasse in, her glorious eyes
> Can make as lightsome, as the fairest chamber
>   in Paris Louvre: come captivitie,
> And chaine me to her lookes; how am I tost?
> Being twice in minde, as twice in body lost.[2]

For her part, Violetta 'stands by marking Fontinell' and observes as follows:

> In troth a very pretty Frenchman, the carriage of his bodie likes me well; so does his footing, so does his face, so does his eye above his face, so does himselfe, above all that can bee above himselfe.
>   Camillo thou hast plaide a foolish part,
>   Thy prisoner makes a slave of thy loves heart.
> Shal Camillo then sing willow, willow, willow? not for the world: no, no, my French prisoner; I will use thee Cupid knowes how, and teach thee to fall into the hands of a woman; if I doe not feede thee with faire lookes, nere let me live. If thou getst out of my fingers til I have thy verie heart, nere let me love; nothing but thy life shall serve my turne, and how otherwise Ile plague thee, Monsieur you and Ile deale; onely this, because Ile be sure he shall not start, Ile locke him in a little low roome besides himselfe, where his wanton eye shall see neither Sunne nor Moone. So, the daunce is done, and my heart has done her worst, made me in love. . . .[3]

[2] I. sig. [A4]-[A4]ᵛ (Bullen: I, 12-13).
[3] I. sigs. [A4]ᵛ-B[1] (Bullen: I, 14).

Although these revelations have been preceded by the kind of drawing-room badinage which usually gives promise of a charming romance, they are curiously, and very significantly, devoid of any of the higher motives to love. This is all the more surprising because Violetta has previously given every sign of being a young woman of excellent sense. In any case, having let us hear so much of ennobling sentiments from the representatives of refinement and gentility, Middleton immediately proceeds to reinforce these first suggestions of universal animality by introducing the following scene, full of the most open references to the basic appetites:

    Enter Lazarillo *melancholy,* and Pilcher *his boy.*
Laz. Boy, I am melancholy because I burne.
Pil. And I am melancholy because I am a colde.
Laz. I pine with the desire of flesh.
Pil. It's neither flesh nor fish that I pine for, but for both.
Laz. Pilcher, Cupid hath got me a stomacke, and I long for lac'd mutton.
Pil. Plaine mutton without a lace would serve me.
Laz. For as your tame Monkey is your onely best, & most onely beast to your Spanish Lady: or, as your Tobacco is your onely smoker away of rewme, and all other rewmeticke diseases: or, as your Irish lowse does bite most naturally foureteene weekes after the change of your Saffron seamed shirt: or, as the commodities which are sent out of the Low-countries (and put in vessels called mother Cornelius dry-fats) are most common in Fraunce: so it pleaseth the destinies, that I should thirst to drinke out of a most sweet Italian vessell, being a Spaniard.
Pil. What vessell is that Signior?
La. A Woman Pilcher, the moyst handed Madona Imperia, a most rare and divine creature.
Pil. A most rascallie damn'd Curtizan![4]

The rest of the play may be briefly summarized as follows. In his annoyance at Violetta's fascination with the effeminate Fontinell, Camillo has the latter thrown into a dungeon (thereby playing 'the wise and venerable bearded Master Constable'[5]), despite the good-natured remonstrances of Hippolito, who takes

[4] I. sig. B[1]–B[1]ᵛ (Bullen: I, 15–16).
[5] Blurt is a relatively insignificant character in the underplot: an illiterate constable much like Shakespeare's Dogberry.

the whole business as a huge joke at first, and would do anything rather than 'scratch so much as the skin off the law of Armes'. He soon conceives a plan for changing his sister's attraction to revulsion by getting the object of her affections involved with a notorious prostitute of his acquaintance, the Madona Imperia referred to earlier by Lazarillo. To whet her appetite he sends Imperia a picture of Fontinell. He persuades Camillo to release that much wronged personage, but Fontinell prefers to languish in his cell:

> O happy persecution I embrace thee,
> With an unfettered soule; so sweete a thing
> Is it to sigh upon the racke of love,
> Where each calamitie is groning witnes
> Of the poore Martirs faith: I never heard
> Of any true affection but t'was nipt
> With care, that [(]like the Catter-piller) eates
> The leaves off the springs sweetest booke, (the Rose).[6]

Part of the scheme works out well, nevertheless, for the Madona is very much taken with Fontinell's likeness, and her servant helps him to escape. Unfortunately for the schemers, however, she also lends her support to a secret midnight marriage between her Frenchman and the infatuated Violetta. The latter are reunited at 'Saint Lorenzos Monasterie'—a detail which suggests Middleton's intention of making a travesty of *Romeo and Juliet*—in a burlesque scene which readers, mistaking Middleton's purpose and trying to see the play as a straightforward romance, have been wont to take seriously:

	Enter Violetta *and a Frier apace.*
Viol.	My dearest Fontinell!
Font.	My Violetta, oh God!
Viol.	Oh God!
Font.	Where is this reverend Frier?
Frier.	Heere, over joy'd young man.
Viol.	How didst thou scape?
	How came Imperiaes man?
Font.	No more of that.
Viol.	When did Imperia? ——

[6] III. sig. [D4] (Bullen: I, 51–2).

> Font.   Questions now are theeves,
> And lyes in Ambush to surprize our joys,
> My most happie starres shine still, shine on,
> Away, come, love beset had neede be gone.[7]
>
> *Exeunt.*

In spite of his ludicrous evasion of Violetta's questions about the complicity of Imperia, Fontinell is not unmindful of his obligations to his ally for her assistance. Not a romantic hero, but rather a complete moral idiot, he returns to the brothel where Imperia has been diverting herself at cards awaiting his arrival, and spends his wedding night in her embraces. By the next morning, he has become so attached to the Madona that he cannot bear the thought of leaving her:

> Imp.   Ah you little effeminate sweete *Cheveleere*, why dost thou not get a loose Periwig of haire on thy chinne, to set thy French face off, by the panting pulse of Venus: thou art welcome a thousand degrees beyond the reach of Arithmaticke: Good, good, good, your lip is moiste & mooving; it hath the truest French close, even like Mapew, la, la, la &c.
> Font.   Deare Ladie, ô life of love, what sweetnes dwels
> In loves varietie? The soule that plods
> In one harsh booke of beautie, but repeates
> The stale and tedious learning, that hath oft
> Faded the sences: when (in reading more)
> We glide in new sweets, and are starv'd with store.
> Now by the heart of love, my Violet
> Is a foule weede (ô pure Italian flower!)
> She, a blacke Negro, to the white compare
> Of this unequal'd beautie: O most accurst!
> That I have given her leave to challenge me.
> But Ladie, poison speakes Italian well,
> And in a loathed kisse, Ile include her hell![8]

Somewhat earlier Hippolito had begun to doubt the efficacy of his plan. In a scene in which he accompanies his friend Camillo to an interview with Violetta, he loses all patience and gives vent to some rather unbrotherly epithets:

[7] III. sigs. E2v–E3 (Bullen: I, 59).
[8] V. sigs. G2v–G3 (Bullen: I, 85).

S'light, she meanes her French *garsoon*!

. . . .

You scurvey Tyt: s'foote, scurvey anything.
Doe you heare Susanna: you, puncke, if I geld not your
Muske-Cat! Ile doo't by Jesu; lets goe Camillo.
Viol. Nay but pure swaggerer, ruffian,[9] doe you thinke
To fright me with your bug-beare threates? Goe by;
Harke tosse-pot in your eare, the Frenchman's mine,
And by these hands Ile have him![10]

But Violetta is finally obliged to go to the brothel to fetch home her property. In her obsession, she puts all pride behind her and pleads obsequiously with Imperia. Several lesser functionaries of the brothel and the object of her desires, understood to be skulking somewhere in a room off-stage, are part of her audience:

> Doe not mocke mee fairest Venetian; come, I knowe hee's heere: good faith I doe not blame him, for your beautie glides over his error. Troth I am right glad that you (my Countrie woman) have received the pawne of my affections. You cannot bee hardharted, loving him, nor hate mee, for I love him too: since wee both love him, let us not leave him, till wee have call'd home the ill husbandrie of a sweet Stragler; prethee (good wench) use him well.

Imp. So, so, so.
Viol. If he deserve not to bee used well (as Ide bee loath he should deserve it) Ile ingage my selfe (deere beauty) to thine honest hart; give me leave to love him, and Ile give him a kinde of leave to love thee. I know he heer's me; I prethee try mine eyes. . . . In troth Ile not chide him: if I speake wordes rougher then soft kisses, my pennaunce shall bee to see him kisse thee, yet to holde my peace.
Fris[co] And that's torment enough, alas poore wench.
Sim[perina] Shee's an Asse, by the crowne of my Mayden-head,
Ide scratch her eyes out, if my man stood in her Tables.
Viol. Good partener, lodge me in thy private bed,
Where (in supposed follie) he may end
Determin'd sinne . . .

. . . .

[9] Spelt 'rufflin' in the quarto.
[10] III. sig. E[1]ᵛ (Bullen: I, 56).

Imp. Good troth (pretty wed-locke) thou makst my little eyes smart, with washing themselves in brine; I keep your Cocke from his owne roost? ... no, no, no, ... your Chamber-fellow is within. ....[11]

In the final scene, the Duke of Venice arrives just in time to prevent Camillo, Hippolito, and several of their friends from entering the brothel and taking a bloody revenge. Blurt and his men then bring Fontinell, Imperia, and Violetta, as well as two culprits from the minor plot, into the Duke's presence, and Violetta is obliged to tell a lie to save Fontinell from the death penalty attending on the crime of adultery. She maintains that the whole affair was her idea, and that Fontinell had not really been unfaithful. By this time she has managed to recaptivate her feckless spouse:

> This was a plot of mine, onelie to trie
> Your loves strange temper ...
> Font. O sweetest Violet; I blush——
> Viol. Good figure,
> Weare still that maiden blush, but still be mine.
> Fon. I seale my selfe thine owne, with both my hands,
> In this true deede of gift. Gallants, heere stands
> This Ladies Champion, at his foote Ile lye
> That dares touch her: who taintes my constancie,
> I am no man for him, fight he with her,
> And yeeld, for shee's a noble conqueror.[12]

With these fatuous remarks the action of the main plot ends with everyone good friends, and it only remains for the Duke to decide that there has been enough of strife and proclaim a morning of merry-making.

Beginning with a casual comment by E. H. C. Oliphant in 1926 to the effect that *Blurt Master-Constable* looked to him like Dekker's work, a controversy arose over the authorship of the play.[13] It may be noted that two responsible modern authorities, Muriel Bradbrook (*The Growth and Structure of Elizabethan Comedy*, 1955) and Una Ellis-Fermor (*The Jacobean Drama*, 4th edn., 1958), do not doubt that it is Middleton's; the former

---

[11] V. sig. [G4]–[G4]ᵛ (Bullen: I, 89–90).
[12] V. sig. H2ᵛ (Bullen: I, 96).
[13] The history of this controversy is summarized by R. H. Barker in *Thomas Middleton* (New York, 1958), pp. 197–9.

makes no question of it, and the latter, while recognizing its precocity, objects to its ascription to Dekker and argues that it is just in Middleton's early style. Also, F. T. Bowers was not sufficiently satisfied with the suggestion of Dekker to feel justified in including it in his recent edition of Dekker's plays. But the remarkable fact is that, just as the character and purpose of Middleton's art in general have never been fully appreciated, there is no evidence that the technique and meaning of this play have ever been understood. The main points which have not been realized are: first, that Middleton was a consummate artist, capable of maintaining aesthetic distance so effectively, when he chose to, that his achievement of the ideal expressed in the aphorism, 'To reveal art and conceal the artist is art's aim', is unparalleled; second, that he had a sense of moral purpose in his writing; and third, that there are recurring themes in his work, expressed in characteristic ways. Had these things been understood, there would have been no difficulty in understanding *Blurt Master-Constable*, or in seeing its place in the nexus of Middleton's works, and there would have been no question about who wrote it.

In the first edition of his *History of English Dramatic Literature*, A. W. Ward had this to say about the play: 'The lightness and gaiety of writing . . . cannot render tolerable a play with so vile a plot. Beginning pleasantly, and indeed prettily enough, with the sudden passion of a lady for the prisoner brought home from the wars by her lover, it ends offensively with the unfaithfulness of the prisoner, who has escaped and married the lady. . . .'[14] The second editor of Middleton's complete works objected strenuously to these words—'Severe censure has been passed, quite undeservedly, on the conclusion of the play.' He chastened Ward benevolently as follows:

I am sorry that Mr. Ward should have misrepresented the plot; but I allow that Middleton ought to have rendered such misrepresentation impossible by supplying more details and leaving less to the reader's imagination. It is not easy to carry in one's head the plots of several hundreds of plays; and so careful a stage-historian as Mr. Ward may well claim indulgence for occasional lapses.[15]

[14] (London, 1875), II, 74.
[15] Introduction to *The Works of Thomas Middleton*, I, xxiii.

Evidently Ward's quite accurate reading of the events of the play offended Bullen's aesthetic sensibilities, because he describes the play as a romance, flagrantly misrepresents its events himself, and even goes so far as to offer the half-line 'at his foote Ile lye' (see p. 16 above) as 'at [t]his foot I'll lie' in his text,[16] with the absurd footnote, inspired by Dyce, 'Used transitively', to lend credibility to his mistaken idea. In the second edition of *A History of English Dramatic Literature* Ward said, '. . . I cannot think that the dramatist intended to represent Fontinelle as really faithful to his young wife, or to furnish in her final speech a really truthful account of his conduct.' To his reprover he said, 'I owe Mr. Bullen many thanks for the extreme courtesy of his censure . . .; but although in the previous edition of this book I gave an unsatisfactory account of the plot of this play, I confess that his correction leaves me still unable to see through it clearly.'[17]

Blurt Master-Constable will be best understood when it is seen in the over-all thematic context of the rest of the canon, but despite the disregard of the 'reader's imagination' of which Bullen accuses Middleton, it is quite possible to discover Middleton's purpose without looking beyond the play itself. Actually Bullen went directly to the core of the problem by using that phrase, because the principal difficulty in understanding this play would stem from the necessity one is under to read it, rather than see it performed; and any tendency towards a special point of view, like the one Lamb develops in his essay 'On the Tragedies of Shakespeare, considered with reference to their fitness for Stage Representation', would greatly intensify that difficulty. For Middleton creates his illusion of artistic detachment through the use of a kind of 'ironic approval', the subtlety of which is heightened in mere reading.

Chaucer's characters in *The Canterbury Tales* are given 'ironic approval' in the authorial comments of the General Prologue. Middleton's genre confined him to the use of dialogue, however, and he was obliged to adopt a less direct, more artistic means of achieving the same effect. His purpose in this play was to discover hypocrisy to his audience, and therefore, before revealing the underlying animality of his characters, he wrote a scene, rightly described by Ward as full of 'lightness and gaiety', in

[16] *Works*, I, 96.
[17] (London, 1899), II, 503, n. 1.

which they appear with their masks of civility in place. Chiding her brother for his warlike proclivities and bravado, Violetta appears to be the soul of wisdom, and in her first exchange of words with Fontinell both she and he are models of dignity:

Viol. Faire stranger droope not, since the chance of wars
Brings to the Soldier death, restraint, or scarres.
Font. Lady, I know the fortune of the field,
Is death with honour, or with shame to yeild,
As I have done.
Viol. In that no scandall lyes,
Who dyes when he may live, he doubly dyes.
Font. My reputation's lost.
Viol. Nay thats not so,
You flee not, but were vanquisht by your foe;
The eye of warre respects not you nor him,
It is our fate will have us loose or win....[18]

How much the absence of the costumes and gestures of actual drama, coupled with a failure to recognize Middleton's purpose, would make the reader miss in Fontinell in this scene may be accurately gauged by Bullen's presumptuous chastisement of Ward, and of Middleton for not 'supplying more details'. In a passage which precedes the one just cited Middleton makes his audience visualize a much different choice of mates for Violetta, a romantic ideal of manhood:

2nd Lady ... I have heard that some men have dyed for love.
Viol. So have I, but I could never see't: I'd ride forty miles to follow such a fellow to Church, and would make more of a sprig of Rosemary at his buriall, than of a gilded Bride-branch at mine owne wedding.
Camil. Take you such delight in men that dye for love?
Viol. Not in the men nor in the death, but in the deed; troth I thinke he is not a sound man that wil dye for a woman, and yet I would never love a man soundlie, that would not knocke at deathes doore for my love.[19]

Ward's perplexity—a perplexity shared by subsequent readers[20] —at having to reconcile dialogue like this and 'so vile a plot' as Middleton sets in motion immediately afterwards, with his preconceived notions of Elizabethan drama is not hard to imagine.

[18] I. sig. [A4] (Bullen: I, 12).
[19] I. sig. A3–A3ᵛ (Bullen: I, 9–10).
[20] For example, see R. H. Barker, *Thomas Middleton*, p. 198.

Nevertheless, the play contains many clues to the author's intentions. Not only is Blurt the name of a minor character, but in Middleton's day the word itself was an expression of contempt. Bullen, following Dyce,[21] tells us that '"Blurt! Master Constable!" appears to have been a proverbial expression'; but neither of them saw that the title of the play is Middleton's contemptuous allusion to the world of appearances which the play exposes, even though he was at pains to command this interpretation of the expression in the dialogue. In Act II Curvetto, the senile lecher, turns on Hippolito and says,

> Right, you swore,
> But oathes are now like Blurt our Constable,
> Standing for nothing, a meere plot, a tricke.[22]

Imperia herself conveys the gist of Middleton's theme when Curvetto objects to her habit of swearing by her 'Virginitie':

Doe not therefore come over me with crosse blows, no, no, no I shall be sicke, if my speech be stopt! By my Virginitie I sweare, and why may not I sweare by that I have not, as well as poore mustie Soldiers doe by their honour; Brides at four & twentie, ha, ha, ha, by their Maidenheads; Cittizens, by their faith; and Brokers as they hope to be saved?[23]

The clues which have gone unnoticed about Violetta and Fontinell are in their assessments of each other in Act I. In an unwary reader's insistence upon seeing them as romantic hero and heroine, he fails to note that they are entirely right about each other, she remarking 'his wanton eye', and he guessing that she has a 'heart of flint' within her 'Angels bodie'. The wilful and wanton Violetta[24] looks forward very significantly to Beatrice-Joanna in *The Changeling*, and to Deflores's observation that

---

[21] Dyce referred to *English Proverbs*, appended to Howell's *Lexicon Tetraglotton*, 1660, but overlooked the significance to the play of what is written there: 'Blurt Mr. Constable: *spoken in derision*'.

[22] Sig. D2–D2ᵛ (Bullen: I, 45). Middleton laments the decline of honour revealed by the emptiness of oaths at greater length in *The Family of Love*, again through a minor character. See below, p. 48.

[23] II. sig. D[1]ᵛ (Bullen: I, 43–4).

[24] To the end of his career, Middleton continued to cherish the high conception of the virtue of chastity to which he had done boyish honour in *The Ghost of Lucrece*. Nevertheless, it is clear from this early play that shortly after his arrival in London he had begun to appreciate the enigmatical nature of woman, and he never ceased to be fascinated by it.

'Some women are odd feeders.' As for Fontinell, the accuracy of Hippolito's observation that he has 'a soft Mermaladie heart' should be borne out, even without a stage and actors, by his effeminate name, his ecstasies of anguish at the beginning of Act III,[25] his dialogue with Imperia, and his idiotic speech before the Duke.

It is from his counterpart in the underplot, Lazarillo, 'the Spanish curtall that in the last battaile fled twenty miles ere he lookt behind him', that the play derives its alternative title. On the night of the wedding Imperia has professional appointments with Curvetto at ten, and Lazarillo at midnight, which she must break in order to accommodate Fontinell. When Curvetto tries to gain access to the Madona by means of a cord depending from a window, he drenches himself with water and provokes the following exclamation from Simperina 'above':

... by my pure Maiden-head heer's a jest: why this was a water-worke to drowne a Ratte that uses to creepe in at this window![26]

At Lazarillo's next appearance he has been started on his 'Nightwalke' by being sent into a strange room: '*Enter* Lazarillo *bare headed in his shirt: a paire of Pantaples on, a Rapier in his hand and a Tobacco pipe: he seems amazed, and walkes so up and downe.*' At Imperia's instance Simperina has opened the stage trap-door, through which Lazarillo duly falls into the fetid cellar of the brothel. When he emerges later on, he is in sorry case:

Thou honest fellow (the man in the Moone) I beseech thee set fire on thy bush of thornes, to light and warme me, for I am dung wet: I fell like Lucifer I thinke into hell, and am crauld out, but in worse pickle than my leane Pilcher: heere about is the Hot-house of my love, ho, ho? why ho there?

[25] Writers who have objected to Middleton's authorship of *Blurt Master-Constable* because they thought that the dialogue was 'too deliberately poetical for Middleton', and 'too self-consciously euphuistic', did not realize that the purpose of that poetry and euphuism was to characterize the false gentility of Fontinell and Violetta. Had they understood Middleton's intention, they might have seen that he was writing the same kind of florid dialogue for Gerardine and Maria, and Lactantio and Aurelia, who are in a direct line of descent from Fontinell and Violetta (see the latter half of I. ii, II. iv from 'Re-enter Maria', III. i, III. vii, and V. ii of *The Family of Love*, and I. i of *More Dissemblers Besides Women*, respectively), and for precisely the same reason.
[26] IV. sig. F2ᵛ (Bullen: I, 71).

Frisco appears and, after calling him 'Fly-blowne rascall', 'Spanish vermine', 'hogs-face', and 'Turpentine pill', he promises to 'wash off [his] teares':

> La. Thou hast sowsed my poor hogs-face! O Frisco, thou art a scurvie Doctor to cast my water no better; it is most rammish Urine! Mars shall not save thee, I will make a browne toaste of thy heart, and drinke it in a pot of thy strong bloud.[27]

Thus Middleton administers poetic justice to the debauchees, in scenes at once droll and appropriately brutal, leaving them to wallow in their own mire. Lazarillo and Curvetto have not only served their purpose as clowns, but have defined the character of lust, and emphasized the ugliness which the animal drives, lurking beneath the thin idealistic veneers of the principals of the main plot, may so readily assume. Violetta's 'Night-walke' in the mire is implicit in the nature of the prize she has won; and the key to an understanding of the whole play lies in the realization that if there is any qualitative distinction at all to be made between Fontinell and Violetta on the one hand, and Lazarillo and Imperia on the other, it must be in favour of the latter. The civil speech which Middleton gives to Fontinell and Violetta in Act I, and the costume of nobility they would wear, would only serve to make their carnality even more grotesque than the moronic but undisguised depravity of the minor characters.[28]

Among the important talents which Middleton brought to play-making was a remarkable power of observation. Truepenny's description of the melancholy lover and the portrait of the harlot in the environment of her brothel in Act II of this play are not caricatures, but candid reproductions of life which could only have been written by a sympathetic observer. Middleton's humanity is a constant factor in his social criticism, and it can be sensed in Curvetto's reminiscences of his days as a gallant, a passage which also shows that Middleton had learned to combine effectively stage direction with dialogue:

> I have a good heart knave; and a good heart
> Is a good face-maker. I am young, quicke, briske,
> I was a Reveller in a long stocke
> (There's not a gallant now filles such a stocke)

---

[27] See sigs. F2^v, [F4]^v–G[1] (Bullen: I, 73, 79–80).
[28] See below, p. 77, n. 45.

Plumpe hose, pain'd, stuft with haire (haire then was held
The lightest stuffing) a faire Cod-peece; hoh,
An Eele-skin sleeve, lasht heere and there with lace,
Hye coller, lasht agen; breeche lasht also;
A little simpring ruffe, a dapper Cloake,
With Spanish button'd Cape: my Rapier heere,
Gloves like a Burgomaster heere; hat heere,
(Stucke with some ten-groate brooch:) and over al,
A goodlie, long thicke Abram-colour'd beard;
Ho God, Ho God, thus did I Revell it![29]

From *Blurt Master-Constable* it can be seen that Middleton had a gift for writing natural, economical, free-flowing dialogue, and for capturing and reproducing the verbal idioms of different classes of society. It is generally acknowledged that he was a master of well-knit play construction, and *Blurt Master-Constable*, though written with an economy that depends on actors and costume,[30] is no exception. Criticism of its structure has arisen directly from the failure of readers to perceive the function of that structure on a stage, and indirectly from a failure to understand its author, who had hit upon a way of imparting to his dramatic writing the ambivalent quality which would make it both meet the practical demands of the theatre and serve his ulterior didactic motive.

[29] II. sig. D[1]ᵛ (Bullen: I, 42–3).
[30] For examples of structural compression in later plays, see below, pp. 76, n. 41; 103, n. 12; 154; 156–7; and 189–90.

III
OTHER EARLY PLAYS

MIDDLETON's point of view as man and artist was omniscient. Nowhere in the canon of his plays is this fact more in evidence than in *The Phoenix*, for when he came to write that play, he chose to abandon his customary concern to 'conceal the artist' and yielded completely to a temptation which every didactically-motivated writer must feel, and which, except in this and a few other instances, none has resisted better: the temptation to make one of his characters—a character who embodies the author's ideals in all respects—his personal spokesman. The series of episodes of which *The Phoenix* consists would have satisfied an Elizabethan audience's demand for entertainment; but for once Middleton allowed the practical end of play-making to become noticeably subordinate to the aim announced in the Epistle to the Reader in *The Black Book*: to protect the virtuous members of society from the insidious inroads of the vicious. For these reasons, consideration of *The Phoenix*, and its structural and thematic relationships with other works that I shall discuss in this chapter, must be fundamental to any attempt to discover the characteristics of Middleton's early philosophy and art.

A basic theme which runs through all Middleton's early drama is the idea that most of the virtuous are uninformed about vice, and that in that unconscious or 'neutral' state they are constantly in imminent danger of corruption; and it was evidently to encourage the innocent to 'shun those two devouring gulfs ... deceit and luxury, which swallow up more mortals than Scylla and Charybdis', that he set about writing plays that emphasize the ugliness of sin.

That this purpose might be most economically and effectively accomplished in *The Phoenix*, he chose to give dramatic form to the structure of the picaresque romance;[1] and, himself the

---

[1] Middleton was later to employ the episodic structure, in variously modified forms, in *The Black Book* and *The Ant and the Nightingale*, and in two other early plays, *Michaelmas Term* and *Your Five Gallants*.

omniscient observer in the first instance, he both provided himself with a mouthpiece, and imparted a mechanical coherence to the play, by placing another omniscient observer in the *dramatis personae*: the ardently virtuous but inexperienced hero from whom the play derives its title, Prince Phoenix, son of an aged Duke of Ferrara. A pretext for the play's series of *exposés* of vice is provided in the opening scene. The Duke, anxious to unburden himself of his authority, proposes to his council that Phoenix should succeed him, but, yielding to the objection of Proditor, a malevolent secret schemer—'... tis the greatest pittie Noble Lord, | He is untraveld'—he agrees to send him abroad first for a time. For all his inexperience, however, there is nothing wrong with Phoenix's intelligence. He chooses his friend Fidelio[2] as travelling companion and confides in him his suspicions and his plan:

> By absence, ile obey the Duke my father,
> And yet not wrong my selfe.
> . . . .
> Ile stay at home, and travaile.[3]

Phoenix and Fidelio then begin their odyssey 'to look into the heart & bowels of this Dukedome, and in disguise, marke all abuses readie for Reformation or Punishment'. Disguised in a less obvious way is Middleton, and there are strong indications that the two travellers merely retrace some of the footsteps of a kind of journey which their playwright-guide had himself been making ever since his arrival in London from Oxford—a journey like those of which Emile Zola was to make so many, with his spectacles and his notebook, in another great city some three hundred years later, and the results of which are recorded in such sociological studies as *L'Assommoir* and *Le Ventre de Paris*, works which bear many similarities to Middleton's early drama. One of these indications is found in Phoenix's reply to his father's surprised exclamation on learning that his son wishes to travel without a retinue: '. . . that's the benefit a private Gentleman | Enjoyes . . . he notes all, | Himselfe unnoted.' Another is given later on when Phoenix reveals his motive to Fidelio:

---

[2] The allegorical significance of the names of Middleton's characters is seldom less obvious than this one's.

[3] I. sig. A3ᵛ (Bullen: I, 107).

... I cannot otherwise thinke but there are infectious dealings in most offices, and foule misteries throughout al Professions: and therefore I nothing doubt but to find travaile ynough within my selfe, and Experience I fear too much: nor will I be curious to fit my bodie to the humblest forme and bearing, so the labor may be fruitfull: for how can abuses that keepe lowe, come to the right view of a Prince, unlesse his lookes lie levell with them . . . ?[4]

There can be little doubt that Middleton came by his detailed knowledge of vicious practices by giving himself frequent occasion to blend into the background of London's underworld.

Some of the results of those investigations are represented in the four loosely-entwined actions of *The Phoenix*. One is concerned with a thieving ex-sea-captain, a chronic bachelor who, in middle age, has made the mistake of marrying ('What lustfull passion came aboord of mee, that I should marrye, was I drunke?'), and is now prepared to sell his virtuous wife, Fidelio's widowed mother, to the lascivious Proditor. Another is a portrayal of an adulterous relationship between a wanton jeweller's wife and one of King James's knights by purchase,[5] a type Middleton attacked several times, as here where the jeweller's wife introduces her parasitical paramour (he calls her 'My sweete Revennewe') to her father Falso, a former highwayman:

Fals. Daughter, what Gentleman might this be?
Jew.   No Gentleman sir, hee's a Knight.
Fals. Is he but a knight? troth, I would a sworne had beene a Gentleman, to see, to see, to see.[6]

A third action is concerned with the attempt of Falso, now a corrupt justice of the peace and keeper of a gang of thieves which he uses his office to protect, to make his orphaned niece (Fidelio's fiancée) his mistress; it includes scenes which portray a litigious humour, Tangle:

... some say hee's as good as a Lawyer, (marrie 'ime sure hee's as bad as a Knave) if you have any suites in lawe, hee's the fittest man for your companie ... hee is able to affoord you more knavish counsell for tenne groates, then another for ten shillings.[7]

---

[4] I. sig. [A4] (Bullen: I, 108).
[5] Although the announced scene is Ferrara, the characters are all Londoners.
[6] I. sigs. D[1]ᵛ–D2 (Bullen: I, 135).
[7] I. sig. B3ᵛ (Bullen: I, 118–19).

Running through the whole is the thin unifying thread of Proditor's plot to usurp the dukedom. Phoenix is a witness to all.

The device of double incognito—the omniscient character disguised from his fellows on the stage, and in that character the author himself disguised from the audience—was an important technical experiment. In the prose pamphlet, *The Black Book*, the authorial mask is effected with irony: Lucifer, disguised in turn in 'a constable's night-gown', 'an usurer's fusty furred jacket', 'a captain's suit', and 'the habit of a covetous barn-cracking farmer', conducts a tour which includes stops at a brothel, the Burse, and an ordinary, and introduces the reader to a wide variety of criminals and debauchees. But so intent was Middleton upon his didactic motive in *The Phoenix* that he did not refrain from investing his spokesman with the nobility of character which would qualify him to point morals; and, sometimes forgetting, or, more probably, ignoring, the requirement that a play should be diverting, he subjected the audience to a number of harangues, some relatively short, others so long as to make his intention unmistakable. An example of the latter is the thirty-two-line monologue on 'Reverend and honourable Matrimony' which follows, like a Sophoclean chorus, the scene wherein the captain's wife is sold to Proditor. Another, of thirty-one lines, beginning 'Thou Angell sent amongst us, sober Law', follows Phoenix's first interview with Tangle.[8] Middleton was attempting to make *The Phoenix* give society the benefit of some of the experience of his own apprenticeship to life, and such passages represent what may be viewed as a deliberate relapse—deliberate because we have seen that there are guises for authorial comment in *The Black Book* and *Blurt Master-Constable*—into something very much like the self-conscious sententiousness of *The Wisdom of Solomon Paraphrased* and *The Ghost of Lucrece*. To Phoenix they give a puppet-like quality, and while his spirit rises, so to speak, very often elsewhere in the canon, in no other play is authorial management or contrivance quite so conspicuous.

The closest parallel is to be found in Fitsgrave, the hero of *Your Five Gallants*, who, though his circumstances differ, has a good deal in common with the Prince of Ferrara. Both are

---

[8] For these two monologues see II. sigs. [D4]ᵛ–E[1] and I. sig. C2–C2ᵛ respectively (Bullen: I, 145–7 and 125–6).

staunchly virtuous young men; and they share a sense of
amazement combined with revulsion, strongly reminiscent of the
young author of *The Ghost of Lucrece*, at the spectacle of a vice-
ridden world:

Phoe.   What monstrous daies are these!
        Not onely to be vicious, most men study,
        But in it to be ugly, strive to exceed
        Each other in the moste deformed deede.[9]
Fits.   . . . o thou world,
        How art thou muffled in deceitfull formes:
        There's such a mist of these,[10] and still hath beene,
        The brightnesse of true Gentry is scarce seene.[11]

Both heroes are used to unify and make coherent a series of more
or less independent episodes, but Fitsgrave has a much less
pervasive presence in them, and the fact that his motive lacks the
altruistic quality of Phoenix's makes him a more oblique authorial
mask. He and the five gallants (Frippery, a broker; Primero, a
bawd; Goldstone, a cheat; Pursenet, a thief; and Tailby, like the
carpet knight in *The Phoenix*, a male prostitute) are rivals for the
hand of Katherine, a wealthy and virtuous orphan. Middleton uses
this situation as his pretext for turning Fitsgrave into another
omniscient observer, and availing himself again of the double
incognito:

Fitsg.   A quiet moneth the Virgin has enclosde
        Unto her selfe: suiters stand without till then,
        In which space cunningly Ile winde my selfe
        Into their Bosomes. I have be-thought the shape;
        Some credulous Scholler, easily infected
        With fashion, time, and humor; unto such
        Their deepest thoughts will like to wanton fishes,
        Play above water, and be all parts seene.
        For since at me their envie pines, ile see
        Whether their lives from touch of blame sit free.[12]

Only once did Middleton give Fitsgrave a lengthy monologue
like those he gave to Phoenix, a disquisition on 'impudence'
inspired by his several observations of his rivals in action. With
its 'Suspectlesse virgin' a counterpart of the 'sober and continent

---

[9] I. sig. C3 (Bullen: I, 127).   [10] Masked robbers.
[11] III. sig. E3 (Bullen: III, 186–7).   [12] I. sig. B3 (Bullen: III, 143).

[but naive] livers' to whose attention 'the world's shadowed villanies' are drawn in *The Black Book*, and its speaker—'Now onely rests, that as to me they'r knowne, | So to the world their base Arts may be showne'—a transparent mask for Middleton, this monologue provides one of the play's most important clues to the didactic thread which runs back to *The Wisdom of Solomon Paraphrased*.[13]

In regard to the use of a hero-presenter imbued with virtue *The Phoenix* and *Your Five Gallants* are companion pieces; but only in *The Phoenix* is the hero concerned with virtue for virtue's sake. Not until he came to write *A Fair Quarrel*, some fourteen years later, did Middleton produce another male paragon. Nevertheless, he often used the other components of these plays, and he used them in such ways as made his didactic motive more effectively ulterior. *Michaelmas Term*, for example, is another dramatic 'frame story', but the hero, while sympathetic, is a foolish and innocent heir from the country rather than a refined nobleman, and his use as a unifying factor is more naturally and skilfully accomplished than is Phoenix's: on arriving in London he becomes the victim of various scoundrels. Gerardine, the young hero of *The Family of Love*, at first appears to have the attributes of a romantic ideal of manhood, but very subtly we are allowed to see that his lofty words, like Fontinell's, are only words. The hero of *A Mad World, My Masters*, like Phoenix and Fitsgrave, adopts an incognito, but for an unworthy purpose. The spirit of a didactic author remains ubiquitous in these plays, but without dependence on an indefectible, animadverting intermediary. Only twice again—in his Captain Agar in *A Fair Quarrel* and Cleanthes in *The Old Law* (not mechanical contrivances such as Phoenix, but rounded characters)—did Middleton choose a relatively transparent *persona*.[14] His more characteristic artistic pose, that in which he was content to make his comments from behind a veil of irony or *montage* and to let his audience draw conclusions where it might, is evident in the induction to *Michaelmas Term*. Here he not only relieves the critic of the task of labelling him a realist by making this fact quite clear himself, but both invites interpretation of his play and expresses a doubt that his underlying intention would be understood:

[13] For the reader's convenience, I quote the monologue in full in Appendix B.
[14] See Chapter VIII.

Why we call this play by such a deere and chargeable Title, Michaelmas
Tearme? Knowe it consents happilye to our purpose, tho perhaps
faintlie to the interpretation of many; for he that expects any great
quarrels in Lawe to bee handled here, will be fondly deceaved. This only
presents those familiar accidents, which happend in Towne in the
circumference of those sixe weekes, whereof Michalemas Terme is
Lord: Sat Sapienti, I hope there's no fooles i'th house!   *Exit.*[15]

Phoenix and Fitsgrave have much in common, but, in a way which was extremely important to Middleton, they differ. Fitsgrave, while not himself vicious, is, like Follywit, the knavish young protagonist of *A Mad World, My Masters*, and Middleton himself, no stranger to vicious practices. Fitsgrave becomes a watcher not for his education, but to gain particular information about his rivals; and while the vices which he discovers offend his sensibilities, they do not come as general revelations. Experience puts him on his guard at the outset, and both academic and practical knowledge determine the form which his justice finally takes. Phoenix, on the other hand, has known only books hitherto; but, happily for him, Middleton gives him a father who knows the limitations of academic training, and Phoenix himself is not affected with foolish pride in his learning:

Duke. We have thought good and meete . . .
       . . . to move you toward Travaile,
       The better to approve you to your selfe
       And give your apter power, foundation:
       To see affections actually praesented,
       Ee'n by those men that owe them, yeeld more profit,
       I more content, then singly to reade of them,
       Since love or feare, make Writers partiall.
       The good and free example which you finde,
       In other Countries, match it with your owne,
       The ill to shame the ill, which will in time,
       Fully instruct you how to set in frame,
       A kingdome all in peeces.[16]

---

[15] Sig. A3 (Bullen: I, 218). Compare Middleton's characteristically whimsical tone when addressing his audience here with that of his Letter to the Reader in *The World Tost at Tennis* (Appendix B).

[16] I. sigs. A2ᵛ–A3 (Bullen: I, 104–5). The inadequacy of academic reading as a sole preparation for life had impressed itself forcibly upon Middleton's mind. It is a point to which he makes frequent allusion. In *Michaelmas Term*, for example, the country wench's father observes that 'Witte by experience bought foyles wit at

It is Phoenix's ignorance of the world of vice that makes him, to some extent, the exemplar of a type of hero through which Middleton gave expression to another of his warning themes. Phoenix has the benefit of wise advice, and a happy predisposition to learn; Easy, the fond and gullible country heir in *Michaelmas Term*, and his counterpart in 'The Ant's Tale when he was a ploughman' in *The Ant and the Nightingale*, entering upon life 'with their eyes closed', are not in such happy case.

The central figure in 'The Ant's Tale when he was a ploughman'[17] is a foolish young prodigal from the country who goes to London, is gulled and fleeced, becomes profligate and, in his turn, a cheat and pander; in the process, he brings about the woeful ruin of all his tenants and retainers. Middleton also revealed his interest in the contemporary socio-economic problem of country gentry and yeomen abandoning their holdings[18] in *The Phoenix*. A speech in which the ex-sea-captain bewails the inconveniences of marriage contains another comment on the ironic combination of productive husbandry and prodigal waste:

... What a fortunate Elder Brother is he, whose father being a Ramish Plough-man, himselfe a perfumde Gentleman, spending the labouring reeke from his Fathers Nosthrils in Tobacco, the sweate of his Fathers bodye in monthlye Phisicke for his pretty quesie Harlot.[19]

These two examples illustrate one aspect of Middleton's idea of the school of experience: its formidable power to perpetuate

Schoole'; and when Fitsgrave has assumed the disguise of a 'credulous Scholler, easily infected | With fashion, time, and humor' in *Your Five Gallants*, Goldstone introduces him to his fellows telling them that he has come 'Piping hotte from the University, he smells of buttered loaves yet, an excellent scholler, but the arrantest Asse!' (a description that aptly fits Tim Yellowhammer, 'the Cambridge Boy' in *A Chaste Maid in Cheapside*).

[17] *The Ant and the Nightingale* or *Father Hubburd's Tales* is a frame story in verse and prose containing three episodes. The speaker is an ant who at various times has taken the shape of a man. At the beginning of the pamphlet he is captured by a nightingale (Philomela). When she realizes that he is not an enemy in disguise, she releases him, and the ant then recounts his adventures in 'The Ant's Tale when he was a ploughman', '...a soldier', and '...a scholar' (referred to above, pp.xvii–xviii). 'The Ant's Tale when he was a soldier' tells of the exploits of a man invalided out of the army and reduced to beggary in Shoreditch.
[18] Evidently country gentry had the choice of facing the city and its hazards or staying at home to bear the brunt of internal revenue demands (see E. P. Cheney's *A History of England from the Defeat of the Armada to the Death of Elizabeth* [New York, 1926], II, p. 13).
[19] I. sig. B[1]ᵛ (Bullen: I, 112).

iniquity, a theme to which I shall refer again later. My immediate reason for citing them is that they show that in the country-bred individual Middleton saw the kind of innocence which was most vulnerable to the dangers of the city environment; and from that background, by different paths, come Easy and the nameless country wench of *Michaelmas Term*, a play that shows how it is possible to emerge from the school of experience either morally unscathed or utterly corrupted.

Even while en route for London Easy has been under the surveillance of a land- and money-hungry wool-draper, Quomodo, who has just returned from a vacation in Essex. Quomodo immediately sets his minion Shortyard to ensnaring the youth, a task which he accomplishes by means much more elaborate and polished than the techniques described by Robert Greene in *A Notable Discovery of Coosenage*. Easy is eventually brought to countersign a bond by which a loan is contracted for his new-found boon companion Blastfield (Shortyard in disguise). Unable to meet the debt, the fixed period having expired and 'Blastfield' having mysteriously disappeared, it appears that Easy must forfeit his estate. Quomodo's eccentric self-indulgence leads to his downfall, however, and Easy escapes from the toils a wiser man. The following excerpt will be sufficient to illustrate Middleton's consummate grasp of the beguiler's method, and his underlying didactic motive. Easy has just lost heavily at dice, and his better instincts tell him to desist from gambling for the future. Rearage and Salewood are two young gentlemen-debauchees:

Sho[rtyard] . . . Come, you shall beare yourselfe Jovially: take heede of setting your lookes to your losses, but rather smile uppon your ill lucke, and invite 'em to morrow to another breakefast of Bones.
Eas. Nay ile foresweare dicing.
Sho. What? peace? I am ashamed to heare you: will you ceasse in the first losse? Shewe mee one Gentleman that ere did it! Fie uppon't I must use you to companie I perceyve, youde be spoilde else: forsweare Dice? I would your friends heard you yfaith.
Eas. Nay I was but in jest sir.
Sho. I hope so, what would Gentlemen say of you? there goes a Gull that keepes his money. I would not have such a report goe on you, for the Worlde as long as you are in my companie. Why man fortune alters in a Minute. I ha knowne those have recovered so much in an houre, their purses were never sicke after.

OTHER EARLY PLAYS 33

Rer[age] Oh worse then consumption of the Liver! consumption of the patrimonie.[20]
Sho. How now? marke their humours master Easie.
Rer. Forgive me, my posteritie, yet ungotten!
Sho. Thats a penitent Maudlen Dicer.
Rer. Few knowe the sweets that the plaine life allowes, Vilde sonne that surfets of his fathers browes.
Sho. Laugh at him master Easie.
Eas. Ha, ha, ha.
Sal[ewood] Ile bee damn'd and these bee not the bones of some queane that couzened me in her life, and now consumes mee after her death.
Sho. Thats the true-wicked blasphemous, and soul-shuddering Dicer, that will curse you all service time, & attribute his ill lucke alwayes to one Drab or other.[21]

In Act III, after Easy's entanglement has been effected, Middleton allows Quomodo to assume the rôle of Easy's teacher directly: he delivers his honest victim a lecture on practical affairs:

... —as often as you give your name to a bond, you must think you christen a child, and take the charge on't too: for as the one, the bigger it growes the more cost it requires: so the other the longer it lies, the more charges it puts you too. Onely heer's the difference a child must bee broke, and a bond must not. The more you breake children, the more you keep 'em under: but the more you breake bondes, the more theyle leape in your face, and therefeore, to conclude, I would never undertake to bee Gossip to that bond which I would not see well brought up.[22]

All of the action which precedes the dénouement is foreshadowed in the description of Easy early in Act I ('. . . a faire free-brested Gentleman, somewhat too open, bad in man, worse in woman, the Gentrye-fault at first . . .');[23] Shortyard points the moral in

---

[20] The abrupt introduction of dialogue, or a scene which comments upon what has immediately preceded it (sometimes by giving it the lie, as here), is one of Middleton's favourite ways of obtaining emphasis or conveying a didactic theme. For other examples see Doctor Glister's remarks on 'egregious ignorance', followed by his interviews with Lipsalve and Gudgeon, in *The Family of Love*, II. sig. C3 ff. (Bullen: III, 40–5), and the Fontinell–Violetta, Lazarillo–Pilcher sequence in *Blurt Master-Constable*, pp. 11–12 above.
[21] II. sig. C2 (Bullen: I, 241–2).
[22] Sig. [F4]ᵛ (Bullen: I, 287).
[23] Sig. [A4] (Bullen: I, 221).

Act IV:

> ... for Easie,
> Onely good confidence did make him foolish,
> And not the lack of Sence, that was not it,
> Tis worldly craft beates downe a Schollars wit.[24]

Both Easy and Phoenix are honestly-disposed young men; but Middleton was equally interested in, and sought approval for, individuals who, though once corrupted, have been capable of seeing the ugliness of their past lives and achieving self-reformation. Noteworthy in this connection are three slightly-developed characters which prefigure the rounded character of the Colonel in *A Fair Quarrel*: Quieto, who undertakes the cure of mad Tangle in *The Phoenix*; the country wench's father in *Michaelmas Term*, who comes to London in search of his wayward daughter; and Penitent Brothel, the lecher who seduces Mistress Harebrain in *A Mad World, My Masters*. The case of Penitent Brothel is not really apropos of the theme now under discussion, because he is merely overcome with a sense of guilt after once achieving his purpose, and persuades Mistress Harebrain that they must hereafter live chaste, in a scene[25] suggestive of the Hippolito-Bellafront interview in the sixth scene of *The Honest Whore, I*. Quieto and the country wench's father, however, relate their present virtuous orientation to life directly to a prolonged previous state of depravity. On his first appearance the latter is given an expository soliloquy, the cardinal point of which he reiterates several times later in the play:

> Where shall I seeke her now?—oh if she knew
> The Dangers that attend on womens lives,
> She would rather lodge under a poore thatcht Roofe
> Then under carved seelings: she was my joy,
> . . . .
> Woe worth th'infected cause that makes me visit
> This man-devouring Cittie—where I spent
> My unshapen youth, to be my ages cursse,
> And surfetted away my name and state
> In swinish Riots, that now being sober,

---

[24] Sig. H[1]ᵛ (Bullen: I, 303). See above, pp. 30–31, n. 16.
[25] See Bullen: III, 327–30.

I doe awake, a Begger,—I may hate her.
Whose youth voides wine, his age is curst with water.
Oh heavens! I know the price of ill, too well,
What the confusions are in whome they dwell . . .[26]

Quieto's involvement in evil has not only been superseded by informed virtue but it has put him in possession of a facility for succouring those who have succumbed to the city sickness:

> Qu. . . . I have been wilde and rash
> Committed many and unnaturall crimes,
> Which I have since repented.
> . . . .
> Yet a mans worth pittie,
> My quiet blood ha's blest me with this guift,
> I have cur'd some, and if his wits be not
> Too deepely cut, I will assay to helpe e'm.
> Phoe. Sufferance does teach you pittie.[27]

As those who sink to the depths and somehow rise again to the surface are rare in life, so are they rare in Middleton's dramatic microcosms. With few exceptions, the innocents shown serving their apprenticeships to life in these early plays only demonstrate the power of iniquity to reproduce itself. The threat of being sent to prison which is directed at Pursenet's boy in *Your Five Gallants*, when he is caught attempting to pick Bungler's pocket, gives rise to a comment, entirely uncalled-for from the standpoints of plot or character development, on the evil influence of penal institutions: '. . . as for Bridewell, that will but make him worse. A will learne more knavery there in one week, then will furnish him and his heirs for a hundreth yeare,'[28] and it is given to a corruptible officer of the watch in *The Phoenix* to make a more general statement of Middleton's idea:

Argo, nay, we have bene Schollars I can tell you, wee could not have beene knaves so soone else, for as in that notable Cittie cald London, stand two most famous Universities, Poultrie and Woodstreet, where some are of twentie yeares standing, and have tooke all their degrees from the Maisters side, downe to the Mistris side. . . .[29]

[26] II. sig. C3–C3ᵛ (Bullen: I, 244–5).
[27] IV. sigs. H[1]ᵛ–H2 (Bullen: I, 184).
[28] III. sig. F[1]ᵛ (Bullen: III, 195).
[29] IV. sig. [H4]–[H4]ᵛ (Bullen: I, 192).

Iniquitous characters and the virtuous but unadvised are often either given opportunities of referring to factors in their backgrounds which have conditioned them to evil, or actually shown in the process of being corrupted. In *Your Five Gallants* Primero explains one way in which infamy perpetuates itself, and Frippery examines a novice prostitute on the fundamental precepts of whoredom, later recounting some details of his own 'raysing'.[30] Like *Blurt Master-Constable*, the sub-plot of *The Family of Love* is a travesty of romantic love: in Act III, with 'Sweet let me give more scope to true desire', the fair-seeming Gerardine seduces his infatuated, inexperienced ('What wouldst thou more then our minds firm contract?') Maria.[31] In *A Mad World, My Masters*, the mother who is bawd to her own daughter is indirectly involved, through the latter, in the corruption of Mistress Harebrain.[32] The case history of the country wench in *Michaelmas Term*, in conjunction with that of Lethe, the depraved son of a tooth-drawer, is an integral part of the play's thematic plan, balancing the action involving Easy. In the last scene of Act I, a scene as clinically verisimilar as it is, characteristically, devoid of sentimentality, Lethe's pander corrupts her by appealing to her rustic cupidity:

Pand: Come, leave your puling and sighing.
Count: Beshrew you now, why did you entice me from my father?
Pand: Why? to thy better advancement. Wouldst thou a pretty beautiful-Juicy squall, live in a poore thrumbd house i'th cuntry in such servile-habiliments, and may well passe for a gentlewoman i'th Citie? Do's not 5 hundred do so thinkst thou, and with worse faces? Oh, now in these latter dayes, the Devill raygning tis an age for cloven creatures! But why sad now? Yet indeed tis the fashion of any Curtizan to be sea-sicke i'th first Voyage, but at next shee proclaimes open wars, like a beaten souldier. Why Northampton-shire Lasse do'st dreame of virginity now? Remember a loose-bodied Gowne wench, & let it goe. Wires, & tyres, bents and bums, felts and falls, thou shalt deceive the world, that Gentlewomen indeed shall not be knowne from others....[33]

[30] See I. sigs. [A4], [A4]ᵛ, and B[1]ᵛ (Bullen: III, 131, 134–5 and 137–8).
[31] See sig. D2 (Bullen: III, 48–50).
[32] I. sigs. [A4] and B[1]ᵛ (Bullen: III, 259–60 and 265–6).
[33] Sigs. B3ᵛ–[B4] (Bullen: I, 232–3).

In her next appearance, attended by a tailor and a tirewoman, the
transformation is completed to the satisfaction of her preceptor:

Helg[ill]   Who would thinke now this fine Sophisticated squal came
    out of the Bosome of a Barne, and the loynes of a Haytosser!
Curt. [wench]   Out you sawcie pestiferous Pander, I scorne that
    yfaith.
Helg.   Excellent, already the true phrase and stile of a strumpet. Stay,
    a little more of the red, and then I take my leave of your Cheeke
    for foure & twenty houres. [*aside*:] Doe you not thinke it im-
    possible that her owne Father should know her now, if he saw
    her?[34]

[34] III. sig. E2 (Bullen: I, 267).

IV
CHARACTERISTICS OF MIDDLETON'S EARLY DRAMA

THE objective and balanced point of view which characterizes Middleton's dramatic writing takes its origin in a theme which pervades his earliest work. In the citation with which the preceding chapter concludes, Hellgill twice expresses his amazement at the altered appearance of the country wench. Such rhetorical questions and exclamations about change and illusion take their place often with direct statements to the same effect. In *A Mad World, My Masters*, for example, the courtesan's mother tells her daughter,

> Tis nothing but a politicke conveyance,
> A sincere carriage, a religious eyebrowe,
> That throwes their charmes over the worldlings senses;
> . . . .
> Be wisely tempered and learne this my wench:
> Who gets th'opinion for a vertuous name
> May sin at pleasure, and nere thinke of shame.[1]

and Goldstone in *Your Five Gallants* observes,

> What cannot wit so it be impudent
> Devise and compasse? I would faine know that fellow now,
> That would suspect me but for what I am.
> He lives not! 'Tis all in the conveyance. . . .[2]

Collectively, they become the general question—what is real? a question for which, despite the implicit answer—nothing, which individual comments upon scenes of depravity convey, Middleton ultimately had a positive reply. We have seen that he was a would-be preserver of civilizing institutions,[3] and there are en-

---
[1] I. sig. [A4] (Bullen: III, 260).
[2] IV. sig. [G4]ᵛ (Bullen: III, 219).
[3] See above, p. 27.

MIDDLETON'S EARLY DRAMA

dorsements of universal justice in the crime and punishment, and virtue and reward, sequences of the plots, and in statements like Shakespeare's 'This shows you are above', | You justicers. . . .' When Follywit discovers, after defrauding his wealthy grandfather in *A Mad World, My Masters*, that the woman he has wooed and won was, until the time of their marriage, his grandfather's mistress, he says, 'Ist come about? Tricks are repaid I see',[4] and Lipsalve, unsuccessful in his attempts to gain access to Maria and Mistress Purge in *The Family of Love*, concludes:

> . . . sure thers some providence
> Which countermaunds libidinous appetites,
> For what we most intend, is countercheckt
> By strange and unexpected accidents.[5]

For Middleton, reality inhered in the operation of a universal justice which directs man towards worthy behaviour and away from sin; and we have seen indications of his personal faith in man's ability to respond to that direction, and of his determination to applaud worthy motives. On one occasion he not only made his answer to the question—what is real?—explicit, but placed it directly in the context of that question:

> None for Religion, all for pleasure burne.
> Hot zeale into hot lust is now transformde,
> Grace into paynting, charity into clothes,
> Faith into false hayre, and put off as often.
> Theres nothing but our vertue knowes a meane.[6]

---

[4] V. sig. I[1]ᵛ (Bullen: III, 357).
[5] IV. sig. [F4]ᵛ (Bullen: III, 84–5).
[6] *A Mad World, My Masters*, IV. sig. G[1]ᵛ (Bullen: III, 329). In the first two lines of this quotation it is very likely that Middleton had in mind the kind of sexual promiscuity (generated and, apparently, sanctified in the minds of the ignorant by religious fervour) which he described in the main plot of *The Family of Love*. Although John Rogers's *The Displaying of an horrible secte of grosse and wicked Heretiques . . . the Familie of Love* (London, 1578) and his *An Answere unto a wicked & infamous Libel made by . . . one of the chiefe Elders of the . . . Family of Love* (London, 1579) make no mention of the erotic excesses of which Middleton accuses this anabaptist sect, it may be noted that its adherents appear to have been generally ignorant, that a new member was 'admitted, with a kisse. vz. All of the company both men, and women, kisse him, one after another', and that a tradition is recorded that their second messiah, Henry Nicholas, was a profligate lecher (see *The Displaying . . .*, Bodleian Wood 795, sig. [Dvi]–[Dvi]ᵛ, 'A confession made by two of the Familie . . .'; ibid., sigs. Iiiiiᵛ and Ivᵛ; and *A Supplication of the Family . . . for grace and favour . . . Examined, and found to be derogatorie in an hie degree . . .* [Cambridge, 1606], Bodleian 4° F 14 Th., pp. 15–16).

But Middleton also had an acute consciousness of the fact that the world, viewed through the eyes of the materialist, has paradoxical and ironic aspects, and it affected his work in several significant ways. I have described one of the results of this consciousness in the preceding chapter: the sane concern with causes which was illustrated there, and the avoidance of misanthropic preoccupation with effects, stem from Midddleton's awareness that life places a wide variety of seeming barriers—barriers which he at least was able to view as potential stepping-stones—in man's path to the realization of positive virtue. Middleton's ability to appreciate the incongruities of the world seen through other men's eyes, and his insistence upon relating effects to causes, are the features of his approach to social criticism which contribute most to his stature in that sphere, and they are the factors which look forward to the deep insights into human character in his later plays. And yet it is an irony in itself that Middleton's faithful representation of paradox and irony in his plays, and his eminently successful concomitant repression of the blatant, and disguising of the dogmatic, tendencies of *The Phoenix* and *Your Five Gallants*, account for the fact that his faith and fundamental philanthropy have often been mistaken for neutrality and cynicism.

Middleton caused the Duke of Ferrara to warn his son about writers whom 'love or fear, make . . . partiall', and it was part of his dedication to the profession of letters in *Micro-cynicon* and *The Black Book* not to be such a writer himself. So essential to his nature was his inclination to realism, and so strong this tendency not to be a writer whom 'love or fear', or, in fact, to the extent of art's power to conceal, his personal principles, made 'partiall', that even in *The Phoenix* and *Your Five Gallants*, plays in which he indulged in bald preachments, the ironies and paradoxes of life as seen through the eyes of others are frequently preserved with all fidelity. When the groom has furnished his thumb-nail sketch of Tangle, the 'Law-worme, that eates holes in poor me[n]s causes', Phoenix asks wonderingly, '. . . but doe you know him to be a Knave, and will lodge him?', whereupon the groom replies drily,

Your worship begins to talke idlely, your bed shall be made presently: if we should not lodge knaves, I wonder how we should bee able to live honestlye. Are there honest men enough thinke you in a Terme time to fill all the Innes in the towne . . . ?[7]

The same kind of appeal to economic pragmatism characterizes the defence presented by Furtivo, one of Falso's thieves, when he is going through a form of trial in Act III;[8] and in *Your Five Gallants*, Pursenet is allowed to provide a rationale for his impudence:

> . . . I have learnt these principles:
> Stoope thou toth' world, 'twill on thy bosome tread,
> It stoopes to thee, if thou advance thy head.
> The minde beeing farre more excellent then fate,
> Tis fit our minde then be above our state;
> Why should I write my extremities in my brow,
> To make them loath me, that respect me now.
> If every man were in his courses knowne,
> Legs that now honor him, might spurne him downe.
> To conclude, nothing seemes as it is but honesty,
> & that makes it so little regarded amongst us.[9]

I have said that Middleton's sensitivity to life's incongruities, and his inclination not to see effects without seeing at the same time, and with equal clarity, the causes which lie behind them,[10] are the aspects of his early outlook which predict the power of characterization to which he attained in later plays. In *The Phoenix* Proditor is represented as an unworthy member of the human race—a menace to society; but there is as little attempt to educe the original causes of his vicious proclivities as there is to explain the factors which have given rise to the virtue of, say, Fidelio's mother or Falso's niece. This kind of black and white dichotomy

---

[7] I. sig. B3ᵛ (Bullen: I, 119).
[8] See sig. G[1]ᵛ (Bullen: I, 171-2).
[9] III. sig. E[1]ᵛ (Bullen: III, 181).
[10] There is one notable exception to this rule. Fontinell and Lazarillo are patently in large part mere caricatures embodying received opinions about Frenchmen and Spaniards, in much the same way, though not with such good humour because not for the same purpose, as Shakespeare's Fluellen, Macmorris, and Jamy represent contemporary generalizations about the Welsh, Irish, and Scotch in *Henry V*. However natural and justifiable it may be that an Elizabethan gentleman should entertain such sentiments, Middleton's contempt for Frenchmen and distrust of Spaniards must be regarded as chinks in his armour of dispassionate objectivity. One might say that his objectivity was limited by his patriotism. The projected marriage of Prince Charles to the Spanish Infanta provoked his most conspicuous submission to this attitude: *A Game at Chess*.

is rare even in these early plays, and in the later ones, while a few of the characters in the minor plots are slightly developed, there are no unvindicated Uriah Heeps among the protagonists. The remarkable power of character portrayal, and the equal distribution of sympathy which we find in such later plays as *A Fair Quarrel, Women Beware Women,* and *The Changeling* are correlative, and they spring directly from Middleton's early interest in the theme of appearance versus reality. That theme is subsumed in his dramatic technique, it is an important aspect of his realism, and it is the key to his thematic expression.

Casual comments upon the world of appearances are pervasive in the early plays. Speaking of Maria in *The Family of Love,* Gerardine says, 'Shees truely vertuous', and Lipsalve replies, 'Tut man outward apparance is no authentick instance of the inward desires. . . .'[11] In *Your Five Gallants* Goldstone has required his man to prepare counterfeits to substitute for the silver tavern-beakers which he means to steal from the Mitre; when he asks whether the forgery has been skilfully performed, he is answered as follows:

> You shall be judge sir. Here be the Taverne Beakers,
> And here peepe out the fine Alchimy knaves,
> looking like, wel sir, most of our Gallants,
> that seeme what they are not.[12]

Such allusions attest frequently to Middleton's awareness of man's facility for the deception of others and readiness to dissemble with himself; it is this awareness that suggests the several avenues of retreat which he found from the direct praise and censure of *The Phoenix*. I have mentioned the intimative mode of thematic expression which he attempted in the plot and character *montage* of *Blurt Master-Constable,* and the ironic guise for authorial comment with which he also experimented in that play.[13] In the almost exclusive use[14] and progressive refinement of the latter device Middleton's natural tendency toward a wide, all-inclusive, objective, and balanced view of the human condition was reinforced and lent impetus. A significant comparison, in this

---

[11] I. sig. [A4]ᵛ (Bullen: III, 20).
[12] II. sig. [C4]ᵛ (Bullen: III, 163).
[13] See above, p. 22.
[14] I have referred to the exceptions in *The Phoenix, Your Five Gallants, A Fair Quarrel,* and *The Old Law* in Chapter III.

regard, can be made between the speech of Fitsgrave which I have quoted in Appendix B,[15] and that of Pursenet on page 41. Both deal with the same subject, and even employ the same image of the forehead; but the former, in the mouth of a virtuous character, amounts to a diatribe, while the latter achieves at least the semblance of an illusion of artistic detachment by being veiled in plausibility and spoken by an arrant thief. Another point must be noted. In Pursenet's speech the thief is allowed to enunciate what was for Middleton an eternal verity—'nothing seemes as it is but honesty': a repetition of the answer to the tacit question— what is real?—expressed in precisely the same context in the lines ('None for...'), lacking an authorial mask, which I have quoted on page 39—an excerpt from Penitent Brothel's speech extolling the virtuous life for the edification of Mistress Harebrain. It is fundamental to an understanding of Middleton to see that allowing the vicious to have logical bases for their actions and ways of life, and even to be in possession of universal truths, was a habit which he fell into naturally: it has implications which go beyond the mere creation of an artistic illusion. Moreover, it is necessary to see this habit in its germinal state in these early plays, because by the time we come to such a play as *Anything for a Quiet Life*, Middleton's tendency to reproduce scenes from life uncoloured by personal bias is so fully realized, and his mode of thematic expression so intimative, that its didactic undercurrents, powerful as they are, may be missed altogether. It is this habit which goes far to explain the appearance of authorial neutrality in Middleton's work. So insistent is the expectation that an author must, like Marston in *The Malcontent* or Jonson in his satires, use the drama to foist off his opinions and prejudices in some obvious way, that Middleton's failure to do so has won him a reputation among those who know him only for his latest work for having been unsympathetic, 'coldly' detached, and opinionless.

The truth is that Middleton was not by nature a mere carping social critic, and he was not a pharisee wallowing in 'the pessimistic spirit of the time'. Middleton was ready to concede, indeed anxious to demonstrate, that whether he makes use of it or not, every man at least has access to the key to his own salvation; for this reason the ironic guise I have been describing was not entirely ironic, nor entirely a guise. His experiments with direct

[15] The soliloquy on 'impudence' in *Your Five Gallants*.

statement in *The Phoenix*, and with a kind of modified direct statement in *Your Five Gallants*, are the antithesis of the indirect modes of thematic expression which are far more characteristic of his dramatic writing, and which, presumably, he found more aesthetically satisfying. In a similar way, it was not in accord with his basic philanthropy to produce an unrelievedly bad character such as Proditor, or to conceive of an individual who was beyond redemption through self-reformation.

Concomitant with Middleton's faith in the operation of universal justice is his affirmation of an innate ability in man to respond, sooner or later, to its directing influences. He did not undertake to damn sinners; he was satisfied simply to repudiate sin, by revealing, ever more dispassionately, its ugliness. It is Middleton's idea, even in these early plays, that justice is essentially a teacher, and not an executioner. The justice which the new Duke of Ferrara metes out at the end of *The Phoenix* is consistent with the lesson in Quieto's testimonial in that play, and the country wench's father's in *Michaelmas Term*: Proditor is permanently banished, '. . . the rest are under reformation, and therefore under pardon.'[16]

In other words, Middleton's justice is hardly distinguishable from his theme of 'apprenticeship to life': the sanctions it imposes on the refractory are both poetic and mnemonic in nature. The cases of Glister, Purge, Lipsalve, and Gudgeon in *The Family of Love*, of Quomodo and Lethe in *Michaelmas Term*, and of Violetta, Lazarillo, and Curvetto in *Blurt Master-Constable*, are all illustrative of this point. In *Your Five Gallants* Middleton combined justice with the theme of appearance versus reality in an interesting experiment in stagecraft.[17] Throughout the play, until the last scene, the five iniquitous gallants masquerade successfully as respectable men. In the last scene, the deception is compounded and reversed: the gallants are presented to the wealthy young orphan, whom each of them hopes to marry, in a formal masque which Fitsgrave has so arranged that they think they appear in a flattering light, whereas in fact their true viciousness is revealed. Their disposition to parasitize their fellow men—'a small mist | Will dazle a fooles eye, and thats the world'—and to hold the

---

[16] V. sig. [14]ᵛ (Bullen: I, 205).
[17] See below, pp. 55–56.

'sober and continent' part of society in contempt is continually emphasized in their dialogue; the dénouement proclaims that such attitudes cannot be held with impunity.

The infallibility of a justice which is insistently disposed to correct, rather than merely to exact 'an eye for an eye', is a constant in Middleton's dramatic writing. Nowhere is this cornerstone of his philosophical synthesis, and his attendant belief that every man must both detect the operation of justice and ultimately see its application to his own life, more clearly discernible than in *A Mad World, My Masters*. The central figure of this play is Follywit, a young rake-hell who brags to his companions of being completely inured to a criminal way of life:

... now I'me quite ... blowne into light colours, let out othes by th'minute, sit up late till it bee early, drinke drunke till I am sober, sincke downe dead in a Taverne, and rise in a Tabacco-shop. Her's a transformation: I was wont yet to pitie the simple, and leave e'm some money. Sl'id, now I gull e'm without conscience. I goe without order, sweare without number, gull without mercie, & drinke without measure.[18]

Follywit's awareness of his own ugliness is implicit in the unglamorous idiom of his bragging, but he is obstinate: in order to enjoy his inheritance before the death of his grandfather, Sir Bounteous Progress, he hoaxes and robs the pretentious old man. In the dénouement he feels the touch of nemesis when he learns that the 'virgin' whom he has wooed and married is his grandfather's former mistress, Frank Gullman; Sir Bounteous observes, '... this makes amends for all. ... Who lives by cunning marke it, his fates cast, | When he has guld all, then is himselfe the last.'[19] The point that is really significant about this in regard to Middleton's philosophical outlook is that Follywit has all the while been aware of the forces of justice which bring about his own embarrassment, but has failed to mark his own susceptibility to their sanctions. In Act III he actually enunciates universal equity as a principle, but only to extenuate his crimes against his grandfather:

... I am sure my Grandsire nere got his money worse in his life, then I got it from him. If ever he did cozen the simple, why I was borne to

[18] I. sig. A2 (Bullen: III, 254).
[19] V. sigs. I[1]ᵛ and [I2] (Bullen: III, 357 and 358). The same general conclusion is reached by Hoard at the end of *A Trick to Catch the Old One*. See below, p. 82.

revenge their quarrell; if ever oppresse the widdow? I, a fatherles child have done as much for him; and so tis through the world either in jest or earnest. Let the userer looke for't, for craft recoyles in the end, like an overcharg'd musket, and maymes the very hand that puts fire too't; there needs no more but a Usurers owne blow to strike him from hence to hell, twil set him forward with a vengeance. . . .[20]

In the dramatic situation of Follywit we see the implications of Middleton's habit of assigning to men living in a state of iniquity, knowledge of universal truths, and the power of reasoning from them, which go beyond the mere desire to provide a mask for authorial comment. In Middleton's view, it was possible for a man to respond favourably to the directing influences of universal justice either with great resolution, like Phoenix and Fitsgrave, or by conformity, like Quieto and the country wench's father; or it was possible to ignore them, either flagrantly, like Quomodo and the five gallants, or blindly, like Follywit; but it was impossible for a man to remain for ever ignorant of their existence, or to escape the responsibilities of that knowledge, once gained. When Douglas Bush referred to an aspect of Platonic thought which inheres in the ethics of Milton's poems, he might equally well have had in mind an underlying precept of Middleton's drama: 'If one may venture, in these days of psychological laboratories when moral responsibility has been shifted to defective glands, to recall again the naive ideas of ancient thinkers, the kernel of the matter is that reason, the highest and most human of human faculties, should control the irrational passions and appetites.'[21]

Like Milton too, Middleton was a great lover of individual liberty, and this humanistic predilection no doubt played a large part in producing the balanced and objective outlook which his dramatic microcosms increasingly reveal. At the same time it must be noted that in regard to sociological questions Middleton's liberalism was considerably 'advanced', and it is rather surprising, in view of this, that he so successfully avoided the pitfall of zealotry. In several of these early plays we find, for example, his repudiations of artificial class barriers; and yet Middleton was not an enemy of the aristocracy, or of any other class; nor was he

[20] Sig. E3ᵛ (Bullen: III, 309).
[21] *The Renaissance and English Humanism* (Toronto, 1962), pp. 117–18. See below, p. 89, n. 19.

MIDDLETON'S EARLY DRAMA   47

opposed to the class system of social organization itself, for that matter. Yet these deliberate remarks—like some of his other incidental comments upon a man-made world of appearances, more or less fortuitous with respect to plot or character development—make it clear that he was intolerant of the humbug in the social structure. I have mentioned his specific contempt for 'hundred-pound knights'. One may also note two statements which are directed, in general terms, against criteria for class distinctions which do not arise from spiritual ideals of moral excellence, but are, on the contrary, merely formal and materialistic. These statements are complementary in a sense, emanating in their dramatic contexts from opposite ends of the social scale, and they provide another illustration of the over-all balance in Middleton's work. In *The Phoenix* Fidelio has an idea of what is socially appropriate which, in one of the nobility, must be regarded as remarkably devoid of class prejudice. In Act I he tells his fiancée of his misgivings about the sea-captain's suitability as a husband for his widowed mother, and he refuses, significantly, to have his meaning misunderstood:

Fid. . . . that marriage, knew nothing of my minde,
It never flourisht in any part of my affection.
Neece. Me thinkes sha's much disgrac'd herselfe.
Fid. Nothing so: if he be good & wil abide the touch, a Captaine may marrie a Lady, if hee can saile into her good will.[22]

That enlightened views about social arrangements are not the special preserve of a cultivated aristocrat, in Middleton's dramatic world, is shown by the apprentice in *The Family of Love*, who applies a Christian teaching to the worldly pragmatism of his mistress:

Club. . . . but what am I then, that does all the drudgerye in your House?
Mi[stress] Pur[ge] Thart born to't! Why boy, I can show thy Indentures. Thou giv'st no other milke: wee know how to use all i'theyr kinde.
Club. Yare my better in Barke and Rhyne, but in pith and substance I may compare with you: y'are above me in flesh mistrisse, and thers your boast, but in my tother part, we are all one before God.[23]

[22] Sig. [A4]ᵛ (Bullen: I, 110).
[23] III. sig. [D4]–[D4]ᵛ (Bullen: III, 56–7).

The proof that Middleton's attribution of wisdom to an apprentice was not merely a whim of the moment lies in the fact that he uses the humble Club as one of his spokesmen elsewhere in the play. In Act I, for example, it is Club who delivers a lecture on the subject of 'swearing', the cumulative parallel structure of which came to be one of Middleton's favourite means of obtaining a kind of sardonic emphasis:

Ther's nothing mistrisse that is sworne out of date that returnes; their first oath in times past was by the Masse. And that they have sworne quite away. Then came they to their Fayth, as by my Faith t'is so. That in a short tyme was sworn away too, for no man beleeves now more then a sees. Then they swore by their honesties, and that Mistrisse you know is sworn quite away. After their honestyes was gone, then came they to their Gentilitie, and swore, as they were Gentlemen, and their Gentilitie they swore away so fast, that they had almost sworne away all the Aunceint Gentrie out of the Land, which indeede are scarce mist, for that Yeomen and Farmars Sonnes, with the helpe of a few welchmen, have undertooke to supplie their places. That at the last they came to Silver, and their Oath was, by the Crosse of this silver, and swore so fast uppon that, that now they have scarce left them a Crosse for to Sweare by.[24]

Middleton did not set himself against the system, but against the false values and sham within the system; and when he took exception to a religious group or social class or profession, it was because of some hypocrisy or notorious abuse attributable to it. In *A Mad World, My Masters* Harebrain is told that his wife 'Fondly and wilfully ... retaines that thought, | That every sinne is dambd', and something of Middleton's general attitude is implicit in the sarcasm of his reply:

Oh fie, fie, wife! ... for shame be converted: theres a diabalocall opinion indeed; then you may think that usury were dambd: you're a fine merchant yfaith; or briberie? you know the law well; or sloth? would some of the Clergy heard you yfaith; or pride? you come at Court; or gluttony? you're not worthie to dine at an Aldermans table.[25]

There is another aspect of the objectivity and balance of Middleton's view of which it is important to note the first indications in these early plays. From the evidence adduced so

---

[24] Sig. B[1]ᵛ (Bullen: III, 22–3).   [25] I. sig. B2ᵛ (Bullen: III, 267).

far, we have seen that Middleton certainly hated sin; but we have also seen what is equally clear and much more remarkable: that he did not hate sinners. Yet in an essay on the collaboration of Middleton and William Rowley, an essay that has enjoyed widespread acceptance for some seventy years,[26] the author attempts to persuade the reader that Rowley's position in the collaboration was an influential one by arguing that Middleton was not only a misanthropist, but a misogynist as well. I hope that the foregoing discussion will have shown that Middleton was much more inclined to be a philanthropist than the reverse, and I believe that the suggestion that he was less favourably disposed towards women than men was a prejudiced and hasty generalization. At least it is a suggestion which cannot be sustained on the evidence of Middleton's writings. Certainly it must be conceded that the scrupulous honesty of Middleton's scrutiny of a sinful world was not compromised or obscured by considerations of chivalry. If there was a 'blind spot' in his realism, it was patriotism; his treatment of Fontinell and Violetta, and Gerardine and Maria, shows that he was inclined to be very suspicious of other romantic ideals. Consequently, he was just as sensitive to the ugliness of sin in women as he was sensitive to the ugliness of sin in men, and he was just as outspoken about it. The sentiments and imagery of such observations as the following may well be found indelicate, and perhaps offensive:

Lip[salve] ... women have sharp faulcons eyes, and can soare aloft, but keepe them like Faulcons from flesh and they soone stoope to a gawdy lure.[27]

Curtiz[an] ... sir Bounteous Progress: hee's my keeper in deed, but ther's many a peece of venison stolne that my keeper wots not on; theres no parke kept so warily, but looses flesh one time or other; and no woman kept so privately, but may watch advantage to make the best of her pleasure: and in common reason one keeper cannot be enough for so proud a parke as a woman.[28]

In fairness to Middleton, however, it must be noted that his descriptions of weakness and sin in men are no less blunt, and are characterized by imagery which is no more prepossessing. In

[26] See below, p. 207, n. 5.
[27] *The Family of Love*, I. sig. [A4]ᵛ (Bullen: III, 20).
[28] *A Mad World, My Masters*, I. sig. [A4] (Bullen: III, 259).

Michaelmas Term, for example, when Quomodo's honest wife Thomasine[29] receives a letter containing an indecent proposal from Andrew Lethe, a debauched lump of affectation, she says,

> ... —a base proud knave—a has forgot how he came up, & brought two of his countrie men to give their words to my husband for a sute of greene Karsey, a has forgot all this. And how does hee appeare to me, when his white Sattin suttes on, but like a Magot crept out of a Nutshell, a faire bodie and a foule necke. Those partes that are covered of him, lookes indifferent well, because we cannot see e'm; else for all his clensing, pruning and paring, hee's not worthy a Brokers Daughter, and so tell him.[30]

Together with this further comment upon the world of appearances, Mistress Glister's admonition of the infatuated Maria in *The Family of Love* is worthy of remark:

> No marvell sure you should regard these men with such reverend opinion, ther's few good faces, and fewer graces in any of them ... and for their behaviour, wit and discourse (except some few that are travelled) it is as imperfectious and silly, as your Schollers new come from the University. By this light I thinke we loose part of our happinesse when we make these weathercocks our equalls.[31]

No writer has held women in higher regard than did the author of *The Ghost of Lucrece*, and his ideal of womanhood lost nothing in noble stature by being defined in the same terms as his ideal of manhood. On the contrary, as Middleton's first ideal of womanhood was to be remoulded and matured through his dedication to realism, so by virtue of the fact that he rejected a double standard and made no distinction between men and women as movers in life, the quality of that reformed ideal was to be more wholesome and meaningful. The thing that is truly remarkable about Middleton in this regard was indicated by Professor Ellis-Fermor with admirable precision when she said, 'He is one of the few ... who is not so obsessed with the differences between the sexes as to be

---

[29] When Quomodo pretends to die in order to test his family's loyalty, Thomasine immediately offers herself to Easy, with whom she has always secretly sympathized, and by marrying him helps him to regain his lost estate. I suspect that making her his namesake was Middleton's way of having a joke with himself about the considerable *deus ex machina* which he was forced to lower in order to secure his hero's happy issue from Quomodo's toils.

[30] II. sig. C3^v (Bullen: I, 246).

[31] II. sig. C2 (Bullen: III, 37).

MIDDLETON'S EARLY DRAMA   51

unable to see the likenesses.'[32] Middleton was not so much a champion of women's rights as he was a proponent of the equality of the sexes, and the emphasis of that equality was not upon rights but upon obligations. He credited women with having equal moral responsibility with men, and he did not subscribe to the vain distinction implied in the male-invented myth of female 'frailty'.

Some of the important structural characteristics of the early plays have already been mentioned in connection with Middleton's themes and artistic point of view. The deliberately intimative mode of thematic expression in *Blurt Master-Constable* is enough in itself to show that he was the kind of writer that E. M. Forster had in mind when he wrote, '. . . the artist is not a bricklayer at all, but a horseman, whose business it is to catch Pegasus at once, not to practise for him by mounting tamer colts.' Other features of the construction of the plays in this first group, interesting in themselves as experiments in stagecraft, and noteworthy because they become part of Middleton's dramaturgical idiom, are briefly referred to in the following notes.

Blurt Master-Constable

The last half of Act III is taken up by a lecture delivered by Lazarillo to a group of city wives intent upon learning how to gain the upper hand over their husbands. The 'putting to school' of idle and mischievously-inclined persons to some such perverse tutor as Lazarillo was a type of scene which Middleton wrote several times to obtain sardonic effects. The courtesan in *A Mad World, My Masters* gives private tuition, in the same subject as that dealt with by Lazarillo, to Mistress Harebrain.[33] An example in a later play is the 'roaring' lesson which takes up nearly the whole of Act IV of *A Fair Quarrel*.

The Phoenix

Toward the end of Act II Tangle pays a call upon Justice Falso for the purpose of obtaining the latter's 'commendation' of a thief who has robbed a church. The reunion of these two old sharpers becomes the occasion for the performance of something in the

[32] *The Jacobean Drama*, p. 150.   [33] See Bullen, III, 263-7.

nature of a ritual dance. As soon as they have greeted each other, Falso calls for 'Rapier and Dagger foyles'. When these are brought, he and Tangle put them to use in a 'law-bout'. This combines the thrust and parry of a stylized fencing match with a verbal duel in legal jargon which tests the combatants' dexterity in the use of the 'weapons' of the law. The battle concludes as follows:

Tang. Now followes a writ of execution, a *Capias ut Legatum*, gives you a wound mortall, trippes up your heeles, and layes you ith Counter.
Fals. O Villaine!
Tang. I crie your worship heartily mercie sir.
I thought we had beene in Lawe together, *Adversarius contra adversarium* by my troth.
Fals. Oh! reach me thy hand. I nere had such an overthrowe in my life.[34]

Although there may have been few who connected its didactic significance with Phoenix's declamation on the deplorable abuse of law in Act I,[35] there can be little doubt but that this ingenious scene gave full satisfaction to an Elizabethan theatre audience. Middleton's love of allegory—a love which he was to indulge to the full in *A Game at Chess*—is another distinct manifestation of his consuming interest in the theme of appearance versus reality.

The Family of Love

When W. D. Dunkel described the similarities between this play and the underplot of *A Fair Quarrel*,[36] he did not mention that both illustrate Middleton's readiness to invent a jargon. The 'magic words' used by Lipsalve and Gudgeon before their poetic discomfiture in Act III are of the same substance as the 'roaring' cant studied by Chaugh and Trimtram in Act IV of *A Fair Quarrel*:

Lip. ... well I must venter: *Clogmathos*.
Gud. My Cue: *Clogmathathos*.

[34] Sig. F3 (Bullen: I, 163).
[35] See above, p. 27.
[36] See W. D. Dunkel's 'Did not Rowley merely Revise Middleton?', *PMLA*, XLVIII (Sept. 1933), 799–800.

Lip.	My Cue: *Garrazin.*
Gud.	*Garragas.*
Lip.	*Garrazinos.*
Gud.	*Ton tetuphon.*
Lip.	*Tes tetuphes.*
Ambo.	With a *Whirley Twinos.*—they lash one another.[37]

Earlier I have described *Blurt Master-Constable* as a travesty of romantic love, and indicated that *Romeo and Juliet* may have been Middleton's special target. I have also mentioned that the Gerardine–Maria plot in *The Family of Love*, with its carnality cloaked in fine words, is another travesty of exactly the same kind; but it is more obvious here that Middleton had *Romeo and Juliet* especially in mind.[38] The corollary of which Middleton's realism was often to demand a strong expression throughout his career was a rejection of romanticism and, what seemed to him to be, its unavoidable attendant hypocrisy.[39]

Michaelmas Term

The most important artistic feature of this play is the rapport which Middleton sets up between the experiences of the two innocents, Easy and the country wench. This is accomplished, as in *Blurt Master-Constable*, by a deliberate juxtaposing or *montage* of scenes. A notable sequence, by way of example, is Shortyard's fleecing of Easy, at the beginning of Act II, following immediately after Hellgill's corruption of the country wench, at the end of Act I. The theme of appearance versus reality is given emphasis by another deliberate parallel. The country wench and Andrew Lethe both come to the city and are so transformed by it that the wench's father and Lethe's mother fail to recognize their children and take service with them as menials.

Another noteworthy feature of the play is its masque-like

---

[37] Sig. E2ᵛ (Bullen: III, 64–5).
[38] The clues have been noted by W. J. Olive in 'Imitation of Shakespeare in Middleton's *Family of Love*', *Philological Quarterly*, XXIX (Jan. 1950), 75–8.
[39] One is reminded that Middleton had once chosen Shakespeare for his model in another genre (see above, pp. 7–8). The antipathetic moods of the two poems on Lucrece give promise that Middleton would be disposed to be suspicious and critical of Shakespeare's motives for the future, and they foreshadow the incompatibility of Middleton's realism and Shakespeare's romance.

induction involving the four terms. It includes a dumb show for which the stage directions are as follows:

Musicke playing { *Enter the other 3. Termes, the first bringing in a fellowe poore, which the other 2. advanceth giving him rich Apparell, a page, and a pandar. Exit.*[40]

This action shows the lamb, so to speak, being prepared for the slaughter which will be effected in due course by Michaelmas Term. In the play proper, the 'fellowe poore' whom two of the terms 'advanceth' is most readily identified as Andrew Lethe. The characteristics of Michaelmas Term are merged in the predatory disposition of Quomodo.

Like *Blurt Master-Constable*, *The Phoenix*, and *The Family of Love*, *Michaelmas Term* concludes with a trial scene.

A Mad World, My Masters

Near the beginning of Act IV a succubus, in the shape of Mistress Harebrain, comes to torment Penitent Brothel when he is attempting to purge himself of his 'deadly follies' and 'adulterous motions'. The scenes in Acts II and III of *The Family of Love* in which Doctor Glister dupes the two lechers, Lipsalve and Gudgeon, by pretending to be able to conjure up the spirit of Mistress Purge, are evidence of Middleton's personal contempt for necromancy. Still the succubus scene in *A Mad World, My Masters* shows that he recognized that the subject had a strong fascination for the general public. He was to ridicule that fascination later with a burlesque of the 'powers of darkness' in *The Witch*.

A Mad World, My Masters is full of the elaborate stratagems of which Middleton was to become so prolific an inventor, and nowhere is this gift for the conception and concise execution of a complex sequence of events better exemplified than in Act V, where Follywit and his companions, disguised as players, visit Sir Bounteous Progress and perform *The Slip*.

Your Five Gallants

Despite its episodic structure, *Your Five Gallants* is a unified and coherent play. Its unity derives from the mutual interest of Fitsgrave and the gallants in Katherine, the wealthy orphan; but

[40] Sig. A2ᵛ (Bullen: I, 216).

Middleton's early confidence with his medium is revealed by the means he devised to make the diverse episodes of the play cohere. One of these was the introduction and periodical reintroduction of certain properties as consolidating threads. Near the end of Act I, for example, Fitsgrave gives Katherine a pearl necklace, which is stolen shortly afterwards and turned over to Pursenet; in Act II Pursenet gives the necklace to his mistress, who passes it on to Tailby, with whom she is infatuated; in Act III Pursenet regains the necklace by robbing Tailby; in Act IV, Pursenet having accidentally dropped it, Goldstone finds the necklace, but it passes back to Pursenet, who pawns it with Frippery; the necklace is returned to Katherine in Act V— Frippery presents it to her during a masque. Fitsgrave's cloak and a precious stone are used in the same way, but less extensively. Middleton's further conscious efforts to keep the play coherent can be seen in his periodical reassembling of the principals. All the gallants except Frippery are first seen together in an abbreviated form of induction. In the play proper, they first appear as a group at Katherine's interview with her suitors in Act I. Their next forgathering, at the beginning of Act II, is occasioned by the desire of Mistress Newcut, a promiscuous city wife, to find a consort at Primero's bawdy house:

Pri.   You see your old spy-hole yonder. Take your stand. Please your owne eye. Ile worke it so, the Gallants shall present themselves before you, and in the most conspicuous fashion.[41]

At the end of Act IV, they are brought together again for a quarrel over their grievances with one another. This concludes with their reconciliation, and Goldstone's proposal of a masque provides the pretext for their final assemblage in Act V.

Of the three outstanding experiments in allegory in this first group of plays—the duel in *The Phoenix*, the masque-induction which introduces the motif of *Michaelmas Term*, and the masque which is the climax of *Your Five Gallants*—the last is the most elaborate. At the end of Act IV Goldstone sues to Fitsgrave, who is disguised as a scholar, as follows:

... now a little of thy braine for a device to present us firme, which wee shall never bee able to do our selves thou knowst that; and with a kind of speech wherein thou mayst express what gallants are, bravely.[42]

[41] Sig. B3ᵛ (Bullen: III, 145).   [42] Sig. H3 (Bullen: III, 228).

Fitsgrave duly invents a fitting emblem and Latin motto for each, obtains the assistance of some friends, and enlists the secret help of the gallants' mistresses by telling them that their consorts want to abandon them for the wealthy Katherine. He even finds a part for Pursenet's boy:

... and to assist them the better, Pursenets boy that little pretious pick-pocket, has a compend[i]ous speech in lattin, and like a Mercury presents their their [sic] dispositions more liberally.[43]

The stage directions for the masque indicate the formal manner in which the revelations are to be made:

Enter the maske, thus ordered. A torchbearer, a sheeld-boy, then a masker, so throughout, then the sheeld boyes fall at one end, the torchbearers at the other, the maskers ith middle. The torchbearers are the five gentlemen [Fitsgrave's accomplices]; *the sheeld boies the whores in boies apparrel; the maskers the five Gallants; they bow to her* [Katherine]; *she rises and shewes the like; they dance but first deliver the sheeldes* [bearing the revelatory emblems and mottoes] *up; shee reades.*[44]

[43] V. sig. I[1] (Bullen: III, 235).   [44] V. sig. I2ᵛ (Bullen: III, 241).

PART TWO
AN INTEREST IN CHARACTER

A Trick to Catch the Old One
The Roaring Girl
A Chaste Maid in Cheapside
No Wit, No Help Like a Woman's
More Dissemblers Besides Women

V

MORE DISSEMBLERS BESIDES WOMEN

O F the five plays, *A Trick to Catch the Old One*, *The Roaring Girl*, *A Chaste Maid in Cheapside*, *No Wit, No Help Like a Woman's*, and *More Dissemblers Besides Women*, the last provides the best illustration of a change in emphasis in Middleton's writing, and of the change in his perspective which that new emphasis implies. In the plays already considered Middleton's curiosity about the people who commit sins is just as much in evidence as his preoccupation with sin itself; but while his knowledge of the external features of evil was soon remarkably detailed, his understanding of its human agency was limited to relationships between observable behaviour and surface conditions of life, and his ideals of virtue were incompletely defined. The works with which the present part of this study are concerned show the growing together of Middleton's curiosity about people and his interest in morality, and the supplementation of his active interest in external cause-effect relationships by a more mature focus on the internal workings of the mind. In the present plays Middleton places more emphasis on the nature of positive virtue, and we find him looking below the surface of environment to discover the sources of outward behaviour, to character.

There are six principals in *More Dissemblers Besides Women*—three men: the Cardinal of Milan, his nephew Lactantio, and a general named Andrugio; and three women: the Duchess of Milan; an unmarried young lady, Aurelia; and Lactantio's mistress. All six are dissemblers in one way or another; and all, except the first and last, are, distinctly, variations or significant progressions on characters who make their appearances in the group of plays already discussed.

Aurelia is beloved of the manly soldier Andrugio, a more sympathetic counterpart of Camillo, the spurned lover of Violetta in *Blurt Master-Constable*. She has also been wooed, with her father's approval, by the governor of the fort; but Aurelia, like Violetta, is promiscuously inclined, and prefers the attentions of the voluptuous Lactantio. In the opening scene, after a maidenly, 'You make me blush Sir', reminiscent of Maria in *The Family of Love*, she agrees, saying that 'the power of Love commands' her, to Lactantio's proposal that she should come to his rooms disguised as a man. Apparently she is unaware that she has a rival in Lactantio's present mistress, who is known only as 'Page'—she has assumed that disguise to facilitate her frequenting of Lactantio's quarters in the Cardinal's palace. However, Aurelia gets no farther with carrying out Lactantio's instructions than the donning of her disguise. Her servant betrays her plans, and her father, pretending a visit to the Cardinal, hastens to disappoint them. He places her forthwith under lock and key in the fort.

In Lactantio are combined the vices of Follywit in *A Mad World, My Masters*, and Fontinell in *Blurt Master-Constable*. Like Follywit, he is greedy and unscrupulous; like Fontinell, a notable lecher. His language in addressing Aurelia early in the play has the same euphuistic character as the wooing language of Fontinell, and the seduction speeches of Gerardine in *The Family of Love*. Of Aurelia's blush he says,

> 'Tis but a star shot from a beauteous cheek,
> It blazes Beauties bounty, and hurts nothing.[1]

and he bids her farewell with the words, 'I shall wither in comforts, till I see thee.' His less poetic speech with his 'page', who has had to report 'I fear Sir I'm with childe', leaves the reader in no doubt about his underlying ugliness:

> I'll ne'r keep such a peece of Touch-wood again,
> And I were rid of thee once. . . .
> Page. If my too much kindness
> Receive your anger onely for reward,
> The harder is my fortune. I must tell you Sir,
> To stir your care up to prevention,
> (Misfortunes must be told as well as blessings)
> When I left all my friends in Mantua,
> For your loves sake alone, then with strange oaths
> You promis'd present marriage.
> Lact. With strange oath's quoth'a?
> They're not so strange to me, I have sworn the same things,
> I am sure forty times over; not so little.[2]

[1] I. p. 3 (Bullen: VI, 379).
[2] III. pp. 30–31 (Bullen: VI, 414–15).

In the first three acts of the play Lactantio is chiefly occupied in preserving a saintly exterior in the presence of his uncle, the Cardinal, upon whom he is completely dependent:

> ... for my Fortunes sake then,
> For I am like to be his onely Heir,
> I must dissemble and appear as fair
> To his opinion, as the brow of Piety,
> As void of all impureness as an Altar.[3]

When Andrugio returns from the wars near the end of Act I, he finds that Aurelia has been placed in the custody of his rival, the governor of the fort. Unaware of her infatuation with Lactantio, he disguises himself and obtains employment as her guard, to help her escape. In the last scene of Act II they converse. She tells him that she has been imprisoned for remaining true to him, and he outlines a plan and takes his leave. Aurelia delivers the soliloquy which ends the act and makes manifest the 'heart of flint' which she has in common with Violetta:

> And after that, farewel sweet Sir for ever.
> A good kinde Gentleman to serve our turn with,
> But not for lasting: I have chose a Stuff
> Will wear out two of him, and one finer too.
> . . . .
> . . . I smile
> To think how I have fitted him with an office;
> His love takes pains to bring our loves [hers and
>   Lactantio's] together,
> Much like your man that labors to get treasure,
> To keep his wife high for anothers pleasure.[4]

The relationships among Lactantio, Aurelia, and Andrugio are the same as those between Fontinell, Violetta, and Camillo in *Blurt Master-Constable*, but Lactantio is not merely a caricature like Fontinell. The significance of his character, and that of Andrugio, in regard to Middleton's maturer view of man, is best seen in relation to Witgood in *A Trick to Catch the Old One*, Philip Twilight in *No Wit, No Help Like a Woman's*, and Allwit in *A Chaste Maid in Cheapside*.[5] The wilful and perverse Aurelia is

---

[3] I. p. 3 (Bullen: VI, 379).   [4] p. 30 (Bullen: VI, 412–13).
[5] See Chapter VI.

a simple extension of Violetta, through Maria in *The Family of Love*;[6] but unlike her predecessors, she is not a chief focus of Middleton's interest—Aurelia's basic purpose in the play is to serve as a foil.[7] In *More Dissemblers Besides Women* the main part of Middleton's attention is devoted to two new kinds of character: the Duchess of Milan, a widow who seven years before the action takes place has promised her dying husband not to remarry, and the Cardinal, her confessor.

The importance that Middleton attached to the moral of the story he was about to tell is made clear by the prominence he gave to the announcement of his theme. The play begins with a song. It is sung by the Duchess, and overheard by Lactantio, who is awaiting the arrival of Aurelia outside the Duchess's lodgings:

<blockquote>
Song

Musick.

To be chaste, is Womans glory,
'Tis her fame and honors story.
Here sits she in Funeral weeds,
Onely bright in vertuous deeds.
Come and read her life and praise,
That singing weeps, and sighing plays.[8]
</blockquote>

Lactantio's ensuing speech is used to emphasize the Duchess's vow—'she has kept the Fort most valiantly'—and to announce a chief eccentricity and preoccupation of the Cardinal:

<blockquote>
... the Lord Cardinal
Wears so severe an eye, so strict and holy,
It not endures the sight of Woman-kinde
About his Lodgings;
Hardly a Matron of Four-score's admitted,
</blockquote>

---

[6] When Aurelia is confined for not falling in with her father's plans for her marriage, she says, 'I would Lactantio | Would seek some means to free me from this place. | 'Tis prisonment enough to be a Maid; | But to be mew'd up too, that case is hard, | As if a toy were kept, by a double guard'—II. p. 27 (Bullen: VI, 409–10); under similar circumstances, Maria exclaims, 'O Sillie men! which seek to keepe in awe | Womens affections, which can know no lawe'—I. sig. A2ᵛ (Bullen: III, 14). Both young women are reacting to parental authority in a conventional way, of course, and neither of their fathers is represented as being a sympathetic or enlightened parent; but although both make an initial pretence of modesty, Aurelia values her virtue no more than a 'toy', and neither of them has any desire to control her animal appetites. See Violetta's speeches on pp. 11 and 15 above.

[7] See below, p. 66, n. 19.

[8] p. 1 (Bullen: VI, [377]).

> Though she be worn to gums, she comes not there,
> To mumble Mattens. All his admiration
> Is plac'd upon the Dutchess; he likes her,
> Because she keeps her vow, and likes not any.[9]

The lives of the Duchess and Cardinal are closely entwined. The Cardinal's celibacy has engendered in him an insensate zeal for sexual abstinence which makes him dote upon the cloistered widowhood of the Duchess. In the first of two important interviews with the Lords of Milan he enjoins them to 'bestow [their] eyes | Upon those abstracts of the Dutchess vertues, | [His] studies ornaments', and goes on to say,

> I make her Constancy
> The holy Mistress of my contemplation.
> Whole volumes have I writ in zealous praise
> Of her eternal vow. I have no power
> To suffer Vertue to go thinly clad,
> I that have ever been in youth, an old man
> To pleasures and to women, and could never love, but pitty 'em,
> And all their momentary frantick follies.

The Lords are then subjected to a verbal encomium, the First Lord's reply to which changes the course of the interview, and establishes the point of departure and direction of the main action of the play, by introducing the specific idea that Middleton was intent upon examining:

> Chaste Sir, the Truth and Justice of her Vow
> To her deceased Lord's able to make poor
> Mans treasury of praises. But methinks
> She that has no temptation set before her,
> Her Vertue has no conquest; then would her constancy
> Shine in the brightest goodness of her glory,
> If she would give admittance, see, and be seen;
> And yet resist, and conquer. There were argument
> For Angles, 'twould out-reach the life of praise
> Set in Mortalities shortness. . . .[10]

The Cardinal takes this challenging rejoinder very much to heart. He forgets himself momentarily and petulantly dares the Lords to use 'all the art, | Temptation, witcheries, sleights, and

[9] I. p. 3 (Bullen: VI, 379).
[10] See I, pp. 3–4 (Bullen: VI, 380–1).

subtleties, | . . . [their] means can practice'. Then he apologizes with the excuse, 'So dear is her white fame to my souls love, | 'Tis an affliction but to hear it question'd; | She's my religious triumph.' The audience is made to understand that the Duchess's seven years' 'constancy' has been strenuously bolstered and fortified by incessant admonitions: in his agitated state of mind, the Cardinal reveals both the intensity of his monomania, and his domineering egotism, in such outbursts as, 'You have put my zeal into a way, my Lord, | I shall not be at peace, till I make perfect; | I'll make her victory harder!' and 'Believe my Judgment, | I never praise in vain, nor ever spent | Opinion idlely, or lost hopes of any, | Where I once plac'd it.'[11]

But the truth about the Cardinal, that 'worthy prelate', as A. W. Ward called him, 'gifted with an eloquence of an extremely unctuous kind', is that his 'Judgment' is remarkably bad. Of his licentious nephew, who has him completely hoodwinked, he says,

> The company of woman is as fearful to him,
> As death to guilty men. I have seen him blush,
> When but a Maid was nam'd. I'm proud of him,
> Heaven be not angry for't.[12]

and adds, ludicrously, but also significantly, 'He's near of kin | In disposition to me.' Filled with self-interested uneasiness at the First Lord's questioning of the perfect firmness and invulnerability of the Duchess's virtue, the Cardinal loses no time in putting her to the suggested test. In I. iii he tells the Duchess that she must re-enter the world to win a 'harder fight', and she agrees—

> . . . I'll come forth
> And show my self to all, the world shall witness
> That like the Sun, my Constancy can look
> On Earth's corruptions, and shine clear it self.[13]

—but before the scene ends, she witnesses the return of the warrior Andrugio, and falls in love with him at first sight.

It is important to note that I. iii is a compressed reproduction of the same general sequence of events as takes place at the beginning of *Blurt Master-Constable*. In a speech addressed to her

[11] See I. p. 5 (Bullen: VI, 381–3).   [12] I. p. 6 (Bullen: VI, 383).
[13] I. pp. 13–14 (Bullen: VI, 392).

maid-servant, prior to her conversation with the Cardinal, the Duchess gives just such an impression of indefectible refinement as does Violetta before Fontinell's arrival on the scene:

> What a contented rest rewards my minde
> For faithfulness; I give it Constancy,
> And it returnes me Peace...
> . . . .
> ... I am arm'd now
> 'Gainst all deserts in man, be't Valor, Wisdom,
> Curtesie, Comeliness, nay, Truth it self,
> Which seldom keeps him company. I commend
> The Vertues highly, as I do an Instrument
> When the Case hangs by th'Wall; but man himself
> Never comes near my heart.[14]

After one look at Andrugio in his martial splendour, she betrays Violetta's same underlying animality:

> I confess I'm mortal,
> There's no defending on't, 'tis cruel flattery
> To make a Lady believe otherways.
> Is not this flesh? Can you drive heat from fire?
> So may you love from this....[15]

These are the similarities which show that in the rough outline of his conception of the character of the Duchess of Milan, Middleton had in mind the same aspect of the theme of appearance versus reality as he had conveyed through his heroine in *Blurt Master-Constable*. But the Duchess is a much rounder, more accomplished study than Violetta, and some important characteristics of Middleton's maturer outlook are revealed in the ways in which she differs from her perverse predecessor. In portraying the Duchess of Milan and her Cardinal, Middleton examined some of his own earlier precepts—held them up to the light, as it were, to inspect them for flaws.

Unlike Violetta, the Duchess is not simply an unmitigated hypocrite. She faces the same situation as Violetta, and makes the same response to it; but by now Middleton had accepted the fact that animal drives are a universal human inheritance, and he had in view a much more realistic definition of virtue than that

[14] I. p. 12 (Bullen: VI, 390-1).   [15] I. p. 16 (Bullen: VI, 395).

which is implicit in the stony, animadverting chastity of the Lucrece of his adolescence. The Duchess's civility is not merely a sentimental romantic veneer—her ideals are Middleton's; but her virtue is insubstantial because it has not been tried under fire. For Middleton, marriage was always one of the most civilized of human institutions. Of it he had made his Phoenix say, 'Thou art the onely and the greatest forme, | That put'st a difference betweene our desires | And the disordered appetites of Beastes';[16] and, beyond the usual commitments of Christian marriage, he seems to have had in mind as the acme of an ideal union of man and woman a monogamy that would be unaffected even by death. In *A Mad World, My Masters* Penitent Brothel admonishes the promiscuously-inclined Mistress Harebrain by saying, 'Shees part a Virgin whom but one man knowes',[17] and in *More Dissemblers Besides Women*, written some ten years later, the last speech of the dying Duke of Milan to his wife contains the same sentiment, with the extended implication, in almost the same words: 'she's part Virgin, who but one man knows.'[18]

Middleton begins his portrayal of the Duchess by making us see that she has made a reasoned acceptance of this ideal, and there is more conviction in her 'How happily | Might woman live, methinks, confin'd within | The knowledge of one Husband!' than in Violetta's purely emotional idealization of the man who would 'knocke at deathes doore for [her] love', and Aurelia's protestation to Lactantio that if he were to die, she would die too, before he could be buried.[19] But while the Duchess is capable of possessing herself of an ideal through a process of reasoning, what happens after she sees Andrugio proves that somewhere in that process there is something wrong; and the flaw, which arises, incidentally, from the same incompleteness of perception as Middleton himself evinced some fifteen years before, in his angry denunciation of Tarquin, is contained in the following speech.

[16] *The Phoenix*, II. sig. [D4]ᵛ (Bullen: I, 146).
[17] IV. sig. G2 (Bullen: III, 330).
[18] II. p. 23 (Bullen: VI, 404).
[19] Aurelia's affected 'Alas Sir, | I should not have the leisure to make Vows, | For dying presently, I should be dead | Before you were laid out', possibly a mocking allusion to the melodramatic conclusion of *Romeo and Juliet*, shows that Middleton intended that his audience should see the Duchess's behaviour in the play in direct relation to Aurelia's. As usual, he wanted them to be aware of the similarities that they might the better appreciate the differences.

MORE DISSEMBLERS BESIDES WOMEN 67

> ... If my vow
> Were yet to make, I would not sleep without it,
> Or make a Faith as perfect to my self
> In resolution, as vow would come to;
> And do as much right so to Constancy,
> As strictness could require. For 'tis our goodness,
> And not our strength that do's it.[20]

Before her emergence from seven years of self-confinement, the Duchess, like the youthful Middleton at Oxford, sees man's animal part only in the abstract; afterwards, she has an immediate, concrete, personal awareness of it, and the rest of her experience in the play teaches her, what years of adult life in London had taught Middleton, that 'goodness' without 'strength' is an empty illusion—that 'goodness', in other words, can only be real when it has gained the power to sustain itself through experience of temptation: savouring it, understanding it, and resisting it.[21] It is typical of Middleton that he should have given it to a distinctly minor character, the First Lord, to introduce this idea into the play, and to the Cardinal, of whom he does not approve, to communicate it to the Duchess.

The Cardinal's speech is marked by a deceptive suavity:

> 'Tis not enough for Tapers to burn bright,
> But to be seen, so to lend others light,
> Yet not impair themselves, their flame as pure,
> As when it shin'd in secret. So t'abide
> Temptations, is the Souls flame truly try'd.[22]

He advocates the First Lord's theory here with the same self-assurance as he has shown previously when boasting of the

---

[20] I. p. 12 (Bullen: VI, 391).
[21] Certain details suggest that Middleton was concerned to make *More Dissemblers Besides Women* comment upon the generalization, 'Frailty, thy name is woman!' In both his interviews with the Lords, the Cardinal, the disclosure of whose own abject, male variety of frailty was one of Middleton's chief interests in the play, shows his acceptance of this notion: in the second, this acceptance is merely implicit in the use of the phrase 'woman's frailty'; but in the first, he says, 'When we finde grace confirm'd, especially | In a creature that's so doubtful as a woman | We'are spirit ravish'd, men of our probation | Feel the Sphears. . . .' When referring to the implications and consequences of a woman's remarriage following the death of her spouse, the Duchess says it 'rather proclaims Desire | Prince of affections, then religious love; | Brings frailty and our weakness into question; | 'Mongst our Male enemies, makes Widows tears, | Rather the cup of laughter then of pity'.
[22] I. p. 13 (Bullen: VI, 392).

Duchess's strict adherence to his own cherished, and diametrically opposed, monastic formula of withdrawal from the world—

> Sh'as kept her vow so strictly and as chaste
> As everlasting life is kept for Vertue,
> Ev'n from the sight of men, to make her oath
> As uncorrupt as th'honor of a Virgin
> That must be strict in thought, or else that title,
> Like one of Frailties ruines, shrinks to dust.[23]

But although the Duchess is deceived, the audience is not. They have heard the Cardinal say that he has 'ever been in youth, an old man | To pleasures and to women', and they realize that concern for his reputation, and not wisdom, accounts for the ardour with which he becomes a traitor to his own principle, and the champion of another, for belief in the efficacy of which he has no more basis in personal experience than his charge. Up to the moment when the Duchess comes face to face with life, she and the Cardinal, whose asceticism has gained him nothing but a grotesque pride in his own celibacy, have it in common that their espousals of moral principles have had no empirical foundations.

The Duchess tells the Cardinal of her fall from grace at their next meeting. She has concluded, beforehand, that 'an ill cause had need of . . . much art', and decided that by telling him it is his own beloved nephew—whom in reality she holds in utter contempt—that she dotes upon, she will induce him to accept her revelation, and at the same time make a 'fair way', that is, create a mask, for her love to Andrugio—without 'suspect' and 'reprehension'. The Cardinal's reception of her 'Sir, I'm in love', that 'spightful ill', as he calls it, which shatters his world, is more explosive than the Duchess anticipated, however. He pours out his indignation

> . . . Have I approved
> Your constancy for this, call'd your Faith noble,
> Writ volumes of your victories and vertues?
> I have undone my judgment, lost my praises,
> Blemish'd the truth of my opinion![24]

and demands that he should be given 'the man', that he may 'pour him out | To all contempt and curses'. For a time it appears that the Cardinal will never swallow the Duchess's 'red herring'—

[23] I. p. 4 (Bullen: VI, 381).   [24] II. p. 24 (Bullen: VI, 405).

although she assures him that Lactantio has been 'innocent' of any overtures to her, his injured vanity makes him ready to condemn his nephew out of hand:

> He that I lov'd so dearly, does he wear
> Such killing poyson in his eye to sanctity?
> He has undone himself for ever by't,
> Has lost a friend of me, and a more sure one.
> Farewel all natural pitty. Though my affection
> Could hardly spare him from my sight an hour,
> I'll lose him now eternally. . . .[25]

He determines that Lactantio 'shall straight to Rome'.

The scene which follows this interview serves as prelude to the action which conveys the full force of the statement in the play's title. It consists of a single speech—a soliloquy, spoken by the Cardinal. Middleton has already shown his audience a man who is consistent only in being invariably wrong.[26] Now he lets them see the operation of that man's mind. Beginning with, 'Let me think upon't, | Set holy anger by a while, there's time | Allow'd for natural argument', the Cardinal composes himself to examine the details of this fresh challenge, with a view to constructing a new framework for his disappointed dream. Despite his blustering in the preceding scene, we see at once that the process of digestion has already proceeded far: although he makes no allusion to the bare fact of the Duchess's disastrous infatuation, he has obviously decided that it is a circumstance which he is powerless to alter. Lactantio, he reflects, has not been the aggressor, merely an innocent victim; and while he laments that the Duchess's glance did not pass over his other favourite paragon and fall upon some other man, he signifies his recognition that that regret is a vain one too, when he says, 'Yet I may erre to wish't'—we realize that he is setting out to transform two painful necessities into one reputation-saving virtue:

---

[25] Ibid. (Bullen: VI, 406).
[26] The Cardinal makes manifest his delusion about Lactantio's 'page' early in Act I: '. . . I have oft took him | Weeping alone (poor Boy) at the remembrance | Of his lost friends; which he says, the Sea | Swallow'd with all their substance.' In these lines, as in the dialogue quoted above on p. 60, there is a poignant quality which reveals Middleton's special interest in the plight of an inexperienced and credulous girl taken in by the lies of a faithless blackguard.

> Yet I may erre to wish't, since it appears
> The hand of Heaven, that onely pickt him out
> To reward vertue in him by this Fortune,
> And through affection I'm half conquer'd now,
> I love his good, as dearly as her vow.[27]

'Yet there [in the Duchess's vow]', he reminds himself, 'my credit lives in works and praises.' In a lifetime of sophisticated mental experience, the perverse disparity between actual facts and cherished theories has never presented him with such a formidable problem: 'I never found a harder fight within me, | Since zeal first taught me war.' Nothing daunted, he resolves to 'bear in pity to [the Duchess's] heart' and 'The rest commend to Fortune and my Art'.

In this soliloquy Middleton made his audience see that the Cardinal is no less accomplished at dissembling with himself than at beguiling others: the irony reaches its highest pitch as he uses the euphemistic phrase, 'I never knew a harder fight within me', to convey to himself a picture of his own mind at work upon a saintly conflict of ideals, adding, 'Since zeal first taught me war', to place the picture more securely within a context of sanctity, when what his mind is really at work upon is the quite profane difficulty of forging the untoward materials of his predicament into an invention sufficiently plausible to enable him to emerge from it with unscathed dignity. He has a well-developed facility for confusing zeal for his personal fame with zeal for religion, and his pious-sounding speech has something in common with the euphuistic dialogue Middleton used to impart fair-seeming to Lactantio and Aurelia, and their superficial counterparts in *Blurt Master-Constable* and *The Family of Love*. Although a much more fully developed artistic conception, basically he represents, like them, a morally incompetent human being, in a more elaborate disguise: he gives sanctimonious lip-service to fluctuating precepts, and concludes the utterance of his private thoughts not, as might be expected of an ostensibly devout man, by appealing to God for His help, but by committing the future to 'Fortune' and his own 'Art'.

We soon learn that the Cardinal is really no longer prepared to leave more to the caprice of 'Fortune' than is absolutely neces-

---

[27] II. p. 26 (Bullen: VI, 407-8).

MORE DISSEMBLERS BESIDES WOMEN 71

sary; henceforth, all will be 'Art', and compared with the dissembling which he is about to engage in, that of Lactantio and his 'page', Andrugio, Aurelia, and the Duchess, is mere child's play.[28] First he seeks out his nephew, and, using as his pretext 'the present barrenness of our name and house | (The onely Famine of succeeding honor)', urges him to give up his once-admired abstinence from women and marry the Duchess:

> She's thine and not her vows—[aside:] the more my sorrow,
> My toil and my destruction.[29]

Lactantio makes a few extravagant protestations—'alas, you know Sir, | I know not what love is, or what you speak of; if woman be amongst it, I shall swoun!'— but, deciding eventually that his eccentric uncle is in earnest, he adroitly changes his performance to a seemly show of reluctance overborne by sense of duty. He seizes his unexpected good fortune, and abandons his recent understanding with Aurelia, in a foppish[30] apostrophe to 'Envy':

> Oh Envy, hadst thou no other means to come by vertue,
> But by such treachery! The Dutchess love!
> Thou wouldst be sure to aim it high enough: ⎫
> Thou knewst full well 'twas no prevailing else. ⎬ [aside]
> Sir, what your will commands, mine shall fulfil: ⎭
> I'll teach my heart in all t'obey your will.[31]

---

[28] The Cardinal bears much the same relation to the other five dissemblers in the play as Fontinell and Violetta bear to the characters in the underplot of *Blurt Master-Constable*. Fontinell's and Violetta's outward display of nobility makes their unbridled animality stand out in stark relief against the depravity of the unpretentious debauchees; likewise, ecclesiastical vestments lend a special ugliness to the Cardinal's vanity, and make his deceitfulness seem more reprehensible than that of simple lay dissemblers.

[29] III. p. 37 (Bullen: VI, 422). Evidently misunderstanding Middleton's Cardinal and his situation, Dilke transferred the words 'the more . . . destruction' to Lactantio in his edition of 1815, probably taking them for part of the latter's affected objection to his uncle's proposal. Unfortunately Dyce followed Dilke in 1840, and Bullen followed Dyce in 1885. The reading of the quarto is correct: the words 'sorrow' and 'destruction' refer respectively to the immediate and apprehended effects upon the Cardinal of the Duchess's having repudiated her vow; 'toil' refers to the pains which he is even now at, in the attempt to save his reputation: 'I shall have as much toil to bring him on. . . .'

[30] The exquisite, impassioned language used by Lactantio when playing the devotee of religion and celibacy before his uncle—'Oh y'ave snatcht my spirit Sir, | From the divinest Meditation | That ever made Soul happy'—is always strongly reminiscent of the languishments of Fontinell. See above, p. 13.

[31] III. pp. 37–8 (Bullen: VI, 423).

Having attended to this necessary preliminary, the Cardinal next reconvenes with the Lords of Milan, and carries out the most remarkable piece of dissimulation in the play. After an elaborate, patronizing form of address, he begins the first of two long speeches by reporting the results of his experiment with the First Lord's suggestion as follows: 'it appears as plain | As knowledge to the eyes of industry, | That neither p[r]ivate motion . . . Nor publick sight . . .

>   hath power to raise
> A heat in her 'bove that which feeds chaste life,
> And gives that cherishing means; she's the same still,
> And seems so seriously imploy'd in soul,
> As if she could not tend to cast an eye
> Upon deserts so low as those in man.

He goes on from this direct lie, without a pause, subtly to prepare the soil for a new seed:

> It merits famous memory I confess;
> Yet many times when I behold her youth,
> And think upon the lost hopes of posterity,
> Succession, and the royal fruits of Beauty,
> All by the rashness of one vow made desperate,
> It goes so near my heart, I feel it painful,
> And wakes me into pity oftentimes,
> When others sleep unmov'd.[32]

The First Lord's sympathetic 'where's the remedy?' gives the Cardinal an opportunity to proceed farther. He elaborates on the lie he has already told to provide himself with a screen, then cunningly combines the introduction of the latest and most drastic modification to his theory of chastity with a vindication of his celebrated writings:

> The Books that I have publish'd in her praise,
> Commend her constancy, and that's Fame-worthy;
> But if you read me o'r with eyes of enemies,
> You cannot justly, and with honor tax me,
> That I disswade her life from marriage there.
> Now Heaven, and fruitfulness forbid, not I:

[32] See III. pp. 38–9 (Bullen: VI, 424).

> She may be constant there, and the hard war
> Of Chastity, is held a vertuous strife,
> As rare in marriage, as in single life;
> Nay, by some writers rarer. Hear their reasons,
> And you'll approve 'em. . . .[33]

The Cardinal continues to develop the thesis that chastity in marriage is rarer, and therefore better, than chastity in single life; dismisses the Duchess's vow as an inefficacious 'thing inforc'd . . . onely to please the Duke', a mere acquiescence for which there is no 'crown prepar'd' in heaven; makes a reference to the Duchess's 'will'—the inconsistency of which the Lords do not appear to notice—, fearing that 'we have sin'd | In too much strictness to uphold her in't'; and finally arrives at his intended destination with

> She cannot be truly call'd constant now,
> If she persever; rather obstinate,
> The Vow appearing forced, as it proves,
> Try'd by our purer thoughts. . . .[34]

He proposes to take his new prescription to the Duchess immediately, and the Lords, completely taken in, promise to 'second' him.

As Lactantio has already been cultivated to serve the Cardinal's purpose, so he 'come[s] now a necessary property' in the Duchess's scheme. After leaving his uncle, he betakes himself directly to the Duchess; his precipitate arrival is announced by the Duchess's maid:

> Madam, 'tis he, with speed.
> I thought he had brought his horse to th'Chamber door,
> He made such haste and noise.[35]

In a humorous scene the Duchess endures Lactantio's swollen impudence and feigns a rapturous devotion to him. Knowing beforehand that he hates Andrugio, she enquires who his enemies are, that she may help him be revenged upon them. When the expected answer comes, she declares that she has grievances

---

[33] III. pp. 39–40 (Bullen: VI, 425).
[34] III. p. 41 (Bullen: VI, 426).
[35] III. pp. 41–2 (Bullen: VI, 428).

against Andrugio too. She pretends a plot to incriminate him, and after getting Lactantio to write a love note to her in Adrugio's handwriting, she sends him off to arrest his supposed victim.

The Duchess really wants the note to serve only as the means of getting Andrugio under her control. When he is brought before her, she dismisses Lactantio and the guard, and accuses him of soliciting her. His earnest denials are met with a pretended refusal to believe, a declaration of her intention to 'requite' him, an explanation of how she has used his enemy Lactantio, and a confession that she loves him above her vow. She refuses to listen to any protest, and has Andrugio confined in her palace.

At this stage, the end of Act IV, there is little to distinguish the Duchess's almost savage determination to have what she wants, from the erotic wilfulness of Violetta, Maria, and Aurelia; one hears echoes of Lipsalve's comments upon women,[36] and of the carpet knight's 'A man so resolute in valour as a Woman in desire, were an absolute Leader.'[37] But a change is soon to take place which will show that the Duchess is really the fulfilment of an ideal of rational, strong, spirited, and dignified womanhood.

At the beginning of the last scene of the play she learns that Andrugio loves someone else; by making the Duchess confront a rival, Middleton continued to follow the outline of the principal action of *Blurt Master-Constable*: Aurelia now becomes the counterpart of Imperia, the object of Fontinell's affections.

The Duchess's response to the situation is much different from the abject wheedling resorted to by Violetta during her visit to the brothel. Aurelia, since her escape, has been masquerading as a gipsy to avoid recapture by her father, and she first appears before the Duchess in that disguise. To begin with, the Duchess is offended to think that 'so base a creature' should be preferred to her; but later she sees Aurelia as herself, and says,

> I confess
> I have no wrong at all; she's yonger, fairer.
> He has not now dishonor'd me in choice;
> I much commend his noble care and judgment.

---

[36] For example, see above, p. 49.
[37] *The Phoenix*, I. sig. C3ᵛ (Bullen: I, 130).

The Duchess not only shows fairness, good sense, and admirable self-possession at this juncture, but goes on to interpret the disappointment of her plot as a manifestation of the directing influence of universal justice, brought on by her failure to resist temptation:

> 'Twas a just cross led in by a temptation,
> For offering but to part from my dear Vow,
> And I'll embrace it cheerfully.[38]

She concludes by giving Andrugio and Aurelia a warm blessing, and Andrugio is momentarily invested with the spirit and office of Prince Phoenix, in order to signalize the Duchess's arrival at a truly noble state of mind, when he replies: 'Vertues crown be yours Madam.'

The dénouement is accomplished in a very short space. Andrugio learns of Aurelia's unfaithfulness, but she, disillusioned by Lactantio's haughty rejection of her, humbles herself, and Andrugio forgives her: 'I have a love | That covers all thy faults.' Lactantio is disappointed of his expectations. The Duchess eventually produces her 'page', whose secret she has discovered, and leaves him with no choice but to acknowledge her as his wife,[39] but before doing so, she impugns the Cardinal, who has proferred him, as follows:

> O Blasphemy
> To Sanctimonious Faith! comes it from you Sir?
> An ill example; know you what you speak,
> Or who you are? Is not my Vow in place?
> How dare you be so bold Sir? Say a woman
> Were tempt with a temptation, must you presently
> Take all th'advantage on't?[40]

The Cardinal's 'Is this in earnest Madam?' points back to a scene in Act IV in which the Duchess had only feigned a loathness to

---

[38] See V. p. 78 (Bullen: VI, 475).
[39] Lactantio observes, 'I'm paid with my own money.' The frustration of his assignation with Aurelia led him to conclude that 'there is no mischief | But brings one Villain or other still | Ev'n close at heels on't', but in the conduct of his subsequent affairs he has failed to take due cognizance of universal justice; now he must recognize that the lessons of experience are not to be ignored. This is a reproduction of the pattern Middleton established with Follywit in *A Mad World, My Masters* (see above, pp. 45-6).
[40] V. pp. 80-1 (Bullen: VI, 477-8).

give up her vow.[41] Her 'Heaven pardon you, if you do not think so Sir; | Y'ave much to answer for', leaves him in no doubt of her present sincerity, however; and the affirmation of the specific thesis that real virtue consists in a readiness to react favourably to knowledge derived from experience of temptation, and the more general theme, 'To be chaste is Womans glory | 'Tis her fame and honors story', is implicit in the rest of her speech—

> But I will leave you;
> Return I humbly now from whence I fell.
> All you blest powers that Register the Vows
> Of Virgins and chaste Matrons, look on me
> With eyes of mercy; seal forgiveness to me
> By signs of inward peace. . . .[42]

The idea that virtue can only be real and effective when it has been tempered by experience was a natural development from Middleton's earlier theme of 'apprenticeship to life'. In *Michaelmas Term* he showed his audience passive young innocents being exposed to society's corrupting influences; and in *Michaelmas Term* and *The Phoenix* he held up to admiration the country wench's father and Quieto as examples of those rare individuals who ultimately derive enlightenment from long involvement in vice. All have shared the helplessness to resist corruption shown by the Cardinal in *More Dissemblers Besides Women*: his predecessors are innocents corrupted from without, and he is an

---

[41] See IV. ii. This pretence is carried out when the Cardinal and Lords approach the Duchess with the suggestion that she should remarry, to bear out the Cardinal's lie about her indefectibility. Middleton did not write a scene to show the Duchess and Cardinal actually coming to the agreement which their joint performance here implies, but the first lines of the soliloquy with which the scene ends—'O there's no art like a religious cunning, | It carries away all things smooth before it. | How subtilly has his wit dealt with the Lords | To fetch in their perswasions . . .'—let the audience see the extent of the Duchess's disillusionment: they understand that what they have just witnessed was the first stage of a prearranged plan, the second stage of which would have been a further embassy, met by, other things being equal, the Duchess's acquiescence to their proposal. Middleton's omission of a scene to connect II. i and IV. ii is another instance of the kind of structural compression found in *Blurt Master-Constable*, and, as in that play, it would be easier for a spectator to make the necessary inference than it is for a reader.
[42] V. p. 81 (Bullen: VI, 478).

innocent corrupted from within.[43] The Duchess of Milan makes a sharp and significant contrast with this earlier pattern. Her behaviour—at the first 'just cross' diverting her energies, unabated, from an unworthy to a worthy cause—indicates that Middleton no longer believed that innocence confronted by evil must always endure a prolonged period of helplessness. The play's concluding lines—

> Oh they that search out mans intents, shall finde
> There's more Dissemblers then of Women kind.[44]

—are spoken by the Duchess, and they show that Middleton wanted his theme to receive emphasis from the juxtaposition of the minds of his two chief characters. The Duchess and Cardinal are equally endowed with native intelligence, and both make pretensions to virtue. At the end of the play the essential difference between them stems from the fact that the Duchess has real experience to bring intelligence and a predisposition to virtue to bear upon, and the Cardinal has not. Consequently the rôles of teacher and pupil reverse: when the Cardinal condemns his unmasked nephew,[45] the Duchess tells him, 'We all have faults; look not so much on his. | Who lives i'th'world that never did amiss?'

[43] While Middleton's specific disapproval of Jesuits is made quite apparent in *A Game at Chess*, his portrayal of the Cardinal in this play, and of the Cardinal in *Women Beware Women*, does little more by way of anti-Roman Catholic criticism than bring in question the monastic principle of withdrawal from the world. The Cardinal in *More Dissemblers Besides Women* is very much an individual. He is cunning and formally learned, but his power of perception is restricted in direct proportion to his ignorance of the world. Yet Middleton depicts him, as he usually does characters of whom he does not approve, without bitter animus. In his soliloquy in I. ii the Cardinal shows a not altogether selfish interest in his nephew, and if his sympathy with the suffering of Lactantio's 'page' is ludicrous, it is also quite genuine.

[44] V. p. 83 (Bullen: VI, 481).

[45] It is interesting to note that the distinction between artless and hidden vice, which is only implicit in *Blurt Master-Constable*, is made explicit in the Cardinal's censure of Lactantio: 'Th'open villain [spelled "villainy" in the early edition] | Goes before thee to mercy, and his Penitency | Is blest with a more sweet and quick return.' See above, p. 22.

VI

OTHER STUDIES IN CONSCIENCE AND CHARACTER

In the Cardinal in *More Dissemblers Besides Women* Middleton presented one of the most intense and sustained character studies in the group of plays now being considered, and by juxtaposing the Cardinal and the Duchess he made his most explicit attempt to give positive definition to virtue; but *A Trick to Catch the Old One*, *A Chaste Maid in Cheapside*, and *No Wit, No Help Like a Woman's* also reveal his efforts to 'search out mans intents', and they contain clear, though somewhat less obvious, evidence of his determination to express ideals of human behaviour.

All these works contribute to the impression of Middleton's growing maturity. All are notable for over-all balanced mood, and for the appearance of detachment which he achieved in greater or lesser degree in his earliest plays. Didactic themes continue to run through Middleton's work however, and occasionally they reach the earlier pitch of urgency. His characters all continue to claim a share of his sympathy, but his proneness to hate ugliness without hating the ugly does not disguise his opinions about them, however effectively it may veil his ulterior motive. He was careful that his distinctions between the characters of whom he approved and disapproved should never be in doubt, and it was partly by means of those distinctions that he imparted his ideals of manhood and womanhood.

We know that unselfishness was among the qualities that Middleton chiefly admired, for example, from the contrast he set up between Andrugio and Lactantio in *More Dissemblers Besides Women*. Andrugio is sensible of some noble obligation to Aurelia, and the fact that he still feels it after learning of her intended unfaithfulness shows that he is being magnanimous, and not merely formal. Lactantio, charitably disposed toward no one, is conspicuously his opposite,[1] and Middleton was at pains to

---

[1] See above, p. 75, and compare p. 60.

represent these opposites as being mutually repellant: much is made of Lactantio's jealous hatred of Andrugio, and Andrugio holds Lactantio, that 'perfum'd parcel of curl'd powder'd hair', as he calls him, in utter contempt. Middleton's alliance with Andrugio is unmistakably revealed when he makes him receive Aurelia's pretended raptures of joy, at their reunion in II. iii, with repugnance; and in IV. ii, the scene in which Andrugio is delivered to the Duchess, the exclamation 'Was ever malice seen yet to gape wider | For man's misfortunes?' is Middleton's appraisal of the gloating Lactantio, as well as Andrugio's. But it is in the constancy he evinces when the Duchess entices him in V. ii, and in the manly generosity with which he accepts his repentant Aurelia, that Andrugio comes into sharpest contrast with Lactantio, and makes his surest claim to Middleton's approval.

Middleton examined selfishness and unselfishness in a variety of situations and relationships. In general, the characters in his plays who possess the virtue make it manifest by showing consciousness of the needs of others, and genuine concern for their welfare. As may be judged from *A Trick to Catch the Old One*, Middleton placed an especially high value on unselfishness in relationships between the sexes, where it takes the form of loyalty—readiness on the part of either partner to accept responsibility for the other.

The relationship between Lactantio and the Cardinal in *More Dissemblers Besides Women*—a degraded, materialistic young man at odds with a wealthy old relative—is a close reproduction of that between Follywit and Sir Bounteous Progress in *A Mad World, My Masters*; Middleton chose the same kind of relationship again for *A Trick to Catch the Old One*, but the dramatic history of the young man, Witgood, is considerably different from Follywit's and Lactantio's. Witgood's opening soliloquy begins, 'All's gone! still thou'rt a Gentleman, that's all; but a poore one, that's nothing'; the rest of it relates his reduced circumstances directly to his profligacy. On the surface, Witgood's situation appears to be more worthy of sympathy than Follywit's, and Lactantio's, because Lucre, his uncle, is not a pretentious squire or an unwise prelate, but a usurer, and a duly unsentimental one. In *A Mad World, My Masters* and *More Dissemblers Besides Women*, age and wealth versus youth and penury is a conflict which gives rise to action, but Middleton made it clear that neither lack of money nor youth extenuated the crimes of the young men against the old—universal justice had an appropriate kind of experience in store for all; the same is true in *A Trick to Catch the Old One*, Lucre's unpopular occupation notwithstanding. Lucre is hard, but his logic is often unexceptionable. Some time before the action begins he has become the instrument of universal justice:

... for my strickt hand toward his morgage that I denie not, I confess I had an Uncles penworth: let me see, halfe in halfe, true, I saw neyther hope of his reclayming, nor comfort in his beeing, and was it not then better bestow'd upon his Uncle, then upon one of his Aunts?[2]

At the beginning of the play there is little to choose between the grasping usurer and his degenerate nephew. Yet although Witgood's methods, like Follywit's and Lactantio's, are deceitful, his enterprise, unlike theirs, meets with success, for Witgood differs from Follywit and Lactantio in an important way. The latter resist the guiding influences of universal justice; but Middleton makes Witgood qualify for his approval by letting him respond favourably to hints to his conscience. Lucre remains unchanged, but Witgood's moral condition begins to improve in the course of the play, and it is this improvement that justifies his success.

Such improving thoughts as enter Witgood's mind are inspired by his mistress, whose capacity for loyalty is the one factor which comes to militate against the squalor of her own life and his. She interrupts his private lamentation at the beginning of the play with a cheerful 'My love!' He returns an ill-tempered 'My lothing!', and gives her the blame for his ruined condition; but the following reply awakens his conscience:

I have beene true unto your pleasure, and all your lands thrice rackt, was never worth the Jewell which I prodigally gave you, my virginity:
Lands morgag'd may returne and more esteemde,
But honesty once pawned, is nere redeemd.[3]

---

[2] II. sig. [B4] (Bullen: II, 267). Lucre goes on to leave no doubt that by 'Aunts' he means prostitutes.

[3] I. sig. A3; (Bullen: II, 253). To this point, the exchange bears a general similarity to that between Lactantio and his 'page' at the beginning of III. i of *More Dissemblers Besides Women* (see the quotations from this scene on p. 60, above).

Witgood says, 'For give, I do thee wrong, | To make thee sinne, and then to chid thee fort', and when she offers to leave him, and thereby relieve his misery, he implores her to stay: 'fate has so cast it that all my meanes I must derive from thee.' Although she knows that he has never regarded her as more than a kind of 'necessary property', she readily offers her help:

> From me? be happy then.
> What lies within the power of my performance,
> Shall be commanded of thee.[4]

This gesture is made entirely in a spirit of comradeship. There is no suggestion of romance in the relationship between Witgood and his mistress; and though not an inveterate prostitute like Frank Gullman, the man who marries Follywit, Witgood's mistress has it in common with the latter that she does not indulge in sentimentality or self-delusion. When she answers Witgood's appeal in this way, it is not with the fond hope that he will eventually marry her—Witgood wishes to marry the niece of his uncle's hated rival, Hoard. In fact, his previous behaviour has given the audience no reason to suppose that she may even expect his gratitude. Yet when he proposes his 'trick' to win back his lost fortune from 'the Old One', she agrees to lend it her support;[5] and her example later inspires a generous feeling in Witgood, which somewhat mollifies the fierce selfishness of his motives. Posing as a rich widow to delude his uncle, she attracts the attention of Lucre's fellow-usurer, Hoard, who is bent upon settling an old grudge. In Act III, when Witgood learns that Hoard has become her suitor, he says,

> Wench, make up thy owne fortunes now. Do thy selfe a good turne once in thy Dayes. Hees rich in money, moveables, and lands,—marry him, he's an old doting foole, and thats worth all. Marry him, twould bee a great comfort to me to see thee do well ifaith,—marry him, twould ease my conscience well to see thee well bestowd.[6] I have a care of thee ifaith.[7]

---

[4] I. sig. A3ᵛ (Bullen: II, 253).
[5] Witgood's mistress is to pose as a wealthy widow while he arranges for it to be brought to his uncle's ears that he is engaged to her, but cannot marry her because of his poverty. He knows that Lucre, thinking him a hopeless waster, will see the possibility of future gain for himself in such a match, and want to go to any length, even to temporarily restoring his nephew's estate, to make it possible.
[6] Spelt 'destowd' in the quarto.   [7] Sig. D3ᵛ (Bullen: II, 291-2).

At the end of the play Witgood's mistress renounces a sinful way of life—'Lo, Gentlemen, before you all, | In true reclaymed forme I fall. | Henceforth . . .'—and Witgood again follows her lead— 'I must confesse my follyes, Ile down to: | And Here for ever I disclaime, | The cause of youths undooing: . . . 'In the final line Hoard speaks for himself and Lucre: 'Who seeme most crafty prove oft times most fooles.'[8]

Probably the most important single feature of *A Trick to Catch the Old One*, in regard to Middleton's maturer view of the human condition, is its reflection of the attitude implicit in the Duchess's reproof of the Cardinal in *More Dissemblers Besides Women*: 'We all have faults; look not so much on his. | Who lives i'th'world that never did amiss?' In *A Mad World, My Masters* Middleton's chief didactic concerns were repudiation of sin, and illustration of the operation of universal justice; with a supplementary motive—a desire to point out saving graces—he took the same basic materials for *A Trick to Catch the Old One* as he had used in the earlier play, and worked them into new forms. Witgood's dramatic experience begins where Follywit's leaves off: with an emphatic lesson from universal justice behind him. His saving grace is a dawning, infant-like ability to respond to wholesome influence; his achievement, a rudimentary discovery of conscience and obligation. His mistress is at a much more advanced stage of moral development. Finding herself abandoned in the world—that is, in the same general circumstances as Follywit's Frank Gullman—she takes Witgood's advice, but once she accepts Hoard's proposal of marriage, she experiences a disturbing conflict of loyalites. In Act IV Witgood, oppressed by his creditors, pretends an intention to go to law for his 'fiancée's' violation of pre-contract, to trick Hoard into paying off his debts. His mistress continues to sympathize with him—'Alasse his creditors so mercilesse, my state beeing yet uncertaine, I deeme it not unconscionable to furder him'—and helps to bear out this additional hoax; but afterwards she expresses her frustration in an aside—

> Ime yet like those, whose riches lie in dreames,
> If I be wakte the're false; such is my fate,
> Who ventures deeper then the desperate state.

[8] V. sig. [H4] (Bullen: II, 352).

CONSCIENCE AND CHARACTER   83

 Though I have sind yet could I become new,
 For where I once vow, I am ever true.[9]

—and she admonishes Witgood as follows: '. . . mee thinkes ifaith you might have made some shift to discharge this your self, having in the morgage, and never have burdned my conscience with it.' In the present group of plays Middleton gave a good deal of attention to filling in the image of nobility in women for which he had provided only a vague outline in Falso's niece, and the sea-captain's wife, in *The Phoenix*; and Witgood's mistress is just as much a part of that image as is the Duchess in *More Dissemblers Besides Women*. The fact that she has sinned is only significant in so far as the experience has served to show her the emptiness of a debased life; a greater emphasis is given to her predisposition to virtue, her growing confirmation in a right way of thinking, and her final resolution to lead a better life. Middleton's desire to find and encourage what is worthy, a desire which is manifested in various degrees in these plays of his early maturity,[10] is evident in her 'Though I have sind yet could I become new, | For where I

---

[9] IV. sig. G[1]ᵛ (Bullen: II, 328).

[10] It is most conspicuous in *More Dissemblers Besides Women*, and least in *A Chaste Maid in Cheapside*, a play more reminiscent of Middleton's original and simpler motive, to condemn sin by revealing its ugliness. Even *A Trick to Catch the Old One*, however, which reflects, hardly less than *More Dissemblers Besides Women*, Middleton's acceptance of the mature idea 'we all have faults', and his tendency to direct more of his attention toward a search for virtue, contains a notable reminder of the *exposés* of vice which preoccupied him in his earliest plays. The final scenes of Acts I, III, and IV, have little ostensible connection with the rest of the play, yet together they provide a grim and concise comment on grasping materialism. In Act I Witgood advises a friend to 'note him well, that Dampit sirrah, hee in the uneven Beard, and the Serge cloake, is the most notorious, usuring, blasphemous, Atheisticall, Brothel-vomiting rascall, that wee have in these latter times now extant . . .', and the audience then hears Dampit explain his sordid origins as a 'law-worme', like mad Tangle in *The Phoenix*. In Act III he is shown arriving home brutishly drunk in the middle of the night. The scene in Act IV is the ugliest of all: the dipsomaniac is discovered in the final stage of decay, chained up in bed, suffering fits of delirium, and surrounded by his demon-like creatures who have come to gape and make sport of him, baiting him like an animal. A speech given to one of them echoes the tone of Follywit's 'in these behold it' soliloquy (see Appendix B), and leaves no doubt of Middleton's didactic intention: 'Note but the misery of this usuring slave. Here hee lies like a noysome dunghill, full of the poyson of his druncken blasphemies, and they to whom he bequeathes all, grudge him the very meate that feedes him, the very pillow that eases him. Here may a usurer behold his end. What profits it to be a slave in this world, and a devil ith next?' By inserting these three scenes as an indirect but telling condemnation of the usury of Lucre and Hoard, Middleton converted a once direct technique to intimative use.

once vow, I am ever true', and in her reassurance of the disabused Hoard: 'She that knowes sinne, knowes best how to hate sinne.'[11]

Mistress Low-water in *No Wit, No Help Like a Woman's*, who has the strength of character to make a lone stand against corruption, as Witgood's mistress does against selfishness, is another of Middleton's studies of dignity in womanhood. Owing to the machinations of a usurer and extortionist now dead, her husband is in a state of financial ruin, and she deplores the injustice of the opulence of the usurer's widow, Lady Goldenfleece, not with selfish envy, but because she sympathizes with her husband's embarrassment, and feels distress at having no dowry or inheritance to bring to his relief. Her soliloquy in Act I hints at an additional cause of anxiety. It begins with a series of rhetorical questions, the first of which, 'Is there no Saving-means? no help Religious | For a distressed Gentlewoman to live by?', implies that some dishonourable 'Saving-means', or 'help' out of her predicament, has been offered. 'Has Virtue no Revenue?' and, later, 'No dowry in the Chamber, beside Wantonness?' leave little doubt as to the course proposed; and the concluding lines express her determination not to follow it:

> Yet stood all miseries in their loathed'st forms
> On this hand of me, thick like a foul[12] mist,
> And here the bright enticements of the world,
> In clearest colours, flattery, and advancement,
> And all the bastard-glories this frame jets in,
> Horror, nor splendor, shadows fair nor foul,[12]
> Should force me shame my husband, wound my soul.[13]

A letter arrives from her would-be seducer shortly afterwards. Sir Gilbert Lambstone, a lecherous blackguard much like Goldstone in *Your Five Gallants*, expects soon to marry Lady Goldenfleece. He knows that the Goldenfleeces have wronged the Lowwaters, and thinks that a chance of revenge will finally induce Mistress Low-water to enter an adulterous relationship with him: '*I'm in the way now to* [do]ub[l]e *the yearly means that first I offered you, and to sti*[r] *you more to me, I'll empty your enemies Bags to maintain you.*' Lambstone's letter has precisely the

---

[11] Note the similarity of the appeal which Aurelia makes to Andrugio under comparable circumstances in *More Dissemblers Besides Women*: 'There's more hope of me | Then of Maid that never yet offended.'
[12] Spelt 'fowl' in the 1657 edition.   [13] I. p. 17 (Bullen: IV, 298).

CONSCIENCE AND CHARACTER

opposite effect from that which he anticipated. On receiving it, Mistress Low-water cries, 'Life, had he not his answer? What strange impudence | Governs in man, when Lust is Lord of him?', and after reading it she observes,

> In this poor Brief, what Volumes has he thrust,
> Of treacherous Perjury, and adulterous Lust!
> So foul a Monster does this wrong appear,
> That I give pitty to mine enemy here.[14]

Mistress Low-water's 'pitty' immediately inspires a plan of action, and constructive mental activity soon makes her previous despair give place to optimism. In an interview with Lambstone she pretends a near-readiness to acquiesce, but asks for another day to make a final decision; then, with the same enthusiasm as that with which Witgood's mistress lends her support to the plan in *A Trick to Catch the Old One*, and awakens Witgood's conscience, and the same initiative as the Duchess assumes in dealing with the Cardinal at the end of *More Dissemblers Besides Women*, Mistress Low-water enlists the aid of her husband:

> Wake, wake, and let not patience keep thee poor,
> Rouze up thy spirit from this falling slumber;
> Make thy distress seem but a weeping dream,
> And this the opening morning of thy comforts,
> Wash the Salt dew off from thy careful eyes,
> And drink a draught of gladness next thy heart,
> T'expel the infection of all poysonous sorrows.[15]

---

[14] I. p. 20 (Bullen: IV, 301). Letters, such as that with which Fontinell makes his wedding rendezvous with Violetta in *Blurt Master-Constable*, the country wench informs her father of her departure for London in *Michaelmas Term*, and the Duchess deludes Lactantio and entices Andrugio in *More Dissemblers Besides Women*, were a favourite device of Middleton's for advancing the action of his plots. Sir Gilbert Lambstone's letter is part of a set of circumstances not unlike that which surrounds Lethe's letter to Quomodo's wife in *Michaelmas Term*. Thomasine, like Mistress Low-water, is a virtuous wife; Lethe, like Lambstone, a debauched man who puts forward a bribe in a letter; and Thomasine shows as much repugnance when she reads Lethe's offer to become her paramour if she will consent to his marriage with her daughter (see above, p. 50), as Mistress Low-water does at Lambstone's proposal; but in *No Wit, No Help Like a Woman's* we see Middleton again taking material from an earlier play and adapting it to more artistic use. The Lethe letter simply helps to emphasize the sender's infamy and the receiver's virtue; the Lambstone letter, explaining at last why Mistress Low-water has spoken of 'whoredom' as an alternative to 'beggery' in her first soliloquy, is the last stage, the release, of a short cycle of suspense.

[15] I. p. 22 (Bullen: IV, 304).

The promise of personal benefit implicit in this exhortation stems from Mistress Low-water's faith in universal justice. Just before Low-water's entrance she expresses this faith in a short soliloquy; in it Middleton turns from his more usual representation of universal justice, as a stumbling-block to vice, to emphasize its function as a prop to virtue:

> There is no happiness but has her season,
> Herein the brightness of her vertue shines,
> The husk falls off in time that long shuts up
> The fruit in a dark prison; so sweeps by
> The cloud of miseries from wretches eyes,
> That yet, though faln, at length they see to rise,
> The secret powers work wondrously, and duly.[16]

Lady Goldenfleece is saved from Lambstone in Act II: Mistress Low-water, disguised as a gallant, becomes a suitor herself, and chooses an appropriate moment to expose Lambstone by showing Lady Goldenfleece the treacherous letter. The restoration of her husband's fortune necessitates Mistress Low-water's continuation of the hoax, and eventually going through a form of marriage with the widow to secure command of her wealth. Beveril, Mistress Low-water's brother, genuinely loves Lady Goldenfleece. On discovering this, Mistress Low-water arranges that the two shall be discovered in adulterous-seeming circumstances on the wedding night, and, after pretending the indignation of a cuckolded husband, and possessing herself of a just share of the widow's fortune, she makes Lady Goldenfleece 'free' by admitting that she is 'married to another'. The deception of Lady Goldenfleece is justified by the fact that 'her whole life . . . | Was ever full of . . . dishonest riddles, | To keep right heirs from knowledge of their own'—she, like other sinners, must go through a process of enlightenment. This begins with the exposure of Lambstone, to whom she says, 'Crawl with they poysons hence, and for thy sake | I'll never covet Titles, and more Riches, | To fall into a gulf of hate and laughter: | 'I'll marry Love hereafter'; and ends after Mistress Low-water has revealed herself:

> I see too late there is a heavy judgment
> Keeps company with Extortion, and foul deeds;

[16] I. p. 21 (Bullen: IV, 304). The comma with which Middleton set off 'and duly' in the last line of this soliloquy, emphasizing the order and reliability of universal justice, is silently omitted in the editions of Dyce and Bullen.

And like a wind which Vengeance has in chase,
Drives back the wrongs into the Injurers face.[17]

Near the end of the play Lady Goldenfleece decides to marry honest Beveril,[18] and she welcomes Mistress Low-water's friendship: 'Hah worthy Sister! | The government of all, I bless thee with.' The principle which operates to bring success to Mistress Low-water's venture, the principle that accounts for the successes of Witgood and his mistress, is enunciated in Act I, when a young friend thanks her for advice: 'In this I thank your help, and may you live | To conquer your own troubles, and cross ends, | As you are ready to supply your friends.'

The 'wit' of which there is none 'like a woman's' is the imagination and resource of Mistress Low-water; the word 'help' in the title applies not only to Mistress Low-water's solution of her husband's financial problem, however, but also to the way Lady Twilight rescues her unworthy son, Philip, from difficulties in the other plot of the play. En route for Guernsey, ten years before the action begins, Lady Twilight and an infant girl, supposedly her daughter Grace, have been captured by pirates, later to be sold and separated. After nine years of silence Sir Oliver Twilight has received a letter from his wife, and immediately dispatched Philip and his servant, Savourwit, to ransom her. In Act I Savourwit recounts how he and his master, 'landing by the way, having a care | To lighten [themselves] of [their] carriage, because Gold | Is such a heavy mettal, eas'd [their] Pockets | In Wenches Aprons', and how Philip, chancing to 'dote finely | Upon a sweet yong Gentlewoman; but one | That would not sell her honor for the Indies, | Till a Priest struck the bargain', married the girl. Devoid of any sense of responsibility, Philip has returned home, passed off his wife as 'his sister that was sold', and told his father that Lady Twilight is dead—'a fair tale of [Savourwit's] own bringing up'. Having been discovered and

[17] V. p. 114 (Bullen: IV, 420–1).
[18] Middleton made some partial borrowings from *Your Five Gallants* for *No Wit, No Help Like a Woman's*. Beveril is a scholar, and like Fitsgrave, who poses as a scholar, he is asked to produce a masque before a lady whom he eventually marries. Lady Goldenfleece's disappointed suitors take part in it at their own instance, as do the suitors whose hopes of marrying a wealthy orphan are disappointed in Fitsgrave's masque; and although the suitors, rather than Beveril, have the upper hand at first, he finally exposes them. In the banquet scene which begins Act II Middleton used the signs of the zodiac in the same figurative way as he had used emblems and mottoes in Act V of *Your Five Gallants*.

ransomed by Beveril, during his travels, Lady Twilight returns home in Act II. She forgives Philip, and, by substantiating Savourwit's 'tale' in Act IV, saves him from the wrath of Sir Oliver. It appears that Philip's wife is indeed the girl his mother took abroad, but she is not his sister. Lady Goldenfleece relieves the anxiety about this by divulging a secret in the final scene: years before, the nurse employed by Lady Twilight had exchanged her own daughter, Jane, for Lady Twilight's Grace, to save her child from poverty. Middleton took the basic framework of this plot from a late sixteenth-century Italian play, della Porta's *La Sorella*, but he departed from his original to impose judgement on Philip, and to express an ideal in Lady Twilight.

In *La Sorella*, it is Attilio, Philip's counterpart, who tells the story told by Savourwit in the opening scene of *No Wit, No Help Like a Woman's*. Middleton made this change because he wanted Philip Twilight to be an unmistakably unheroic character, which Attilio is not. Savourwit, who is far more prominent in the play than Philip, and always dominates the conversation in the scenes in which they appear together, is undisguisedly crude and unscrupulous, and his telling the story of Philip's shabby exploit in front of two of his social betters, one of whom is Philip himself, emphasizes Philip's baseness in much the same way that the juxtaposing of Lazarillo and Imperia emphasizes the baseness of Fontinell and Violetta in *Blurt Master-Constable*. Philip, never speaking remorsefully of his flagrant delinquency until his mother's unexpected return fills him with fear of exposure, is a complete moral idiot, like Fontinell; and with Fontinell, because della Porta's Attilio excited Middleton's special disapproval, Philip shares the distinction of being the most unprepossessing of Middleton's self-indulgent young men. The absolute antithesis of the manly, resourceful, and generous Andrugio in *More Dissemblers Besides Women*, Philip is hardly capable of thought of any kind. Savourwit has to tell him to apologize to his mother and beg her forgiveness, and when her testimony finally frees him from his father's suspicions, he indulges in a petulant, hypocritical display of outraged dignity, interjecting sarcastically, 'I'm unfit to carry a ransom!' and 'My faith is blemish'd, I'm no man of trust Sir!' Savourwit is his will, and when Savourwit's wit seems unequal to the difficulty of the moment, Philip languishes, like Fontinell, and inclines to suicide. When his friend Sandfield is angry with him at the outset of the play, he first offers him his breast to stab, and then trembles, displaying Fontinell's 'soft Mermaladie heart', when Sandfield draws his sword. Overcome by the sense of his own tragedy at two other crises, he offers to kill himself, only to be indulgently prevented by his mercurial Savourwit.

Although Philip is among the least-deserving of sons, Lady Twilight is among the most benign and charitable of mothers. The contrast Middleton establishes between them, accentuating at once the mother's love and sense of parental obligation, and the degradation and filial incompetence of the son, is intensified when Lady Twilight defends Philip's cause with a lie in Act IV, and says, 'Love is a Mothers duty to a son, | As a sons duty is both love and fear.'[19] The mother's excusing of the son in *No Wit, No Help Like a Woman's* is a significant modification of della Porta's plot,[20] for though a slightly developed character, Lady Twilight has a place in the development of Middleton's ideal of womanhood. Her act looks directly forward to his fuller characterization of another devoted mother, Lady Agar, in *A Fair Quarrel*: Lady Agar, like Lady Twilight, does not hesitate to tell a lie to save her son, even a lie that involves the sacrifice of her reputation.[21]

[19] Lady Twilight is charitable, but not gullible: these lines convey a denunciation of fililal delinquency which is clear to the audience, if not to Philip, to whom they are addressed. Middleton expresses the ideal, which comments upon Philip's animal voluptuousness, in Beveril's reflective 'A wise man makes affections but his slaves. | Break 'em in time, let 'em not master thee.'

[20] Another of Middleton's alterations to the original treatment of the story should be mentioned in connection with one of A. W. Ward's comments on the play. Alluding to the suggestion of incest which precedes Lady Goldenfleece's revelation about the secret exchange of infants, Ward criticized Middleton as follows: '. . . the author had not good taste enough to avoid, or at least to pass quietly over, an exceedingly painful situation . . . wholly unfit for comedy' (*English Dramatic Literature*, 2nd edn., II, 524). Ward may not have been familiar with Middleton's source (J. E. Spingarn was first to record a reference to it: see *Critical Essays of the Seventeenth Century* [Oxford, 1908], II, 335), and, needless to say, Middleton could hardly have availed himself of della Porta's plot without including the situation Ward objects to. In any case, it may be noted that, without referring to Ward, D. J. Gordon, who made a comparison of the two plays, remarked, 'There are two scenes in *La Sorella* that are mostly taken up with Attilio's ravings (IV. v. vi). Philip is given much less time to display his emotions. . . . We do not feel in these speeches that Middleton is lingering over the fact [i.e., idea] of incest, as della Porta certainly does' ('Middleton's *No Wit, No Help Like a Woman's* and della Porta's *La Sorella*', *Review of English Studies*, XVII [October 1941], 411).

[21] See below, pp. 114 and 116.

The title, *A Chaste Maid in Cheapside*, seems to give promise of another celebration of womanly virtue, but nothing could be farther from the case. Moll Yellowhammer, daughter of a goldsmith, is the 'chaste maid', but she is a minor character. Middleton gave much more of his attention to two character studies of men in *A Chaste Maid in Cheapside*: to Allwit, a professional wittol,[22] and to Sir Walter Whorehound, who exchanges his money for unlimited proprietary rights in the household nominally Allwit's.

There are several subsidiary streams of action in the play, but the main plot centres on Sir Walter. The family Allwit has been enjoying his support for some time before the action commences, and Allwit explains both himself, and one of the two basic situations of the play, which have Sir Walter as their common factor, in Act I. News of Sir Walter's recent arrival in London occasions the long soliloquy which begins as follows:

The Founders come to Towne. I am like a Man finding a Table furnish't to his hand, as mine is still to me, prayes for the Founder: blesse the right Worshipfull, the good Founders life! I thanke him, h'as maintain'd my House this ten yeeres, not onely keepes my Wife, but a keepes me, and all my Family. I am at his Table: he gets me all my Children, and payes the Nurse, monthly, or weekely, puts me to nothing, rent, nor Church duties, not so much as the Scavenger—the happiest state that ever Man was borne to.[23]

Allwit goes on to give a few details of his luxury—'breake-fast' and 'excellent Cheere' after his morning walk, and 'a good Fier in Winter'; his coal-house full by midsummer, and 'a steeple made up with Kentish Fagots' in his back-yard—and a thumb-nail sketch of his chief asset, Mistress Allwit:

---

[22] In Middleton's day the word 'wittol' denoted both a knowing and a complaisant cuckold, and, with a pun on 'wit-all', a person of 'little sense' (*OED*). Thus it seems that Middleton wished the name 'Allwit' both to acknowledge the cunning of the wittol in *A Chaste Maid in Cheapside*, and indirectly to emphasize the moral halfwittedness that would make such a condition of life seem not merely tolerable, but desirable.

[23] p. 8 (Bullen: V, 17). E. L. Buckingham suggests that Middleton may have taken his inspiration for the Allwit–Whorehound situation from an epigram, describing a like situation, in Thomas Campion's *Observations in the Art of English Poesie*, published in 1602. See 'Campion's *Art of English Poesie* and Middleton's *Chaste Maid in Cheapside*', *PMLA*, XLIII (Sept. 1928), 784–92, and R. C. Bald's 'The Sources of Middleton's City Comedies', *Journal of English and Germanic Philology*, XXXIII (July 1934), 375–7.

>   . . . I say nothing,
> But smile, and pin the doore, when she lies in,
> As now she's even upon the point of grunting.
> A Lady lyes not in like her, there's her imbossings,
> Embrodrings, spanglings, and I know not what,
> As if she lay with all the gaudy Shops
> In Gressams Burse about her; then her restoratives,
> Able to set up a young Pothecarie,
> And richly stocke, the Foreman of a Drug-shop;
> Her Sugar by whole Loaves; her Wines by Rundlets.
> I see these things, but like a happy Man,
> I pay for none at all. . . .[24]

In his concluding remarks Allwit boasts of being 'as cleere from jealousie of a Wife, as from the charge [of supporting one]'; Sir Walter has taken upon himself even that 'labour'—'watches her steps, sets spyes . . . has both the cost and torment'.

It remains a secret to Allwit until the middle of Act III that Sir Walter's main reason for coming to London has not been to visit his ménage, but to marry Moll Yellowhammer. Yellowhammer and his wife, requiring no other recommendation than wealth, welcome the prospective bridegroom in the opening scene of the play. They are doubly jubilant because he has brought with him 'a proper faire young Gentlewoman . . . which Tim [their] Sonne (the Cambridge Boy) must marry'. Yellowhammer believes this 'Gentlewoman' to be Whorehound's 'landed Neece, brought out of Wales', and tells his wife, "Tis a match of Sir Walters owne making, to bind us to him'; but Sir Walter makes her known to the audience as a mistress for whom he has no further use: 'I bring thee up to turne thee into Gold, Wench, and make thy fortune shine like your bright Trade—a Gold-Smithes Shop sets out a Citie Mayd.'

Since each has an active interest in Sir Walter, the basic conflict of the play is between Yellowhammer and Allwit. The former wants to marry off his daughter to the wealthy man; the latter is equally determined to keep 'the Founder' single:

>   I'le stop that gap
> Where e're I find it open. I have poysoned
> His hopes in marriage already:

[24] I. p. 9 (Bullen: V, 17–18).

Some old rich Widdowes, and some landed Virgines,
And I'le fall to worke still before I'le lose him.
He's yet too sweet to part from.[25]

An important part of the action turns on a second conflict which arises from Sir Walter's suitorship, however. When Moll Yellowhammer sees Sir Walter for the first time, she gasps 'O Death!' and runs off the stage. It appears shortly afterwards that her affections have already been won by Touchwood Junior, a young gentleman whose poverty forces him to woo in secret.[26] Allwit and Yellowhammer are both disappointed of their hopes. Sir Walter and Touchwood Junior fight in Act IV, and each survives his wounds; but while Sir Walter is resting at Allwit's house, news is brought that he is about to lose title to his wealth: his kinsman, Sir Oliver Kix, is soon to have an heir, and so become established in a superior claim to the estates Sir Walter now enjoys. On learning this, Allwit turns him out. Sir Walter admits defeat—'if ever Eyes were open, these are they. | Gam[e]sters farewell, I have nothing left to play', and Touchwood Junior manages to marry Moll.

Middleton's study of Allwit is one of his masterpieces of artistic detachment. Despite the enormity of the wittol's personal compromise with life, there is no hint of authorial disapproval in the long expository soliloquy in Act I. Rather, Middleton attempts to represent the compunctionless, materialistic thought-processes and shabby raptures of the wittol objectively, and he achieves, in the process, a natural and effective form of understatement. The prosaic details of Allwit's animal comforts—the 'excellent Cheere', the 'good Fier', the ample supply of fuel for the winter—and the grotesque portrait of the contented wife, emphasize the simple brutishness of the exchange of human dignity for ease and effortless security—Middleton insists that the wittol's ugliness shall speak for itself. Allwit's moral idiocy makes his affinity with Fontinell and Philip Twilight obvious; but he also has a share of the cunning of Follywit and Lactantio, and, like Lactantio, he has made a careful Machiavellian study of his maintainer's vanity: '... 'tis but observing a Mans humour

---

[25] I. p. 11 (Bullen: V, 21).
[26] The Yellowhammer–Touchwood Junior–Moll complication is one of Middleton's several versions of the Dr. Glister–Gerardine–Maria pattern in *The Family of Love*.

once, and he may ha' him by the Nose all his life.' Allwit's rival Yellowhammer is equally shrewd, and Yellowhammer's readiness to marry his daughter to a notorious lecher is parallel with Allwit's perverse concession to materialism. On being apprised of Sir Walter's connection with the Allwits, Yellowhammer says to himself,

> Well grant all this, say now his deeds are blacke,
> . . . .
> The Knight is rich: he shall be my Sonne-in-Law.
> No matter, so the Whore he keepes be wholesome,
> My Daughter takes no hurt then. So let them wed;
> I'le have him sweat well e're they goe to Bed.[27]

The venality of Allwit and Yellowhammer is not far removed from the treachery of Proditor in *The Phoenix*, and the rapacity of Quomodo in *Michaelmas Term*; and Purge, the apothecary who claims that 'jealousie is a hell, and they that will thrive must utter their wares as they can, and winke at small faults', in *The Family of Love*, differs from Allwit only in that he cannot bring himself to 'winke' at his wife's promiscuity, once he discovers it. Yet although the degeneracy of Allwit and Yellowhammer makes the general tone of *A Chaste Maid in Cheapside*[28] resemble that of Middleton's earliest work more closely than any of the other plays in the present group, his desire to discover the operation of conscience is evident in his characterization of Sir Walter Whorehound.

When Sir Walter returns to Allwit's house after his fight with Touchwood Junior, he is a much changed man. The wound given him by his rival has awakened his conscience, and he bitterly repulses his host's solicitous advances: 'Touch me not Villaine! My wound akes at thee, | Thou poyson to my Heart.' The features of Sir Walter's character which anticipate this change may be easily overlooked, overshadowed as they are by the spectacle of his licentiousness; but a moral awakening in such a man is not impossible in Middleton's view, and he prepares for

---

[27] IV. p. 52 (Bullen: V, 85).
[28] For an interesting discussion of 'a level of significant comparisons and contrasts which are developed among the four plots and used to relate them to each other' see Richard Levin's 'The Four Plots of *A Chaste Maid in Cheapside*', *Review of English Studies*, XVI (1965), 14–24.

it in characteristic ways. It is very significant, for example, that
when Sir Walter comes to London bent on marriage, instead of
simply casting his Welsh mistress aside, he brings her with him,
and contrives to marry her to his prospective brother-in-law, to
'make [her] fortune shine'. The fact that Sir Walter has no
selfish motive for this gesture shows that he already possesses, at
the beginning of the play, the primitive sense of obligation to
others which does not begin to dawn in Witgood, in *A Trick to
Catch the Old One*, until Act III;[29] and the case of Sir Walter
demonstrates, no less than that of Witgood, the importance
which Middleton attached to even the rudiment of charitable
feeling. The wish, 'may you live | To conquer your own troubles,
and cross ends, | As you are ready to supply your friends', be-
comes a law in Middleton's dramatic microcosm: its operation
accounts for the success of Witgood's mistress in *A Trick to
Catch the Old One*, and it predicts that of Mistress Low-water in
No Wit, No Help Like a Woman's. Similarly, the crude manifestations of fellow-feeling in Witgood and Sir Walter Whorehound
look forward to moral revival. The dramatic histories of Witgood
and Sir Walter demonstrate that Middleton viewed any generous
tendency as being symptomatic of a dormant predisposition to
virtue, requiring only some stimulus, such as a good example or a
shock, to excite it into active life.

Sir Walter displays a further promising sign. Having already
made him, and the servants, openly contemptuous of the wittol in
Act I, Middleton makes Sir Walter comment upon Allwit's lack
of concern for his reputation in Act II—

> When Man turnes base, out goes his Soules pure flame,
> The fat of ease o're-throwes the eyes of shame.[30]

—to indicate that the contempt the knight has shown before is
not all arrogance and suspiciousness. Yet, while there is an
element of natural disgust in his contempt, Sir Walter's expression of the truth about Allwit, in Act II, is a compound irony.
There is first the superficial irony that iniquitous men should be
in possession of the truth, and able to express it in the form of
categorical propositions;[31] and second, the deeper irony that any

---

[29] See above, p. 81. [30] p. 20 (Bullen: V, 35).
[31] See above, pp. 42–43.

man should both possess the truth and at the same time be careless, or completely unaware, of its continuing relevance to his own life. Both these ironies arise in the histories of Follywit and Lactantio,[32] as well as in that of Sir Walter; but the deeper irony has a new aspect in Sir Walter's case. With Follywit and Lactantio, Middleton was trying to draw attention to the sanctions imposed upon sinners by universal justice, a regulating influence from without; and he was calling for common-sense responses to that inescapable influence. With Sir Walter he is on different ground, however, for now he is not saying that individuals should be persuaded to live virtuously merely from fear of sanctions, but that they should develop, and be guided by, a regulating influence from within. Follywit, Lactantio, and Sir Walter Whorehound all begin their dramatic histories in a state of semi-enlightenment; Follywit and Lactantio about the operation of universal justice, but Sir Walter on the subject of 'shame'. It is to Sir Walter's credit that he recognizes what only the moral idiot would not— that wittolry is shameful. However, that his disgust with Allwit is not inspired directly by the latter's condition, but rather by his inattention to precautions for keeping his wittolry a secret, is deeply ironical, as is also the fact that Sir Walter's precautions for concealing his own condition have hidden its infamy not only from the world but from Sir Walter himself. When Sir Walter speaks of 'the eyes of shame' in Act II, he is only conscious of the eyes of the world; but, just as Middleton takes the part of universal justice and arranges for the completion of Follywit's and Lactantio's educations, so he makes Touchwood Junior's sword remove the veil which obscures Sir Walter's vision of himself, even as it wounds him.

Middleton effects the change in Sir Walter in a short space, and he makes the contrast sharp. The fight takes place at the end of Act IV. Sir Walter expresses his confidence about the imminent success of his enterprise immediately before Touchwood Junior's entrance; at the same time, he leaves no doubt that his own 'Soules pure flame' is wellnigh 'out'. By making him place a monetary value on Moll Yellowhammer's chastity, relating it, in the most brutal terms, to the amount of gold he expects to receive through the marriage, Middleton emphasizes that before

[32] See above, pp. 45–6, and p. 75, n. 39.

the fight Sir Walter is ruled, as Allwit and Yellowhammer are, by the sense of values that goes with a wholly materialistic orientation to life:

> I never was so neere my wish . . .
> . . . ere to morrow noone,
> I shall receive two thousand pound in Gold,
> And a sweet Mayden-head,
> Worth fourtie.[33]

Immediately after the fight, however, Allwit and Yellowhammer are no longer counterparts but foils for Sir Walter: Sir Walter becomes Middleton's moral spokesman, in earnest, at the beginning of Act V.

After repulsing his advances, Sir Walter reproaches Allwit for never having taken him to task for his iniquity, and Middleton did not intend that this reproach should appear absurd. Sir Walter feels a genuine sense of gratitude to Touchwood Junior for having brought him to his moral senses,[34] and Allwit suffers in his estimation by contrast. Here, as in Sir Walter's earlier, but only partially informed, criticism of Allwit, there is a reference to watching eyes:

> Thou know'st me to be wicked, for thy basenesse
> Kept the Eyes open still on all my sinnes.
> None knew the deere account my soule stood charg'd with
> So well as thou, yet like Hels flattering Angel,
> Would'st never tell me an't, let'st me goe on
> And joyne with Death in sleepe, that if I had not wak't
> Now by chance, even by a strangers pittie,
> I had everlastingly slept out all hope
> Of grace and mercie.[35]

The wittol retreats from this unexpected censure, sends forward his wife to take his place, and Middleton goes on to express the rest of the disapproval that he repressed when writing Allwit's soliloquy in Act I.

Wife.   How ist with you Sir?
S. Walt. Not as with you,
          Thou loathsome strumpet. . . .

. . . .

[33] p. 56 (Bullen: V, 91).   [34] See below, p. 115.
[35] V. p. 58 (Bullen: V, 94).

CONSCIENCE AND CHARACTER

> ... Is this a time,
> Unconscionable Woman, to see thee,
> Art thou so cruell to the peace of Man,
> Not to give libertie now?
> . . . .
> ... Prethee shew thy modestie,
> If the least graine be left, and get thee from me.
> Thou should'st be rather lock't many Roomes hence
> From the poore miserable sight of me,
> If either love or grace had part in thee.[36]

Of Mistress Allwit's copious tears Sir Walter says,

> ... What teares are those?
> Get you away with them. I shall fare the worse,
> As long as they are weeping. They worke against me.
> There's nothing but thy appetite in that sorrow—
> Thou weep'st for Lust, ...

and, having identified her tears as manifestations of animal remorse, rather than rational penitence, he points out Mistress Allwit's hypocrisy with a similitude that emphasizes the moral responsibility of women:

> This shewes like the fruitlesse sorrow of a carelesse mother
> That brings her Sonne with diallance to the Gallowes,
> And then stands by, and weepes to see him suffer.[37]

When his children by Mistress Allwit are brought forward, Sir Walter sees them as living evidence of his iniquity—

> O ... let me for ever hide my cursed Face
> From sight of those that darkens all my hopes,
> And stands betweene me and the sight of Heaven.
> Who sees me now ...
> May rightly say, I am o're-growne with sinne.[38]

There are enough points of resemblance between the scene just described and parts of Act IV of *A Mad World, My Masters* to show that Middleton was reworking an old idea. With Penitent Brothel, as with Sir Walter, Middleton makes issue of the idea that 'Adulterie | Drawes the divorce twixt heaven and the

---

[36] V. p. 58 (Bullen: V, 95). [37] V. p. 59 (Bullen: V, 95-6).
[38] V. p. 59 (Bullen: V, 96).

soule';³⁹ Penitent Brothel is tormented by a succubus in the shape of Mistress Harebrain as Sir Walter is by the sight of Mistress Allwit and his illegitimate children; and Penitent Brothel and Sir Walter both remonstrate with their mistresses, making similar references to the devil.⁴⁰ Self-knowledge affects the two debauchees differently, however. Penitent Brothel, fully conscious of his degeneracy from the first, questions himself as follows in Act I: 'why in others doe I checke wilde passions, | And retaine deadly follies in my self?'; not until Act IV, after he has once seduced Mistress Harebrain, does it occur to him to give up his self-indulgent way of life. Sir Walter, on the other hand, is a stranger to his conscience until Touchwood Junior wounds him; and what he realizes about himself afterwards guides him immediately and irresistibly away from iniquity. Middleton has now come to view the conception of conscience implicit in Penitent Brothel's 'When mens intents are wicked, their guilt haunts em' as a mere illusion—a superficiality, like Mistress Allwit's tears. With Sir Walter, and later with the Colonel in *A Fair Quarrel*, he represents conscience as a much more potent force—a force at once overpowering and all-seeing, like universal justice itself, that, once truly awakened, admits of no self-deception and no struggle, and inspires in the possessor not morbid brooding but a sense of gratitude. In *A Chaste Maid in Cheapside* Middleton conveys this ideal of conscience, in part, with imagery—'the eyes of shame'— and Sir Walter, with those 'eyes' at last turned inward, makes a final allusion to them to conclude his service as Middleton's moral spokesman. About to move from Allwit's house, and 'the fat of ease', to the debtors' prison, he remarks, 'If ever Eyes were open, these are they.'

Middleton balanced the serious aspects of *More Dissemblers Besides Women*, *No Wit, No Help Like a Woman's*, and *A Chaste Maid in Cheapside*, with passages and scenes intended chiefly to amuse.⁴¹ By writing the penetrating scenes of the Dampit

³⁹ Penitent Brothel reads this precept to the audience from a book. Sir Walter says, 'Her [Mistress Allwit's] pleasing pleasures now hath poyson'd me, | Which I exchang'd my Soule for.'
⁴⁰ Penitent Brothel's 'Be honest; then the Divell will nere assume thee' is echoed by Sir Walter's 'when Man with-drawes from him, he [the Devil] leaves the place.'
⁴¹ In I. ii and IV. i of *More Dissemblers Besides Women* Middleton exploits the comic and derisory value of an absurd jargon. In the following scenes he uses, or imitates, a foreign language for comic effects: *No Wit, No Help Like a Woman's*, I. iii, and *A Chaste Maid in Cheapside*, I. i and IV. i.

sequence into Acts I, III, and IV of *A Trick to Catch the Old One*,[42] on the other hand, he appears to have been trying to balance his charitable treatment of Witgood and his mistress. Yet Middleton's disposition to allow a worthy motive or unselfish tendency to outweigh, or the suffering of injustice to neutralize, the shortcomings of a character makes itself evident, in less obvious ways, in the other three plays as well. Middleton's uncritical acceptance of a shortcoming in a character implies that that character, though partly wrong, is less wrong than the force that opposes him—as Witgood and his mistress, though partly wrong, are less wrong than Lucre and Hoard; or that that character's worthy motive extenuates the sin that serves his end—as Lady Twilight's mother love extenuates the lie she tells for Philip. This inclination to judge equitably, and hopefully—by letting an individual's virtue help to compensate for his deficiencies—enters into the characterization of the heroine in *The Roaring Girl*.

[42] See above, p. 83, n. 10.

VII

THE ROARING GIRL OR MOLL CUT-PURSE

The Roaring Girl was printed in quarto in 1611 with a title-page ascription to 'T. Middleton and T. Dekkar'. Dekker took a special interest in the cant language of the underworld the heroine frequented, and it is generally agreed that the extensive display of canting in the first scene of Act V is his work.[1] Although this canting scene has the appearance of an insertion[2]—a piece Middleton might have asked his friend specially to write to give the play an additional note of realism, Dekker very likely wrote some of the dialogue in other scenes as well. The plots, characters, and themes bear Middleton's mark, however, and the over-all plan was clearly his. A. W. Ward, conscious of Middleton's pre-eminence in the play, particularly in regard to the characterization of the heroine, wrote as follows:

> In *The Roaring Girle* . . . in which . . . Dekker was associated with Middleton, there seems every reason to assign to the latter a principal share. . . . There are touches in it of that pathetic force which Dekker could on occasion reveal; but the bright vivacity which gives something like a charm to this strange figure may be confidently ascribed to Middleton's happier touch.[3]

But if there are 'touches . . . of that pathetic force which Dekker could on occasion reveal', there is also a remarkable didactic force, not in 'touches', but running through the very texture of the play, that is distinctly Middleton's; and the pervasiveness of that didactic force shows, more clearly than any other feature, that

---

[1] Quotations from Dekker's tracts, *The Belman of London*, 1608, and *Lanthorne and Candlelight*, 1612, are provided in Dyce's edition, and repeated in Bullen's, to explain the cant terms used in the scene.
[2] See below, pp. 109–10.
[3] *History of English Dramatic Literature*, 2nd edn., II, 519.

whichever of the authors did more of the actual writing,[4] the development of the whole was under Middleton's direction. Ward sensed the presence of this force as well, for he went on to write, 'The idea of enforcing by means of an example boldly taken from real life the truth that virtue may be found in the most unexpected quarters, had not become hackneyed in the Elisabethan [*sic*] age.'[5]

In the other plays in the present group Middleton revealed faults in certain of his imaginary characters, introduced circumstances to extenuate or virtues to overshadow these faults, and withheld his criticism; in his Letter to the Reader in *The Roaring Girl* he enunciates this liberal procedure as an artistic principle, and acknowledges that he has followed it in depicting Moll Frith, or Moll Cut-purse as she was commonly known, his 'roaring girl' contemporary:

... worse things, I must needs confesse, the world ha's taxt her for, then has beene written of her; but 'tis the excellency of a Writer, to leave things better then he finds 'em; though some obscoene fellow (that cares not what he writes against others, yet keepes a mysticall baudy-house himselfe, and entertaines drunkards, to make use of their pockets, and vent his private bottle-ale at midnight), though such a one would have ript up the most nasty vice, that ever hell belcht forth, and presented it to a modest Assembly, yet we rather wish in such discoveries, where reputation lies bleeding, a slacknesse of truth, then fulnesse of slander.[6]

Evidently Moll Frith's faults were sufficiently well known to Middleton's audience. Her nickname makes it clear that at some time in her career she was a criminal; but there is evidence that she later used her knowledge of the underworld in the service of

---

[4] R. H. Barker summarizes the opinions of those who have attempted to divide the play on p. 170 of *Thomas Middleton*. The larger share is usually assigned to Middleton. F. G. Fleay assigns only three scenes to Middleton (*A Biographical Chronicle of the English Drama, 1559–1642* [London 1891], I, 132), without mentioning a reason, and F. T. Bowers gives no explanation for his leaning to Fleay's views (*The Dramatic Works of Thomas Dekker*, III [Cambridge 1958], 8). Professor Bowers conjectures that it was Dekker who made the fair copy from which he thinks the printer's copy for the quarto of 1611 derived: '... this hypothesis', he writes, 'helps to explain a scene or two in which the authorship seems somewhat mixed.'
[5] *History of English Dramatic Literature*, 2nd edn., II, 519–20.
[6] Sig. A3–A3ᵛ (Bullen: IV, 8).

law and order,[7] and this vindicates Middleton's judgement of her, and his 'slacknesse of truth'—his minimizing of the unpleasant side of her reputation by allowing Sir Alexander Wengrave, an unattractive character in the play, to be the one to allude to it. Moll Frith's peculiarities are revealed in a woodcut on the title-page of the quarto—she is shown in male attire, smoking a pipe, and holding a sword. She was a man-like woman, and noted for this eccentricity,[8] but Middleton, 'who was able', as Professor Ellis-Fermor observed, 'to perceive not only superficial differences of manner but fundamental differences of mental processes',[9] saw and admired a heroic quality in this 'strange figure', and he emphasized it in his portrayal of her.

There is one structurally simple plot in *The Roaring Girl*, that with which the play begins and ends, and a more complex plot, or nexus of plots with a common motif, that is set in motion at the beginning of Act II and concluded at the end of Act IV. The simple plot and the complex plot are both composed of materials found in Middleton's other early drama. Their actions are independent, but Moll Frith has a part to play in both, and each accentuates a different aspect of her character.

The simple plot concerns a pair of lovers, Sebastian Wengrave and Mary Fitzallard, whose union, like that of Touchwood Junior and Moll Yellowhammer in *A Chaste Maid in Cheapside*, is thwarted by a materialistic parent. At some time before the action begins Sebastian's father, Sir Alexander, and Mary's, Sir Guy, have agreed that the two young people shall be married; but since Mary's dowry is to be small, Sir Alexander has later changed his mind—he is capable of the largess of Sir Bounteous Progress (*A Mad World, My Masters*) when entertaining guests, but, like Sir Oliver Twilight in *No Wit, No Help Like a Woman's*, he is loath to give up any of his money in the marriage

---

[7] From the records of a lawsuit in 1621, it appears that Moll Frith held a royal commission to examine persons arrested for petty crimes. See M. Dowling's 'A Note on Moll Cutpurse—*The Roaring Girl*', *Review of English Studies*, X (Jan. 1934), 67–71.

[8] An anonymous biographical tract of 1662 states that 'stave and toyl, instead of *spinning* and *realing* was her delight[:] tell her of Housewiveing, *Pish, let us live by our Wits* replyed she, *I was never born under a Bushel*' (*The Womans Champion . . . Mrs. Mary Frith . . . from her Cradle to her Winding-Sheet*, Bodleian Wood 654ᵃ 22, p. 2).

[9] *The Jacobean Drama*, p. 124.

of an offspring.[10] To make his father anxious to keep to his original agreement, Sebastian pretends to dote upon Moll Frith, and deciding that 'twixt lovers hearts' Moll is 'a fit instrument', eventually obtains her help in contriving a meeting with Mary, Moll posing as Sebastian's music teacher and Mary disguised as a page. By rendering this aid Moll wins a measure of sympathy, as Touchwood Senior does by helping the thwarted lovers in *A Chaste Maid in Cheapside*. She does not act as intermediary for a vicious purpose, as Frank Gullman does in *A Mad World, My Masters*; on the contrary, her capacity is more that of chaperon. The conception of marriage Middleton expressed through the hero of *The Phoenix*—'Mother of lawfull sweetes, unshamed mornings, | Dangerlesse pleasures, thou that mak'st the bed | Both pleasant, and legitimately fruitfull'—helps to shape a basic theme in the other plot of *The Roaring Girl*, and Moll, imbued with the sense of decency from which that conception arises, makes Sebastian and Mary understand that she would not have lent them her assistance had she not been persuaded that their relationship was an honourable one:

Seb.   Thou hast done me a kind office, without touch
       Either of sinne or shame, our loves are honest.
Mol.   I'de scorne to make such shift to bring you together else.[11]

Sir Alexander is taken in by Sebastian's pretended infatuation, but instead of relenting, he tries to ruin Moll. He misjudges her character, however, and his schemes fail. Moll secretly brings about the marriage of Sebastian and Mary, and conspires with Sir Guy Fitzallard to trick Sir Alexander into estating Sebastian 'in those possessions . . . once pointed out for him.'[12] Like Fitsgrave, who hoaxes the malefactors in *Your Five Gallants* in order to expose them, Moll and Sir Guy are agents of universal justice, and no blame attaches to them for their deception. The shocks that they arrange for Sir Alexander, like those endured by Penitent Brothel in *A Mad World, My Masters*, Sir Walter

---

[10] Sir Alexander also shares Sir Oliver's sentiments in regard to undutiful sons. See Bullen, IV, 23 and 316.
[11] IV. sig. H2 (Bullen: IV, 93).
[12] The trick is played in the final scene, and, as in the conspiracy between the Duchess and the Cardinal in *More Dissemblers Besides Women* (see above, p. 76, n. 2), the actual conspiring is omitted; the audience must infer prearranged co-operation from witnessing the trick itself.

Whorehound in *A Chaste Maid in Cheapside*, and Lady Goldenfleece in *No Wit, No Help Like a Woman's*, have a salutary effect: Sir Alexander is brought to a state of contrition.

Moll Frith's sympathy and co-operation with Sebastian Wengrave and Mary Fitzallard show that she is possessed of the qualities Middleton approved of in Witgood's mistress in *A Trick to Catch the Old One*, and Mistress Low-water in *No Wit, No Help Like a Woman's*. The failure of one of Sir Alexander's malicious schemes helps to establish her integrity. Hoping to have her hanged as a thief, Sir Alexander tries to tempt her to steal in the first scene of Act IV. Moll notices the bait and remarks, 'Here were a brave booty for an evening-theefe now', but is only moved to make a reflective observation on the subject of 'mens secret youthfull faults'.[13] Sir Alexander's purpose for the scheme is quite different from Middleton's. Sir Alexander sets a trap; but Middleton imposes a test, like that which the First Lord proposes for trying the virtue of the Duchess in *More Dissemblers Besides Women*.[14] Middleton's aim was to demonstrate that his heroine's reputation for dishonesty was undeserved. This kind of test of honesty is a basic element in the composition of the second plot of *The Roaring Girl*.

Like some of Middleton's earliest plays, the second plot comprises several episodes, each related to the activities of a central figure. In this case, the central figure, Moll, takes an active part in only one of the constituent plots; her presence is felt, rather than seen, in the other two. The following stage direction describes the setting before which the three streams of action begin, and mentions most of the principal characters:

The three shops open in a ranke: the first a Poticaries shop, the next a Fether shop, the third a Sempsters shop: Mistresse Gallipot *in the first, Mistresse* Tiltyard *in the next, Maister* Openworke *and his wife in the third, to them enters* Laxton, Goshawke *and* Greenewit.[15]

Laxton, Goshawk, and Greenwit are gallants. Laxton is involved with the Gallipots in one of the minor plots, and with Moll Frith in another. Goshawk and the Openworks are the principals in the remaining plot. Middleton may have initially intended to involve Greenwit with the Tiltyards in still another plot and then

[13] Sig. H3 (Bullen: IV, 97). [14] See above, p. 63.
[15] II. sig. C3 (Bullen: IV, 31).

abandoned the idea. Moll has an aside which gives promise of a test of Mistress Tiltyard's chastity,[16] but the promise is never fulfilled. Greenwit and the Tiltyards remain characters of minor importance. The three minor plots are united by a common element: each emphasizes women's capacity for self-determination. In two of the plots lecherous gallants become involved with married women. Laxton is a parasite, a debauchee, and a cheat. Like the carpet knight in *The Phoenix*, who calls his mistress, the jeweller's wife, 'my sweete Revennewe', he has attached himself to the wife of a prosperous tradesman. His victim, Mistress Gallipot, has all the wilfulness of Violetta in *Blurt Master-Constable*, Maria in *The Family of Love*, and Aurelia in *More Dissemblers Besides Women*. She is bored with her over-solicitous husband, and takes a perverse pleasure in deceiving him. Laxton brags of her infatuation, and of how he takes money from her without fulfilling her expectations of him—'I'le keepe her honest, as long as I can, to make the poore man [Gallipot] some part of amends—an honest minde of a whooremaister, how thinke you amongst you?'; but Mistress Gallipot is beginning to tire of being put off:

Mist. Gal.   What's the summe would pleasure ye sir? Tho you deserve nothing, lesse at my hands.
Lax.   Why 'tis but for want of opportunitie thou know'st. [aside:] I put her off with opportunitie still: by this light I hate her, but for meanes to keepe me in fashion with gallants. For what I take from her, I spend upon other wenches, beare her in hand still; shee has wit enough to rob her husband, and I waies enough to consume the money.[17]

Mistress Gallipot practises her last deception for Laxton in Act III.[18] In Act IV, while conferring with Mistress Openwork, whom Goshawk has attempted to delude, she makes it clear that

---

[16] See II. sig. D3ᵛ (Bullen: IV, 45).
[17] II. sig. [C4] (Bullen: IV, 34–5). In *No Wit, No Help Like a Woman's* Mistress Low-water comments on a similar kind of situation as follows: 'What a most fearful love raigns in some hearts, | That dare oppose all Judgment to get means, | And wed rich widows, onely to keep Queans' (see I. pp. 19–20 (Bullen: IV, 301–2)).
[18] To obtain thirty pounds for Laxton, she pretends to have been pre-contracted to him; Gallipot gives him the money to buy him off. Witgood uses the same device to deceive Hoard in *A Trick to Catch the Old One* (see above, p. 82).

she is determined to have nothing more to do with Laxton. Mistress Openwork points the moral: 'Happy is the woman can bee ridde of 'em all; 'las what are your whisking gallants to our husbands, weigh 'em rightly man for man?' Laxton approaches Mistress Gallipot shortly afterwards. She refuses to listen to him, and uses him with the contempt with which she had formerly used her husband. When Laxton resorts to extortion, she denounces him, and confesses her trickery.

Mistress Openwork is as self-willed as Mistress Gallipot, but much less peccable, and Openwork, despite his wife's scolding and groundless jealousy, is as devoted a husband as Gallipot, but a much less gullible one. Openwork is suspicious of Goshawk's intentions toward Mistress Openwork, and has decided to 'try [his] honesty'. Taking Goshawk aside, he asks him to intercede and 'make all whole' with his wife, who has just been scolding him; while making this request he imparts the false information that he keeps 'a whore ith subburbs'. Goshawk has 'a guift of trechery . . . to betray [his] friend whe[n] he puts most trust in [him]', and he uses the information to provoke Mistress Openwork's jealous anger, hoping that she will be induced to enter an adulterous relationship with him by a desire for revenge. Instead, she reproaches Openwork for his supposed infidelity and learns the truth. Together, they bring about Goshawk's discomfiture in Act IV. Goshawk has arranged to go to Brentford with Mistress Openwork, ostensibly to catch Openwork in compromising circumstances there, but really to attempt her seduction. Shortly after their meeting prior to departure, Openwork accosts them, seemingly by chance, and Mistress Openwork pretends to charge him with having just returned from a visit to his mistress. Goshawk is fearful of exposure, and Openwork deliberately intensifies his agitation: he feigns a violent rage, demands to be told the name of his accuser, and draws his sword—

. . . if the fiend I meet (in myne owne house)
I'le kill him: —— [in] the streete
Or at the Church dore: —— there —— (cause he seekes to unty
The knot God fastens) he deserves most to dy.[19]

Mistress Openwork then denounces Goshawk, and he makes an

[19] IV. sig. 13–13ᵛ (Bullen: IV, 110–11).

apology; but when Openwork, after expressing his disappointment in him, offers him forgiveness, Goshawk remains sullen. The Laxton–Gallipots plot and the Goshawk–Openworks plot together emphasize the contrast between the shabbiness of lechery and the dignity of marriage. The Gallipots display the weakness of character that places marriage in jeopardy, and the Openworks the strength that makes it secure; and Laxton and Goshawk represent the force that 'seekes to unty the knot God fastens'. Gallipot is foolish, and does not know, as Mistress Gallipot says, 'how to handle a woman in her kind'. Openwork, on the other hand, is like Andrugio in *More Dissemblers Besides Women*: judicious, and, at the same time, generously disposed to forgive;[20] when he tries 'the soundness of [his] judgement' in respect of Goshawk, he also delivers a check to his wife's morbid jealousy—he remarks, after they have taught Goshawk his lesson, '... wife nothing is perfect borne', and she replies, 'I thought you had bene borne perfect.' Mistress Gallipot's deficiencies, deceitfulness, and proneness to corruption, contrast with Mistress Openwork's plain dealing and moral hardihood. Mistress Openwork's jealous disposition makes her ready to believe the report that Openwork has a mistress, but instead of going through with the plan slyly suggested by Goshawk, she lives up to her name by confronting her husband and testing the validity of the report openly—'I up and opened all.' After Openwork has explained his purpose, she understands Goshawk's real motive for suggesting that he should go with her to Brentford. In one of Middleton's earliest plays, *The Family of Love*, Lipsalve and Gudgeon, intent upon Mistress Glister's seduction, use the same approach as Goshawk, though without subtlety, and Mistress Glister shows a readiness to retaliate upon her promiscuous husband by gratifying their desires;[21] but the contempt which Mistress Openwork expresses for Goshawk, in her conversation with Mistress Gallipot, shows that she would be scarcely more inclined to commit adultery for the sake of revenge than Mistress Low-water in *No Wit, No Help Like a Woman's*.[22] Middleton made the relationship between the Laxton–Gallipots plot and the Goshawk–Openworks plot obvious by bringing Mistress Gallipot and Mistress Openwork together for their conversation in

[20] See above, p. 79 and Bullen, IV, 112.
[21] See Bullen, III, 94–6.   [22] See above, pp. 84–5.

Act IV. The relationship between the Laxton–Moll Frith plot and the experience of the Gallipots and Openworks depends almost entirely upon analogy. It is, nevertheless, an equally clear relationship, and the didactic force of the Laxton–Moll Frith plot, the climax of which precedes the development of the other minor plots, goes far to sustain the theme of the action in which the Gallipots and Openworks are involved.

While the gallants stand gossiping before the shops in the opening scene of Act II, Moll Frith enters to make a purchase from the sempster. Her sex is not disguised on this occasion, and her appearance immediately arouses libidinous desire in Laxton: he says, in an aside, 'Hart I would give but too much money to be nibling with that wench!... I'll lay hard siege to her. Mon[e]y is that *Aqua fortis* that eates into many a maidenhead; where the wals are flesh & bloud, Ile ever pierce through with a golden auger.'[23] Laxton looks on while Moll castigates a gallant who has insulted her on some previous occasion, but fails to take the hint the incident affords him. He accosts her, boldly proposes that they 'go out a towne ... [to] bee merry and lye together', and gives her 'ten Angels in faire gold' to prove he is in earnest. She answers his importunity with 'Tis hard but we shall meete sir', and they agree upon a time and place of meeting. Moll keeps the appointment, but Laxton does not recognize her at first because of her male attire.

Lax.   ... Ile sweare I knew thee not.
Mol.   Ile sweare you did not: but you shall know me now.[24]

Moll draws her sword, puts an equal amount of her own money with the gold that he gave her when the appointment was made, and bids him fight a duel with her for the sum. Laxton protests, and she warns him, 'Draw or Ile serve an execution on thee | Shall lay thee up till doomes day.' When he asks '... why what dost meane Mol?', she replies, 'To teach thy base thoughts manners', and delivers a long speech decrying the impudence of lechers. Moll then fights with Laxton, wounds him, and, when he begs for his life, lets him go. She concludes the episode with the following soliloquy:

---

[23] Spelt 'auguer' in the quarto.
[24] III. sig. [E4] (Bullen: IV, 60).

> If I could meete my enemies one by one thus,
> I might...
> ... make 'em know, shee that has wit, and spirit,
> May scorne to live beholding to her body for meate,
> Or for apparell like your common dame,
> That makes shame get her cloathes, to cover shame.
> Base is that minde, that kneels unto her body,
> As if a husband stood in awe on's wife.
> My spirit shall be Mistresse of this house,
> As long as I have time in't.[25]

Middleton intended that Moll Frith's attitude and behaviour in this episode should serve as standards by which his audience might judge the attitudes and behaviour of Mistress Gallipot and Mistress Openwork in subsequent scenes, and he alludes to the Openworks and Mistress Gallipot when he makes Moll liken a lecher to a ravening animal that watches for his 'prey' in 'quarrelling wedlockes' and 'poore shifting sisters'. The juxtaposition of the Laxton–Moll Frith plot and the experience of the two wives is a striking example of Middleton's *montage* technique,[26] but Middleton's chief purpose was not to enforce 'by means of an example boldly taken from real life the truth that virtue may be found in the most unexpected quarters';[27] rather he wished to emphasize that strength of will in women need not manifest itself in perversity, but may be used to preserve a virtuous way of life.

The first scene of Act V of *The Roaring Girl* was clearly a special enterprise, mainly intended to exploit the novelty of the cant language of the underworld, and most of the characters in it do not appear earlier. The canting scene has little connection with the rest of the play, and the action involving the Gallipots and Openworks seems to have been brought to a hasty conclusion[28] to make way for it before the dénouement of the Sebastian Wengrave–Mary Fitzallard plot. In my opinion, Dekker, with his special interest in canting, wrote most of it, and Middleton filled

---

[25] III. sig. F[1] (Bullen: IV, 64).
[26] See above, p. 10.   [27] See above, p. 101.
[28] After Mistress Gallipot's confession Gallipot calls Laxton 'villaine', and Laxton makes an incoherent defence. He begins by representing Mistress Gallipot as a virtuous woman, who only gave him money to keep him from indulging in malicious slander, and ends by contradicting himself and returning Gallipot's gold. Gallipot then invites all the assembled company to dinner. See sig. K[1]–K[1]ᵛ (Bullen: IV, 116–18).

in the concluding speeches in which Moll is given an opportunity to justify her knowledge of 'ill things'.

It was natural that Moll Frith, a self-determined individual who had served an 'apprenticeship to life' in London's underworld should have appealed to Middleton strongly. She may not have had all the wisdom Middleton credits her with, but her forceful personality inspired him to use her as a moral spokesman, and to give her a dramatic position similar to that of his hero-presenters in *The Phoenix* and *Your Five Gallants*.

Before he began his career as a playwright, Middleton celebrated the chastity of Lucrece in an ardent poem,[29] and the image of Lucrece is detectable in the virtuous but vulnerable women in *The Phoenix*, Falso's niece and the sea-captain's wife, and in the wealthy, suspectless virgin Katherine in *Your Five Gallants*, who is completely indebted to Fitsgrave ('. . . ile see | Whether their lives from touch of blame sit free') for her knowledge of the depravity of her other suitors. The heroines of the present group of plays are experienced and capable women, however, as Fitsgrave is an experienced and capable man: they are imbued with some of the spirit of Middleton's idealized 'roaring girl'. Middleton's Moll Frith is well-informed, shrewd ('. . . faith he seemes | A man without; I'le try what he is within'), and, like the Duchess in *More Dissemblers Besides Women* after her encounter with reality, independent. Moreover, like Mistress Low-water, who disguises herself as a man in *No Wit, No Help Like a Woman's*, she has an aggressive spirit that makes her ready to offer active resistance to adversaries, and the necessary strength and resource to overcome them.

[29] See above, pp. 7–8.

PART THREE

VARIATIONS ON THEMES

A Fair Quarrel
The Mayor of Queenborough
The Old Law
The Widow
The Witch

VIII

A FAIR QUARREL AND THE OLD LAW

In or about 1616 Middleton wrote *A Fair Quarrel* and *The Old Law*,[1] plays in which he tended to allow his philosophical preoccupations and sense of moral purpose to take precedence over the motive to entertain, as he did in his early plays, *The Phoenix* and *Your Five Gallants*. In the latter plays the action centres on a virtuous young man whom Middleton uses as a moral spokesman. The same is true of *A Fair Quarrel* and *The Old Law*, but the heroes of these plays are somewhat less conspicuous as moral spokesmen than their predecessors, Phoenix and Fitsgrave, because, unlike them, they do not have detached, intermediary positions as 'omniscient observers' who 'search out mans intents'.

The male principals of the main plot of *A Fair Quarrel* are two soldiers who have just returned from the wars. One of them is known only as 'the Colonell'; the other is Captain Agar, the young hero of the play.

The central event of the action of the main plot is a duel between Agar and the Colonel. A dispute between two of their friends precedes the first appearance of the principals, and serves as prelude to the larger conflict. The dispute is concerned with which of the two, the captain or the colonel, is the nobler and more courageous man, and the supporter of Captain Agar mentions his friend's essential qualities:

[1] The name of William Rowley appears below Middleton's on the early editions of these and two other plays. From the evidence of characterization, structure, themes, and mode of thematic expression, it is clear that Middleton both conceived and dominated the execution of three of the four plays, the two treated in this chapter, and *The Changeling*, which is discussed below in Chapter XI. It has been suggested that the title-page ascription of the fourth play, *The Spanish Gipsy*, is fraudulent, but there is reason to think that Middleton may have had a direct or indirect connection with the drama. The relationship between Middleton and Rowley, and *The Spanish Gipsy*, are discussed below in Appendix C. From the available evidence, it appears likely that Middleton befriended Rowley and made him his pupil-assistant. Philip Massinger's name also appears on the title-page of *The Old Law*, but it is generally agreed that if he had anything to do with the play at all, it was in the capacity of reviser.

> Yong? Why, do you make youth stand for an imputation?
> That which you now produce for his disgrace,
> Infers his noblenes, that being yong
> Should have an anger more inclind to courage
> And moderation then the Colonell:
> A vertue as rare as chastitie in youth.
> And let the cause be good (conscience in him
> Which ever crownes his acts, and is indeed,
> Valours prosperity), he dares then as much
> As ever made him famous that you plead for.²

But whereas Captain Agar insists that the 'cause be good' before he fights, the Colonel is headstrong and contentious—like the soldier Shakespeare describes in *As You Like It*, he is 'jealous in honour, sudden and quick in quarrel'. In a subsequent scene Captain Agar attempts to curb the Colonel's abuse of his uncle, and the Colonel calls him 'the son of a whore'. The young man immediately responds with 'Ha! Whore! plagues and furies Ile thrust that backe, | Or pluck thy heart out after, sonne of a whore?'; but, confident of the validity of the code under which a duel is considered a trial of truth before God, he hesitates to fight until he can obtain assurance from his mother that there is no substance in the Colonel's taunt.

Lady Agar at first wrathfully denies the slur upon her honour, but when she realizes that her son intends to fight a duel over the matter, she pretends to have been 'betrayde to a most sinfull howre | By a corrupted soule [she] put in trust once'. When Captain Agar's friends arrive to accompany him to the duel, he tells them that he does not intend to fight. He withstands their protests, and, at the place appointed for the duel, makes overtures of peace. The Colonel meets these with open contempt, and calls Agar a coward. The latter then feels that he has a morally justifiable reason to fight:

> Oh, heaven has pittied my excessive patience,
> And sent me a cause. . . .
> A coward I was never: —— Come you backe sir?³

In the ensuing duel the Colonel is overcome, and Captain Agar interprets his victory as a vindication of his faith—'Truth never fayles her servant, sir, nor leaves him | With the daies shame

---

² I. sig. A3ᵛ (Bullen: IV, 163).   ³ III. sig. E4ᵛ (Bullen: IV, 210).

upon him.' Just as Sir Walter Whorehound's 'eyes of shame' are opened by a wound from Touchwood Junior's sword in *A Chaste Maid in Cheapside*, so the Colonel's are by a wound from Captain Agar's. Before Agar leaves the field, the Colonel says,

> Oh, just Heaven has found me
> And turnde the stings[4] of my too hastie Injuries
> Into my owne bloud. I pursude my ruin
> And urgde him past the patience of an Angell.
> Could mans revenge extend beyond mans life,
> This would ha' wak't it. If this flame will light me
> But till I see my sister, tis a kinde one.
> More I expect not from't. Noble deserver,
> Farewell, most valiant, and most wrong'd of men.
> Do but forgive me, and I am Victor then.[5]

Charles Lamb praised the moral vigour of *A Fair Quarrel*, and decried the 'hypocritical meekness' of the drama of his own day. Lamb was particularly impressed with the behaviour of Captain Agar.[6] To Middleton the experience of the Colonel was equally important.

Sir Walter Whorehound's gratitude for his moral awakening is implicit in his reference to Touchwood Junior's having wounded him as 'a strangers pittie'.[7] In *A Fair Quarrel* Middleton elaborated the grateful reaction of the newly enlightened man. In Act IV the Colonel answers his sister's 'How cheere you sir?' as follows:

> In soule never better.
> I feele an excellent health there, such a stoutnes,
> My invisible enemy flies me. Seeing me armde
> With penitence and forgivenes, they fall backeward,
> Whether through admiration, not imagining
> There were such armory in a Souldiers soule
> As pardon and repentance, or through power
> Of ghostly valour. But I have beene Lord
> Of a more happy conquest in nine houres now,
> Then in nine yeare before.[8]

The Colonel is so deeply impressed by Captain Agar's virtue that he persuades his sister to offer herself to Agar in marriage. There is a reconciliation between the two men at the end of the play.

[4] Spelt 'strings' in the quartos. [5] III. sig. F[1]ᵛ (Bullen: IV, 214).
[6] See Lamb's *Specimens of English Dramatic Poets* (London, 1808), p. 136.
[7] See above, p. 96. [8] Sig. H[1] (Bullen: IV, 237).

In *No Wit, No Help Like a Woman's* Lady Twilight tells a painful lie to save her son ('Now', she tells him, 'see me take a poyson with great joy, | Which but for thy sake, I should swoun to touch'); but Lady Agar's mother love is more impressive: her lie entails the sacrifice of her cherished reputation (like the Duchess in *More Dissemblers Besides Women*, she has vowed to remain a widow). The experiences of Captain Agar and Lady Agar are parallel—he places 'truth' before his worldly reputation as a soldier, and she places her son's life before her reputation as a chaste woman. It is interesting to note that Lady Agar is made to relate her motherly devotion to her determination to remain a widow:

> . . . when I thinke on him,
> His deerenesse, and his worth, it earnes me more.
> They that know riches tremble to be poore.
> My passion is not every womans sorrow.
> She must be truly honest feeles my griefe,
> And onely known to One. If such there be,
> They know the sorrow that oppresseth mee.[9]

The theme of the main plot of *A Fair Quarrel* has an ambivalent quality. The play was 'Acted before the King', and there can be little doubt that Middleton knew that the following speech by the enlightened Colonel would please James:

> O kinde Lieftenants,
> This is the onely[10] warre we should provide for,
> Where he that forgives largest, and sighes strongest
> Is a tride Souldier, a true man in deed,
> And winnes the best field, makes his owne heart bleed.[11]

Yet the play does not make the sweeping condemnation of fighting that these words suggest. Middleton did not even go as far in his attempt to flatter James as to let the speaker live up to them. In the final scene the Colonel gives his entire estate to Agar, and says,

> For me,
> I never meane to change my mistris,
> And warre is able to maintaine her servant.[12]

---

[9] III. sig. G[1] (Bullen: IV, 224). See above, p. 66.
[10] So the 1617 quarto; the reading of the 1622 quarto is 'one'.
[11] IV. sig. H[1] (Bullen: IV, 237).
[12] V. sig. K4ᵛ (Bullen: IV, 275).

Like the Colonel, Andrugio in *More Dissemblers Besides Women* has war for a mistress, and the graphic terms in which Aurelia explains why this circumstance makes his suit uninteresting not only emphasize her coarseness, but show that Middleton was fully conscious of the horrors of war:

> I like not him that has two Mistresses,
> War, and his sweet-heart; he can ne'r please both.
> And War's a soaker; she's no friend to us—
> Turns a man home sometimes to his Mistress
> Some forty ounces poorer then he went.
> All his discourse out of the Book of Surgery,
> Seer-cloth, and Salve, and lies you, all in Tents,
> Like your Camp-Victlers. Out upon't![13]

Middleton, however, did not share King James's aversion to warriors.[14] The question that occupies Captain Agar's mind is not whether or not to fight, but whether or not there is good and sufficient cause to fight. Middleton does not attack the 'law at Armes' in *A Fair Quarrel*, but the espousal of that law by men of feeble conscience. Before the duel the Colonel knows only two criteria of 'manhood'—warlike prowess, and what Agar calls 'titular shaddowes', and he cannot accept Agar's idea that 'twixt friend, and friend, | There is so even and levell a degree, | It will admit of no superlative'; after the duel the Colonel holds moral courage in higher regard than physical courage, and he 'would not change [his] brotherhood [with Captain Agar] with a Monarch'. Middleton impugns all that is implicit in the phrase 'a quarrelling reputation' in *A Fair Quarrel*, but he clearly approves of Captain Agar's readiness to fight for truth.[15]

---

[13] II. p. 30 (Bullen: VI, 412–13).

[14] G. M. Trevelyan writes: 'James disliked "men of war" whether by land or sea. Until in his declining years he let the initiative pass to the volatile and ambitious Buckingham, he was the most thorough-going pacifist who ever bore rule in England. He wielded the sceptre and the pen, and held them both to be mightier than the sword. Of naked steel he had a physical horror . . .' (*Illustrated History of England* [London, 1956], pp. 385–6).

[15] *A Fair Quarrel* first appeared in print in 1617. In the following year, Middleton obtained King James's approval for the publication of a pamphlet entitled *The Peace-Maker*. In the part of *The Peace-Maker* that deals with duelling, Middleton chose to use a few passages from *The Charge of Sir Francis Bacon Knight*, published in 1614, and it is quite clear that certain of Bacon's remarks inspired the central idea that Captain Agar stands for in *A Fair Quarrel*, the idea that in certain circumstances a man of conscience is justified in engaging in a duel. See Appendix E.

Middleton reworked and expanded elements from *A Chaste Made in Cheapside* and *No Wit, No Help Like a Woman's* in the main plot of *A Fair Quarrel*: the fight that brings about the moral awakening of one of the antagonists, from the former play, and the exemplar of maternal devotion from the latter; and he used materials from earlier plays in the underplot as well. One of the conflicts in the underplot is between Lady Agar's brother, Master Russell, and Fitzallen, a young man who wishes to marry Russell's daughter, Jane: Russell does not approve of the match. W. D. Dunkel has pointed out the similarities between this situation and that involving Doctor Glister, Gerardine, and Maria, in Middleton's early play *The Family of Love*.[16] Some differences between the two situations are also worthy of notice.

An important feature of Middleton's treatment of Gerardine and Maria, as of his treatment of Fontinell and Violetta in *Blurt Master-Constable*, and Lactantio and Aurelia in *More Dissemblers Besides Women*, is his determination to emphasize the fact that the attraction between the sexes is essentially animal in nature, and to attack the use of romantic notions of love to veil that fact and impart an appearance of propriety to illicit sexual intimacy. In portraying the lovers in *A Fair Quarrel*, however, Middleton was not motivated by a desire to expose hypocrisy, but by a desire to emphasize virtues.

Fitzallen and Jane have been no less prone to indulge their animal instincts than Gerardine and Maria, but Middleton does not stress this point in *A Fair Quarrel* as he does in *The Family of Love*. In Act I Russell, who is unaware that Jane is pregnant, temporarily rids himself of Fitzallen by having him falsely arrested for debt ('Let Beggers beware to love Rich mens Daughters. | Ile teach 'um the new morrice; I learn't it | My selfe of another carefull Father'). The simple honesty of Fitzallen and Jane is evident in their dialogue just after Fitzallen's arrest:

Jane. Oh my Fitzallen what is to be done?
Fitz. To be still thine is all my part to be, whether in freedome or
       captivity.
Jane. But art thou so ingag'd as this pretends?
Fitz. By heav'n, sweet Jane 'tis all a hellish plot.
       Your cruell smiling father all this while

---

[16] See above, p. 52, n. 36.

> Has candied o're a bitter pill for me,
> Thinking by my remove to plant some other,
> And then let goe his fangs.
Jane. Plant some other?
> Thou hast too firmely stampd me for thine owne,
> Ever to be rast out. I am not currant
> In any others hand; I feare too soone
> I shall discover it.
Fitz. Let come the worst,
> Binde but this knot with an unloosed line,
> I will be still thine owne.
Jane. And Ile be thine.[17]

In place of the ludicrous romantic language of Gerardine and Maria, Middleton substituted the unaffected, straightforward language of people who take a realistic view of life.

It may also be noted that Middleton treats Jane in much the same way that he treats Witgood's mistress in *A Trick to Catch the Old One*: he lays more stress on her worth than on her indiscretion. Consequently Jane becomes a much more appealing character than the wilful, self-indulgent Maria in *The Family of Love*. After Fitzallen is taken away, Jane complains that she is 'not well', and Russell has a physician sent to her to discover her 'griefe' and 'practise remedie'. Middleton seems to have intended the conflict that arises from this action to be the 'fair quarrel' of the underplot of *A Fair Quarrel*. Jane is eventually delivered of her child without her secret being discovered, but the depraved physician tries to force her to yield to his lust by threatening to divulge it. As in the cases of Captain Agar and Lady Agar in the main plot, the paradoxical consequence of making a creditable decision will be loss of 'reputation'. Jane refuses to submit. The physician then withdraws and sends his sister, Anne, to act as his procuress. Earlier Anne has referred to herself as her brother's 'creature'; now, she explains, 'Who lives (commanded) must obey his Keeper: | I must perswade you to this act of woman.' When Jane expresses her indignation, Anne is affected by it much as the Colonel is affected by the virtue of Captain Agar. Her own spirit is aroused, and she supports Jane in her opposition to the physician. The physician's subsequent disclosure of Jane's secret

[17] I. sigs. C2ᵛ–C3 (Bullen: IV, 179–80).

saves Jane from marriage with her father's candidate, Chaugh, a Cornishman with nothing but wealth to recommend him, and brings about her reunion with Fitzallen.

Middleton's continuing interest in the theme of appearance versus reality is evident in the Jane–physician episode. Immediately before the physician makes his lewd proposal, he officiates at the handing over of Jane's infant to a nurse; he commends it to her 'most indulgent care', and observes,

> ... you know Nurse,
> These are above the quantitie of price.[18]
> Where is the glory of the goodliest trees
> But in the fruit and branches? The old stocke
> Must decay, and sprigs, syens such as these
> Must become new stockes from us to glorie,
> In their fruitfull issue, so we are made
> Immortall on[e] by other.[19]

This fair seeming contrasts sharply with the physician's subsequent behaviour, and the contrast provides an effective background for Jane's denunciation speech:

> Away, y'are a Blackamore, you love me?
> I hate you for your love. Are you the man
> That in your painted outside seem'd so white?
> Oh, y'are a foule dissembling Hypocrite.
> You sav'd me from a thiefe that your selfe might rob me,
> Skin'd ore a greene wound to breed an ulcer.[20]

Chaugh and his man Trimtram, descendants of the lecherous buffoons, Lazarillo in *Blurt Master-Constable*, and Lipsalve and Gudgeon in *The Family of Love*, receive instruction in an inane jargon called 'roaring' in the first scene of Act IV.[21] When Middleton wrote the 'new Additions'[22] for *A Fair Quarrel*, he

---

[18] Spelt 'prise' in the quartos.   [19] III. sig. F2 (Bullen: IV, 215).
[20] III. sig. F3ᵛ (Bullen: IV, 219).
[21] Scenes for which Middleton invented a jargon are noted above, pp. 52–3 and 98, n. 41.
[22] A. H. Bullen writes: 'The unsold copies [of the 1617 edition] were re-issued in the same year with a new title-page:— *A Faire Quarrell. With new Additions.* . . . The additions consisted of three leaves, which the binder was directed to place "at the latter end of the fourth act" ' (IV, [155]). There are allusions to the practice of making additions to completed plays in *The Mayor of Queenborough* (see Bullen, II, 93 and 102).

made Chaugh and Trimtram turn their 'roaring' to effect in an attack on a pander, a bawd, and a whore. At the end of the attack Trimtram decides to 'bury 'um altogether, and give 'um an Epitaph'; the epitaph concludes with 'By three trees . . . these three, Pander, Baude, Whore: | Now stinke below ground, stunke long above before.' The added scene shares the squalid atmosphere of Imperia's brothel in *Blurt Master-Constable*, and Dampit's sick-room in *A Trick to Catch the Old One*.

In *The Old Law* Middleton gave his whole attention to the treatment of problems that arise in relationships between the young and the old. His method in the play is a modified form of that which he used in *The Phoenix* and *Your Five Gallants*. As in the latter plays, the action depends upon the determination of one of the characters to secretly 'search out mans intents'. The 'omniscient observer' in *The Old Law* is not the hero, however, but a relatively inconspicuous figure in the background, Evander, the Duke of Epire. Middleton also varied his procedure by not making the 'omniscient observer' identify himself as such in the opening action. Evander does not begin to manage the situation openly until the last act, and the audience must wait until the end of the play to hear him announce his motive: 'We have our end | . . .: we have now seene | The flowers and weeds that grew about our Court.' Evander's end, and Middleton's artistic purposes, are all neatly served by a law that Evander has had proclaimed before the action begins:

That all men living in our Dominions of Epire in their decayd nature, to the age of foure score, or women to the age of three score, shall on the same day bee instantly put to death. . . .[23]

At the beginning of the play Middleton represents Evander as a tyrant whose decision to do away with his aged subjects has been motivated by concern 'for the care and good of the Commonwealth'—his law has 'divers necessary reasons' to support it:

[Men of eighty are] past their bearing Armes, to aide and defend their Countrey, past their manhood and livelihood, to propogate any further issue . . ., and as well past their councells (which overgrown gravity is now run into dotage) to assist their Countrey . . . [and] women . . . [who] never were defence to their Countrey, never by Counsell

[23] I. p. 5 (Bullen: II, 127).

admitted to the assist of government . . ., onely necessary to the propagation of posterity, . . . now at the age of three-score [are] past that good, and all their goodnesse.[24]

Middleton wished to treat two kinds of relationship in *The Old Law*, that between parent and offspring, and that between husband and wife, and he was particularly concerned to deal with the obligations of the young to the old in these relationships. To obtain these ends he used Evander's law, and he used it in the same way as he used the 'law at Armes' in *A Fair Quarrel*: the law provides the principal characters—a number of exemplars and their foils—with a source of motivation, and it provides Middleton with a pretext for evoking from them the particular responses that he wishes either to praise or to condemn.

In the opening scene Simonides, the unworthy son of Creon and Antigona, seeks reassurance from two lawyers that the law is 'firm'. Like Lactantio in *More Dissemblers Besides Women*, Simonides is a shrewd, materialistic, lecherous hypocrite; like Philip Twilight in *No Wit, No Help Like a Woman's*, he is devoid of any natural regard for his parents' welfare. 'My father must be next,' he tells the lawyers, 'this day compleats | Full fourscore years upon him.' In his characteristic manner, Middleton allows Simonides, who is not really a philosopher, to see Evander's law through the eyes of a thoughtful pragmatist. To the First Lawyer's 'heers a good age now | For those that have old parents, and rich inheritance!' Simonides replies,

> And Sir tis profitable for others too:
> Are there not fellows that lie bed-rid in their offices
> That yonger men would walk lustily in,
> Churchmen, that even the second infancy
> Hath silenc'd, yet hath spun out their lives so long
> That many pregnant and ingenious spirits
> Have languishd in their hop'd reversions,
> And died upon the thought? . . .[25]

When Cleanthes, the hero and principal moral spokesman, enters the scene, Middleton begins at once to establish the contrast between the two young men:

[24] I. p. 5 (Bullen: II, 127).
[25] I. p. 2 (Bullen: II, 122).

A FAIR QUARREL AND THE OLD LAW

Sim.   . . . Cleanthes!
         Oh lad heers a spring for yong plants to flourish—
         The old trees must down kept the sun from us!
         We shall rise now boy.
Clean.   Whither[26] Sir I pray?
         To the bleak air of storms, among those trees,
         Which w[e] had shelter from?[27]

Cleanthes, who is devoted to his aged, widowed father, Leonides, wishes to find out whether there is some way 'to demurr the Law upon occasion'. In the following passage Middleton contrasts the simple rectitude of Cleanthes with the worldliness of a lawyer in the same way as he contrasts these qualities in Phoenix and the groom in *The Phoenix*:

Cle.   Pray you say,
             How doe you allow of this strange Edict?
1st Law.   . . . by my faith Sir,
             The happiest Edict that ever was in Epire.
Cle.   What, to kill innocents Sir, it cannot be,
             It is no rule in justice there to punish.
1. Law.   Oh Sir,
             You understand a conscience, but not law.
Cle.   Why sir, is there so main a difference?
1. Law.   You'l never be good Lawyer if you understand not that.
Cle.   I think then tis the best to be a bad one.[28]

Cleanthes' conversation with the lawyers is interrupted by the entrance of Simonides' parents. Creon comments on the irony of his having spent his life facing the dangers and hardships of military service, only to find death 'treacherously at home'. Antigona tells him,

> The bell of this sharp edict towls for me
> As it rings out for you; Ile be as ready
> With one hours stay to goe along with you.
>   . . . .
> Tis fit that you and I being man and wife
> Should walke together arme in arme.[29]

---

[26] Spelt 'Whether' in the quarto.
[27] I. p. 3 (Bullen: II, 124).
[28] I. p. [4] (Bullen: II, 125). See above, pp. 40–41.
[29] I. p. 8 (Bullen: II, 132 and 133).

The solicitous 'passions' that Simonides affects before his parents in this scene are of the same order as the protestations of Lactantio to the Cardinal in *More Dissemblers Besides Women*, and the ecstatic outpourings of Fontinell in *Blurt Master-Constable* and Gerardine in *The Family of Love*. Middleton makes Cleanthes comment on Simonides' performance in a series of asides; for example, Simonides' reference to his tears as 'true filiall tears' is followed by Cleanthes' aside 'Hypocrite! | A disease of drought dry up all pity from him | That can dissemble pity with wet eyes.' Eventually Cleanthes is left alone on the stage, and he brings the first part of Act I to a close with a soliloquy. Like the soliloquies of Middleton's moral spokesmen in *The Phoenix* and *Your Five Gallants*,[30] Cleanthes' soliloquy is a summing up of preceding events; in it, Middleton gave full development to the tree metaphor that he used in the initial dialogue between Simonides and Cleanthes:[31]

> Why heres a villaine,
> Able to corrupt a thousand by example!
> Does the kind root bleede out his livelihood
> In parent distribution to his branches,
> Adorning them with all his glorious fruits,
> Proud that his pride is seen when hees unseen,
> And must not gratitude discend agen
> To comfort his old limbs in fruitlesse winter?[32]

At the end of the soliloquy Leonides enters in company with Cleanthes' virtuous wife, Hippolita. In the remaining part of Act I Cleanthes and Hippolita persuade the old man to take refuge from the law in a forest retreat, while they pretend that he has died and conduct a mock funeral.

With his customary sureness, Middleton established firm foundations in Act I for the themes that he wished to develop and reinforce in the rest of the play. The old couple, Creon and Antigona, and the young couple, Cleanthes and Hippolita ('one soule, one body, one heart, that think all one thought'), represent his ideal of marriage; Antigona and Hippolita, his ideal of

---

[30] See Bullen, I, 125–6, 145–7, and III, 208.
[31] See above, p. 123. Middleton also uses this metaphor in *A Fair Quarrel* (see above, p. 120).
[32] I. p. 9 (Bullen: II, 134–5).

A FAIR QUARREL AND THE OLD LAW   125

womanhood; and Creon, Leonides, and Cleanthes, his ideal of manhood. To emphasize these ideals Middleton introduces two unsatisfactory marriages, that of Eugenia and Lysander in Act II, and that of Gnothos and Agatha in Act III. The foibles of Eugenia, a young woman who has married an old widower, are in direct contrast with the virtues of faithful and generous Hippolita, whose genuine compassion for old Leonides inspires him to refer to her as 'a treasure invaluable'. On her first appearance Eugenia assigns the preparation of her husband Lysander's 'spoone meat' and the warming of his nightcaps to her step-daughter, and then explains her position in a soliloquy:

> Out apont!
> The meer conceit turns a yong womans stomack.
> His slippers must be warmd in August too,
> And his gowne girt to him in the very dog daies
> When every Mastiffe lols outs tongue for heat.
> . . . .
> This is a life for nineteene! But tis justice,
> For old men, whose great acts stand in their minds
> And nothing in their bodies, doe nere think
> A woman yong enough for their desire,
> And we yong wenches that have mother wits,
> And love to marry muck first, and man after,
> Doe never thinke old men are old enough
> That we may soon be rid on em, theres our quittance.[33]

Middleton uses the same blunt and brutal form of expression to characterize Eugenia's animality in this soliloquy as he uses to characterize Aurelia's in the soliloquy at the end of Act II of *More Dissemblers Besides Women*.[34] Next he introduces two impudent courtiers and Simonides, who come to woo Eugenia in anticipation of Lysander's approaching death. Simonides tells Lysander, '... pray tend your booke sir, | We have nothing to say to you, you may go die, | For heere be those in place that can supply.'

---

[33] II. p. 23 (Bullen: II, 156-7). For other illustrations of Middleton's technique of introducing a character for the first time at the beginning of a scene by giving him a soliloquy in which characterization and exposition are skilfully combined, see Witgood's soliloquy at the beginning of *A Trick to Catch the Old One* (Bullen: II, [251]-52), Mistress Low-water's at the beginning of I. ii of *No Wit, No Help Like a Woman's* (IV, 297-8), and Master Russell's at the beginning of *A Fair Quarrel* (IV, [161]-62).
[34] See Bullen, VI, 412-13.

Lysander senses the operation of universal justice ('These are the plagues of fondnesse to old men | Wee'r punisht home with what we doat upon'[35]), but Middleton goes on to make him a foil to the dignified old age of Creon and Leonides. Having taken 'Counsell with the secrets of all art | To make himselfe youthfull agen', Lysander overcomes the 'impious blood hounds' in contests of dancing, fencing, and drinking.[36] In the last two lines of Lysander's speech after the contests Middleton uses the same imagery to describe the courtiers and Simonides as he uses in Thomasine's speech regarding Andrew Lethe in *Michaelmas Term*:

> What shall we put downe youth at her owne vertues?
> . . . .
> . . . such spring Butterflies . . . are gawdie wingd,
> But no more substance then those Shamble flies
> Which Butchers boyes snap betweene sleepe and waking;
> Come but to crush you once, you are all but maggots,
> For all your beamy out sides.[37]

At the end of the scene Cleanthes first remonstrates with Lysander for having made himself ridiculous, and then rebukes Eugenia—'Immodesty like thine was never equald!'

In the Gnothos–Agatha marriage it is the husband who is the younger and unworthy partner. In the first scene of Act III Gnothos, another descendant of Lazarillo, bribes a clerk to alter Agatha's birth record in the parish register, to 'set forward the Clock a little . . . to helpe the old woman out of her paine.' Just as there are exemplars of virtue of both sexes in the play, so, characteristically, Middleton preserves a balanced view of the sexes as regards predisposition to vice. He makes Gnothos a male counterpart of Eugenia: 'I have another bespoke already; though a peece of old beefe will serve to breakfast, yet a man would be glad of a Chicken to supper.' 'Go get thy sheet ready,' Gnothos tells Agatha in Act IV, 'wee'l see thee buried as we go to Church to be married.'

Middleton devotes the first scene of Act II to development of

---

[35] Middleton redevelops this theme through Sir Francis Cressingham in *Anything for a Quiet Life* (see Chapter X).
[36] The last contest is reminiscent of that between Falso and Tangle in *The Phoenix* (see Bullen, I, 159–63, and II, 187–9).
[37] III. p. 42 (Bullen: II, 189–90). See above, p. 50.

A FAIR QUARREL AND THE OLD LAW 127

the action involving Simonides and Cleanthes and their parents. At Evander's command Creon is taken away, apparently to be 'cast... into the sea'. Next Cleanthes and Hippolita appear and pretend that Leonides has 'beguil'd cruell Law' by dying a natural death. At the end of the act Middleton brings the two main streams of action together. Hippolita meets Eugenia, and the latter affects a state of grief ('the time | Of my dear Love and Husband now drawes on'). Hippolita, who has the sympathetic disposition that distinguishes Witgood's mistress in *A Trick to Catch the Old One*, and Mistress Low-water in *No Wit, No Help Like a Woman's*, realizes that the trick that has saved Leonides could also save Lysander, and she decides to share her secret:

> Fain would I keep it in, but twill not be;
> She is my kinswoman, and I'me pitifull.
> I must impart a good if I knowt once,
> To them that stand in need ont; I'me like one
> Loves not to banquet with a joy alone,
> My friends must partake too.[38]

To obtain revenge for the rebuke that Cleanthes gives her at the end of Act III Eugenia passes the secret on to Simonides. The latter informs the Duke, and Leonides and Cleanthes are arrested at the end of Act IV.

The Old Law, like four of Middleton's early plays, concludes with a trial scene. During the first half of it Simonides and other 'shames of nature' sit in judgement on Leonides and Cleanthes, and make a further display of their callousness. Then Evander intervenes—'Tis time I now begin...'—with surprises reminiscent of those that Phoenix and Fitsgrave give the culprits in *The Phoenix* and *Your Five Gallants*. He has all the condemned old men brought forward from the place of seclusion where they have been kept during the course of his investigation, and pronounces Cleanthes 'judge and censure of youth and the absolute reference of life and manners':

> I find thee cleare, but these Delinquents guilty.
> You must change places for tis so decreed;
> Such just preheminence hath thy goodness gaind,
> Thou art the judge now, they the men arraignd.[39]

[38] II. p. 27 (Bullen: 163–4).   [39] V. p. 66 (Bullen: II, 231).

128   VARIATIONS ON THEMES

Evander's new ordinance requires that in future all sons 'relate their triall and approbation from Cleanthes', and places wives who 'entertaine suitors in their husbands life time' under the jurisdiction of Hippolita.

In treating the themes of filial obligation and obligation in marriage in *The Old Law*, Middleton often gives expression to some of his more general ideas. His Cleanthes and Hippolita testify to his faith in the effectiveness of good examples, as do the Witgood's mistress–Witgood situation in *A Trick to Catch the Old One*, and the Captain Agar–Colonel situation in *A Fair Quarrel*; his Simonides inspired him to recur to a related idea, emphasized in his early writing, when he wrote Cleanthes' soliloquy in Act I—the idea that iniquity, with its vicious examples, has the power to perpetuate itself by corrupting the innocent:[40] 'Why heres a villaine, | Able to corrupt a thousand by example!' 'Nature as thou art old, | . . .', Cleanthes concludes his soliloquy,

> Make some the patern of thy piety,
> Lest all do turn unnaturally against thee,
> And thou be blam'd for our oblivions
> And brutish reluctations.[41]

Middleton's interest in law is in evidence throughout the play; the reverence that he expresses for an ideal of law in *The Phoenix* is echoed in the final lines: 'the good needs feare no Law, | It is his safety, and the bad mans aw.' His perennial theme of appearance versus reality is also pervasive in *The Old Law*. It is expressed in characteristic ways in the lines from a speech of Lysander's, quoted above on page 126, and in the speech in which Cleanthes pretends that Leonides is dead.[42] In the opening action of Act II Evander makes a comment that momentarily renders the latter's guise as an insensate tyrant rather transparent. The Duke is surrounded by youths who, like Simonides, have been quick to take advantage of the Old Law. One of them assures him 'Weel spare for no cost to appeare worthy', and Evander replies,

> Why y'are i'th noble way then, for the most
> Are but appearers; worth it selfe it is lost
> And bravery stands fort.[43]

[40] See above, pp. 24, 31–2, and 35–7.   [41] I. p. 10 (Bullen: II, 135).
See II. p. 20 (Bullen: II, 151–2).   [43] II. p. 17 (Bullen: II, 146).

A FAIR QUARREL AND THE OLD LAW 129

Middleton comments on the world of appearances indirectly when he emphasizes the moral insensibility of the 'weeds' in Epire by their giving hypocritical utterance to the ideals that ennoble the 'flowers'. In a somewhat similar vein, he emphasizes the virtue of Cleanthes at the beginning of IV. ii. As Cleanthes stands musing before the forest retreat of Leonides, he interprets an ideal of filial devotion in terms of an economic principle, and when he alludes to Leonides, at the beginning and end of the soliloquy, he uses the manner of expression of a miser:

> I cannot be too circumspect, too carefull,
> For in these woods lies hid all my life's[44] treasure,
> . . . .
> Psha, I'me too fearful fie, fie, who can hurt me?
> But tis a general cowardice that shakes
> The nerves of confidence: he that hides treasure
> [I]magins every one thinks of that place
> When tis a thing least minded; nay let him change
> The place continually where it keeps,
> There will the feare keepe stil.[45]

Suggestions of Middleton's characters in *The Old Law* are contained in his earlier plays. Eugenia, for example, is partly prefigured in the promiscuous jeweller's wife in *The Phoenix*, and Gnothos, as has been mentioned, descends from Lazarillo in *Blurt Master-Constable*. The relationship between Sir Oliver Twilight and Philip in *No Wit, No Help Like a Woman's* ('the mans in a good case, being old and weary, | He dares not lean his arm on his sons shoulder, | For fear he lie i'th dirt') looks forward to the relationship between Creon and his son Simonides. An intimation of the ideal of filial devotion represented by Cleanthes is found in *The Phoenix*, but it points more particularly to Captain Agar in *A Fair Quarrel*: Fidelio says, 'rather then the poore Ladie my mother should fall upon the common side of rumour to begger her name, I would . . . in the stainlesse quarrel of her reputation, alter my shape for ever.'

[44] Spelt 'lives' in the quarto.
[45] IV. p. 50 (Bullen: II, 203–4).

IX

THE MAYOR OF QUEENBOROUGH, THE WIDOW, AND THE WITCH

IN *The Mayor of Queenborough* Middleton treats the story of Vortigern, or Vortiger as he is called in the play, the legendary King of Britain who usurped the crown from Constantius, the eldest son of Constantine, and later invited the Jutes to England to help fight the Picts.[1] At three junctures in the play Middleton combines expository passages spoken by his presenter, Ranulph, the fourteenth-century Benedictine chronicler, with dumb shows to compress parts of the action, but he gives a full treatment to events in the story that interest him, supplementing them freely with elements of his own invention, and he comments on the main plot by means of the underplot in characteristic manner.

Had Middleton wished to give Vortiger the grand stature of a tragic hero in this play, he could easily have done so. Instead, he chose to show him simply as a treacherous, brutal, inglorious tyrant. He clearly had no intention that Vortiger's actions should inspire awe, and no wish to evoke the audience's sympathy for him. The mood of *The Mayor of Queenborough* is anti-heroic throughout.

Act I and the first scene of Act II deal with the reign of Constantius, whose father had considered him 'unfit for Government and Rule, | And [had] therefore prais'd[2] [him] into [entering a religious order]'. Middleton knew from his sources that it was at Vortiger's instance that Constantius 'was taken out of the abbie of Winchester ... and ... streightwaies created king, as lawfull inheritour to his father',[3] and also that Vortiger later conspired in

---

[1] For an account of the early development of the legend, and Middleton's sources (the chronicles of Holinshed and Fabyan), see R. C. Bald's edition of the play, *Hengist, King of Kent or The Mayor of Queenborough* (New York, 1938), pp. 127–36, and xxxvii–xlii.

[2] Bullen, following a suggestion by Dyce, reads 'pressed'.

[3] Holinshed's *Chronicles of England, Scotland, and Ireland* (London, 1807), I, 552. The first edns. were dated 1577 and 1586.

THE MAYOR OF QUEENBOROUGH   131

Constantius's murder; but the details of Constantius's coronation and reign in *The Mayor of Queenborough* are of Middleton's own invention. In his opening soliloquy Vortiger inveighs against the mob—'Will that wide throated Beast, the multitude, | Never leave bellowing?'—for having 'With their infectious Acclamations | Poyson'd [his] Fortunes for Constantine's sons', and he promises 'though I rise not King, I'le seek the means | To grow as close to one as policy can, | And choak their expectations.' Middleton makes Vortiger's crowning of pious Constantius a ludicrously brutal scene. Much of the drollery arises from the impudence with which Vortiger assumes authority over Constantius, and from the emphatic contrast between the two men. As Constantius and two of his religious colleagues pass by, Vortiger, accompanied by his henchmen, Devonshire and Stafford, waylays the 'vessels of sanctity':

> Constantius, eldest son of Constantine,
> We here seize on thee for the general good,
> And in thy right of Birth.[4]

Constantius exclaims and attempts to pass on, but Vortiger prevents him with 'You must not.' In a short time Constantius, and Vortiger, Devonshire, and Stafford are all kneeling absurdly on the stage, Constantius to plead, 'Bring not my cares into the world again', and Vortiger to 'beg':

> We beg the freeness of your own consent
> Which else must be constrain'd; and time it were
> Either agreed or forc'd.[5]

Vortiger, Devonshire, and Stafford rise, raise Constantius up from his knees, and eventually clap the crown onto his head even while he stands protesting:

Con. Nor is there want of me, your selves can witness—
      Heaven hath provided largely for your peace,
      And bless'd you with the lives of my two Brothers:
      Fix your obedience there, leave me a Servant.
All.   Long live Constantius, son of Constantine,
      King of Great Britain!

[4] I. p. 6 (Bullen: II, 7).   [5] I. p. 7 (Bullen: II, 9).

Con. I do feel a want
     And extream poverty of Joy within;
     The peace I had is parted 'mongst rude men;
     To keep them quiet I have lost it all.[6]

Constantius's credulity is a source of amusement in the play, but his ingenuousness makes him an appealing character. The contrast between the artlessness of Constantius and the cunning of Vortiger operates to the latter's disadvantage. That Middleton intended to minimize Vortiger's stature, and to counteract the tendency of an audience to view acts of boldness with awe and admiration, is indicated not only when Vortiger makes his boldness manifest in the form of absurd impudence in the crowning scene, but by the fact that he departs from the traditional account of Constantius's reign and substitutes a special version of his own. Middleton's sources told him that Vortiger's plan—to put a weak king on the throne and have the effective rule of Britain for himself—was successful from the outset: '... Constantius bare but the name of king: for Vortigerne abusing his innocencie and simple discretion to order things as was requisite, had all the rule of the land, and did what pleased him'.[7] In *The Mayor of Queenborough*, however, Vortiger must endure the humiliation of seeing his initial attempts to secure kingly authority fail, even though Constantius remains innocently unaware of his real intentions throughout; and the failure of these attempts to appropriate the prerogatives of so naïve a king as Constantius leaves Vortiger with little claim to the reverence that he would have inspired, in the eyes of those prone to be infatuated by the spectacle of audacity, had Middleton chosen to allow him to flourish from the beginning.

Vortiger tries a subtlety as soon as the coronation is accomplished, pretending solicitous regard for the King when the latter professes his incompetence for 'temporal Rule' and suggests 'well may the weight kill me':

> Not so, great King, here stoops a faithful servant
> Would sooner perish under it with cheerfulness
> Then your meek Soul should feel oppression
> Of ruder cares; such common coarse employments
> Cast upon me, your servant, upon Vortiger.[8]

[6] I. p. 8 (Bullen: II, 10).   [7] Holinshed's *Chronicles*, I, 552.
[8] I. pp. 8–9 (Bullen: II, 11).

Unwittingly, credulous Constantius makes 'the great motion of Ambition stand' by replying, '... though I cannot bear the weight my self, | I cannot have that barrenness of remorse | To see another groan under my burthen.' Thus Vortiger is 'quite blown up', as he puts it, 'a conscionable way', and he sees 'the death of all [his] hopes ... already'. Nevertheless, he soon decides 'To vex authority from [Constantius], and in all | Study what most may discontent his bloud'. One way of tormenting Constantius presents itself immediately. Two graziers approach Vortiger and tell him that they are his petitioners. With a display of spleen and an absurd reproach, he sends them to worry the King:

> For what? depart, Petitioners to me!
> You have well deserved my grace and favour—
>   have you not a Ruler
> After your own Election? Hye you to Court,
> Get neer and close, be loud and bold enough,
> You cannot chuse but speed.[9]

Vortiger places other petitioners in the King's path, and the latter presents a droll figure when he duly confronts them; but it is Vortiger who is given the final discomfiture and made to appear supremely ridiculous. Knowing that 'a profess'd abstinence | Hath set a Virgin Seal upon [Constantius's] bloud', Vortiger persuades his fiancée, Castiza, to pose as Constantius's prospective queen, and just when Constantius thinks that he has found 'the sweetness of a calm ... a wish'd hour for contemplation', Vortiger intrudes and announces, 'You must forthwith | Settle your mind to marry.' Like Witgood's mistress in Act IV of *A Trick to Catch the Old One*, Castiza is torn between two commendable tendencies. She wishes to be loyal to Vortiger, but dislikes taking part in his 'vexation politique'—'I love Lord Vortiger, | But not these practices; th'are too uncharitable.' Once she and Constantius are alone together, Constantius gains the same influence over her that the Cardinal has over the Duchess at the beginning of *More Dissemblers Besides Women*:

Con. Are you a Virgin?
Cast. Never yet, my Lord,
       Known to the will of man.

[9] I. p. 10 (Bullen: II, 13–14).

Con. O blessed Creature!
. . . .
                         . . . disdain as much
      To let mortality know you, as stars to kiss the pavements;
        y'have a substance
      As excellent as theirs, holding your pureness.
      They look upon corruption, as you do,
      But are stars still; be you a Virgin too.
Cast. I'le never marry. What though my truth be engag'd
      To Vortiger? Forsaking all the world
      I save it well, and do my faith no wrong.[10]

Middleton's intention that Vortiger should appear in an absurd light in the play is nowhere more evident than it is at the conclusion of this interview:

Cast. Y'have mightily prevail'd, great vertuous Sir—
      I am bound eternally to praise your goodness.
      My thoughts henceforth shall be as pure from man
      As ever made a Virgins name immortal.
Con. I will do that for joy   *As he kisses her, enter*
        I never did   Vortiger *and Gentlemen.*
      Nor ever will again.
Gent. My Lord, he's taken.
Vor. I am sorry for't, I like not that so well:
      Th'are something too familiar for their time methinks.
      This way of kissing is no way to vex him;
      Why I, that have a weaker faith and patience,
      Could endure more then that, coming from a woman.[11]

Vortiger's laughable jealousy is replaced by another form of frustration when he learns that Castiza means to enter a monastery, in the first scene of Act II—'My Lord, I am resolv'd,' she tells him, 'tempt me no farther.' His bombastic anguish is unavailing:

Vor. Oh my passion!
Cast. I see you something yielding to Infirmity; Sir,
      I take my leave.[12]

Finding himself again 'quite blown up a conscionable way' ('How am I serv'd in this? I offer a vexation to the King, | He sends it home into my bloud with vantage'), Middleton's Vortiger

[10] I. pp. 15–16 (Bullen: II, 21–2).   [11] I. p. 16 (Bullen: II, 22).
[12] p. 18 (Bullen: II, 26).

sees that he cannot have power while the King lives; in the words of the chorus, 'nothing could prevail to tire the good Kings patience.' In a dumb show Vortiger has Constantius murdered, himself crowned, and the reluctant Castiza fetched from her monastery to become his queen—

> ... they ... force the Maid,
> That vow'd a Virgin-life, to wed;
> . . . .
> And since Fates pleas'd to change her life,
> She proves as holy in a Wife.[13]

Hengist, the second 'Monster of Ambition' in the play, and Horsus, his fellow-Saxon, who must help him 'lead out men' from Germany, are seen taking leave of Roxena, Hengist's daughter and Horsus's secret paramour, in a dumb show in Act I. They arrive at Vortiger's court just after Vortiger has learned that 'the people are up in Armes' against him for 'the Murther of Constantius'. Vortiger at once makes the Saxons his mercenaries, they put down the insurrection, and Hengist begs 'a little earth to thrive on' in payment for his services. Middleton embellishes the legend[14] here by making the adventitious entrance of one Simon the tanner, carrying a hide, the inspiration of Hengist's 'be it but so little | As yon poor Hide will compass'.

Hengist, like Vortiger, is a laughing-stock in the play, but Middleton casts him in an anti-heroic mould without making him unappealing. The Machiavellian side of Hengist's character is balanced by a disarming bluntness of perception, akin to the credulity of Constantius, which keeps him unaware of the liaison between Horsus and Roxena.[15] Hengist also displays an amusing fondness for Simon, which would have kept him in favour with Middleton's audience; his warm feeling for Simon is inspired by gratitude for Simon's having appeared so opportunely with his hide. 'Now let me perish in my first aspiring', he exclaims on learning that Simon has been 'set up' by 'a rich Tanners wife',

---

[13] II. p. 20 (Bullen: II, 28).
[14] 'Some have written that Hengist required of Vortigerne so much ground as he might compas with an oxe hide, and having that granted, he tooke a mightie oxe hide, and cut it into small thongs, and so compassing about a right strong plot of ground with those thongs line wise, began there the foundation of a castell . . .' (Holinshed's *Chronicles*, V, 142).
[15] See Bullen, II, 36-7.

> If the pretty simplicity of his fortune
> Do not most highly take me! 'tis a presage, methinks,
> Of bright succeeding happiness to mine
> When my Fates Gloworm casts forth such a shine.[16]

By letting Hengist show tolerance for Simon and 'his Brethren' Middleton indirectly increases his audience's aversion to Vortiger, in whom the common people, that 'wide throated Beast, the multitude' or those 'Ulcers of Realms' as he calls them, invariably excite feelings of anger. Hengist's genial reception of the tradesmen who seek his assistance in a civic election, in III. iii, for example, contrasts directly with Vortiger's splenetic outburst when Simon, in his capacity as mayor, welcomes him to Hengist's castle at the beginning of Act IV:

> Forbear your tedious and ridiculous duties!
> I hate them, as I do the roots of your
> Inconstant Rabble. I have felt your fits—
> Sheath up your Bounties with your Iron wits![17]

Yet while Middleton makes Hengist's relationship with the populace a foil to Vortiger's in this way, it is important to note that he does not attempt to gloss over Hengist's selfish ambition. Hengist makes it clear in a soliloquy that it is in policy, and not in humanity, that he is Vortiger's superior:

> 'Tis no safe wisdom in a rising man
> To slight off such as these; nay rather these
> Are the foundations of a lofty work:
> We cannot build without them, and stand sure.[18]

From the arrival in Britain of Roxena, near the end of Act II, to the end of the second scene of Act IV Middleton devotes most of his attention to representing Vortiger's infatuation with Roxena, Roxena's secret relationship with Horsus, and Vortiger's putting away of Castiza in order that he may marry Roxena. The legend gave Middleton only a few hints for these episodes: that Vortiger 'was much given to sensuall lust', that Roxena was of a flirtatious disposition, and that Vortiger 'felt himselfe so farre in love with hir person . . . that . . . he forsooke his own wife . . . and

---

[16] III. p. 41 (Bullen: II, 58).
[17] p. 47 (Bullen: II, 69).
[18] III. p. 38 (Bullen: II, 55).

THE MAYOR OF QUEENBOROUGH 137

required of Hengist to have his daughter . . . in marriage'.[19] The character of Castiza, the liaison of Horsus and Roxena, and the connection between Horsus and Vortiger in the play are all elements of Middleton's own invention. Middleton's departures from the legend in representing the relationship between Vortiger and Roxena, like those that he makes in representing the reign of Constantius, have the effect of nullifying Vortiger's claim to admiration as a tragic hero. According to the legend, Vortiger simply yielded to the enticing behaviour of Roxena, put away his wife on some unspecified pretext, and married Roxena; by introducing an intrigue between Horsus and Roxena into the story Middleton again imposes a limitation on Vortiger's success.

Middleton was as conscious of the readiness of his audience to sympathize with lovers as he was of their readiness to be awed by a tyrant, and, not wishing them to give sentimental approval to the liaison of Horsus and Roxena, he concentrated on showing that Horsus and Roxena are not lovers, in the romantic or sentimental sense, at all, but merely hypocritical libertines. Middleton's determination to discourage his audience from viewing Horsus as a romantic lover is clearly evident from the point when Horsus demands of Hengist, with ludicrous impudence, that he should 'Send over for more Saxons. . . . Especially for Roxena.' Horsus's behaviour after the announcement that Roxena has arrived, and that Vortiger has been smitten by her, is reminiscent of the 'Mermaladie heart' of Fontinell in *Blurt Master-Constable*,[20] but the incongruousness of such behaviour in a Saxon warrior adds a good deal to its laughable absurdity. Horsus exclaims aside, 'O this ends bitter now—our close hid flame | Will break out of my heart! I cannot keep it!', and then begins 'yielding to Infirmity', as Vortiger does when he learns that Castiza has decided to become a recluse:

Heng. Gave you attention, Captain?—how now man?
Hors. A kind of grief about these times of the Moon still—
    I feel a pain like a Convulsion,
    A Cramp at heart, I know not what name fits it.
Heng. Nor never seek one for it, let it go
    Without a name—would all griefs were serv'd so.[21]

---

[19] See Holinshed's *Chronicles*, I, 556.   [20] See above, p. 13.
[21] II. p. 27 (Bullen: II, 38).

In the action that follows, Vortiger ingratiatingly creates Hengist Earl of Kent, and Horsus is sure that 'that will doe't'—persuade Hengist to let Vortiger have Roxena. He falls down in a tantrum, and Roxena, calling the fit 'his Epilepsy', and claiming miraculous healing power for 'a Virgins right hand strookt upon his heart', stoops to his assistance. At first Horsus peevishly refuses to play a part in Roxena's ruse 'to bring in Royal credit [her] crackt Virginity', but Roxena hints, with her high-sounding 'Dost think I'le ever wrong thee?', that her marriage to Vortiger will not bring an end to her intimacy with Horsus. Eventually, after it has taken an uncommonly long time for the potency of Roxena's 'Virgins right hand' to manifest itself, Horsus decides that he is 'content for this time to recover'.

In the first scene of Act III, which begins with Horsus and Roxena in private conference, Middleton again dispels the atmosphere of romance from their relationship; both make inflated, ludicrously hypocritical utterances, and occasional shrewd observations, in dry rejoinders, which emphasize their perversity. Horsus has only to be assured of ready access to Roxena for the gratification of his lust; he then offers her his assistance in attaining 'the fair certainties of Britains Queen'. The relationship that Middleton develops between Horsus and Vortiger in the latter half of the scene resembles that between Savourwit and Philip Twilight in *No Wit, No Help Like a Woman's*: pretending to be completely devoted to Vortiger's interest ('My Lord I grieve for you, I scarce fetch breath | But a sigh hangs at the end of it'), Horsus places himself in Vortiger's service and becomes, like Savourwit, an indispensable prop to his master's deficient wit—

Vor. . . . ignorance is safe;
    I then slept happily; if knowledge mend me not
    Thou hast committed a most cruel sin,
    To wake me into judgement and then leave me.
Hor. I will not leave you, Sir, that were rudely done.[22]

It is with Horsus's advice and assistance that Vortiger obtains a pretext for putting away Castiza and marries Roxena. Horsus and Vortiger suggest Savourwit and Philip Twilight again when Vortiger absurdly '*offers to run on his sword*' and '*Horsus prevents him, and perswades him*' in the dumb show at the end of IV. ii.[23]

[22] III. p. 32 (Bullen: II, 46).   [23] See above, pp. 88–9.

Middleton writes in the same derisory vein to emphasize the ugliness of the degenerate relationship of Horsus and Roxena as he uses to induce his audience to acknowledge the animality of Fontinell and Violetta in *Blurt Master-Constable*, Gerardine and Maria in *The Family of Love*, Philip Twilight in *No Wit, No Help Like a Woman's*, Lactantio and Aurelia in *More Dissemblers Besides Women*, and Simonides and Gnothos in *The Old Law*. Middleton's chief aim in *The Mayor of Queenborough* is to deflate the 'Monster of Ambition', however, and he continues to trouble Vortiger's 'dream of glory' to the end of the play. His derisive treatment reaches a peak in the catastrophe, in which Horsus, Roxena, and Vortiger all die in a flaming castle.[24] Vortiger learns that he is a cuckold, and gives vent to such ridiculous ravings as 'Burst me open the violence of whirl-winds!' and 'Defend me | Thou most imperious noise that starts the world!'

Middleton reinforces his theme in the main plot of *The Mayor of Queenborough* with the underplot. At the beginning of Act IV Simon offers Vortiger and Roxena gifts symbolic of the merely animal nature of their relationship, and in the first scene of Act V Middleton makes him play the tyrant. 'What think you of me my Masters?' he asks some rascally players, reminiscent of Follywit and his companions in *A Mad World, My Masters*,[25]

> Hum; have you audacity enough
> To play before so high a person as my self? Will not
> My countenance daunt you?[26]

While the players don their costumes, 'Oliver the Puritan', Simon's erstwhile rival for the mayorship, is brought in captive, for having lived up to his promise to 'prove a Rebel all [Simon's] year'. Although Oliver pleads 'Send me away quickly, this is no biding place— | I understand there are Players in thy house!' Simon is unmoved: 'Nay now proud Rebel, I will make thee stay, | And to thy greater torment see a Play!' But Simon's glory is marred when one of the players throws meal in his face and robs him.

[24] '... at length Aurelius Ambrosius, and Uter, [Constantius's avenging brothers,] came over out of little Britaine, and besieging Vortigerne in a castell, burnt him with the house and all, when they could not otherwise come by him, according to that which Merline the British soothsaier had prophesied before' (Holinshed's *Chronicles*, V, 146).
[25] See Bullen, III, 345-56.
[26] p. 62 (Bullen: II, 92).

The sustained anti-romantic mood of *The Mayor of Queenborough* makes it a companion piece to *Blurt Master-Constable*: the latter play is a travesty of the sentimental treatment given to love in romantic drama, and *The Mayor of Queenborough* is a travesty of the tragedy of ambition. In his distinctive manner Middleton has again employed comic technique to achieve a serious purpose.[27]

The Widow is a blending of many elements from Middleton's earlier plays.[28] Chiefly important among them are the ideal of human behaviour represented by Cleanthes in *The Old Law*, applied here to relationships between the sexes, and the theme of universal justice as a guiding force.

Valeria, 'the widow', is the only one of the four chief characters who does not experience a change in moral outlook in the play. Like Katherine in *Your Five Gallants*, she is a wealthy, 'simple dealing' woman beset with grasping suitors, but she needs no Fitsgrave to protect her; from the beginning she has a sound

---

[27] It was possibly in part because he sensed the underlying serious mood of the play that R. C. Bald ignored the description 'a Comedy' on the title-page of the early edition and stated that it was 'a tragedy and, like *Macbeth*, a tragedy of ambition' (his edition, p. xlvi). But Bald does Middleton an injustice when he tries to see *The Mayor of Queenborough* in terms of *Macbeth*. That he overlooks a fundamental feature of Middleton's art is apparent when he speaks of 'the two incongruous plots' of *The Changeling* (p. xlv), and of the underplot of *The Mayor of Queenborough* as 'a concession to the demand for a double plot which . . . was encouraged by the success of the plays of Beaumont and Fletcher, and which only writers like Shakespeare, Jonson, and Webster were strong enough to resist' (p. xliv). In a similar vein Barker states that *The Mayor of Queenborough* 'has faults which are only too obvious', referring to scenes 'of great brilliance' mixed with 'scenes that are purely perfunctory' (*Thomas Middleton*, p. 120); and Schoenbaum says that it is 'the result of a divided artistic purpose. It is something of an anomaly—a curious union of psychological tragedy, pseudo-history, and comic buffoonery' (*Middleton's Tragedies*, p. 70). The point is that the emphasis in *The Mayor of Queenborough* is different from that in *Macbeth*. Middleton's aim is to prevent his audience from becoming infatuated with the spectacle of brutal audacity or 'magnificence in sin', and it is partly through the use of comic elements (none of which is incongruous, merely conventional, perfunctory, or anomalous when correctly understood) to achieve this end. Shakespeare's appeal in characterizing Macbeth is partly to reason and partly to emotion; Middleton's appeal in characterizing Vortiger is wholly to reason, and no sound understanding of Middleton's work can be achieved which overlooks the concentrated thematic relevance and unity of all of the elements of his dramatic structures.

[28] The pervasiveness of these elements sustains the generally accepted view that if Jonson and Fletcher, whose names appear with Middleton's on the title-page of the 1652 quarto, had any connection with the play, which is doubtful, it was only as revisers. For a summary of individual opinions see R. H. Barker, *Thomas Middleton*, p. 182.

sense of values, the independence of mind that the Duchess learns in *More Dissemblers Besides Women*, and a sufficient amount of the 'wit' that Mistress Low-water displays in *No Wit, No Help Like a Woman's* to find a solution to her own problem. Her remarks about a suitor who has just taken his leave before her first appearance reveal the contempt she feels, in common with many of Middleton's earlier spokesmen, for false outward show:

Val. Servellio.
Ser. Mistris?
Val. If that fellow come agen,
    Answer him without me. Ile not speak with him.
Ser. He in the Nutmeg-colourd band forsooth?
Val. I, that spic'd-Coxcomb Sir. Never may I marry agen
    If his right worshipfull idolatrous face
    Be not most fearfully painted—painted, so hope comfort me!
    I might perceive it peel in many places,
    And under's eye lay a betraying fowlness
    As Maids sweep dust o'th'house all to one corner.
    It shewd me enough there—prodigious pride,
    That cannot but fall scornfully. I'm a woman,
    Yet I praise heaven, I never had the ambition
    To goe about to mend a better Workman.[29]

Valeria's idea of 'a wise man' is one who 'likes that best, that is it self, | Not that which onely seems, though it look fairer', and she intends, by 'great tryall', to find 'one that loves [her] for [her] self . . ., not for [her] wealth'. Valeria is another of Middleton's searchers-out of 'mans intents', and, like her predecessors, she establishes a standard by which the behaviour of other characters may be judged.

Ricardo, 'a decayd young Gent[leman]', is the suitor whom Valeria eventually accepts, but initially he is not motivated entirely by love, though by 'love chiefly', and does not meet her requirement. Ricardo is rash, and like Follywit in *A Mad World, My Masters*, he is the author of all his own difficulties: because he is loath to suffer a repulse ('. . . I am like the Actor that you spoke on: | I must have the part that overcomes the Lady— | I never like the Play else'), he conspires 'to catch [Valeria] in a Contract', but only succeeds in arousing her hostility. Yet Ricardo bears a closer resemblance to Witgood in *A Trick to*

[29] II. p. 14 (Bullen: V, 147).

Catch the Old One than to Follywit, for he has qualities that militate against his faults and look forward to his improvement. Despite his 'subtle trick', he makes no attempt to conceal his 'decayd' condition from Valeria; he shares her dislike of artificiality; and he is not indifferent to the interests of his friends. In the course of the play Ricardo acquires 'a greater mind to [Valeria] . . . than e'r he had', and finally passes her 'great tryall' by not forsaking her when she appears to be penniless.

The other two principals, Valeria's married sister Philippa, and Ricardo's friend Francisco, begin the play as Ricardo does, with defective moral vision. Each is intent upon establishing a liaison with the other, but Middleton interposes some 'strange and unexpected accidents', such as those that force Lipsalve to conclude, in *The Family of Love*, 'sure thers some providence | Which countermaunds libidinous appetites.' Francisco is a callow youth with a responsive conscience. On his way to a secret meeting, arranged by Philippa with a letter of the sort that the Duchess uses to attract Andrugio in *More Dissemblers Besides Women*, he is first arrested and 'set . . . back two mangey hours at least', and then attacked by 'a roguy flight of Thieves'. By the time he arrives at his destination he has decided that

>   . . . these wenching businesses
> Are strange unlucky things, and fatal fooleries.
> No mar'l so many gallants die ere thirtie:
> 'Tis able to vex out a mans heart in five year,
> The crosses that belong to't![30]

A further shock, reminiscent of the salutary fright that Penitent Brothel is given by a succubus in *A Mad World, My Masters*,[31] completes Francisco's education: he sees what he thinks is a ghost standing in the gateway before him:

> 'Life, what should that be! A prodigious thing
> Stands just as I should enter, in that shape too,
> Which alwaies appears terrible.[32]
> What ere it be, it is made strong against me

---

[30] III. p. 31 (Bullen: V, 177).
[31] See Bullen, III, 316–20.
[32] The 'prodigious thing' is really a victim of the thieves who has been robbed of everything but a shirt and left to wander in the night.

By my ill purpose. For 'tis mans own sin
That puts on armor upon all his evils,
And gives them strength to strike him. Were it less
Then what it is, my guilt would make it serve.[33]

Francisco's reflections on the implications of his experience lead him to the conclusion that 'he keeps his promise best that breaks with hell', and he makes his departure. Philippa's disappointments, like Francisco's 'crosses', are interpreted as manifestations of the operation of a supernatural agency that attempts to guide men away from iniquity[34]—near the end of the play she responds favourably to the counsel of Francisco and Martia, the young woman with whom Francisco begins his 'acquaintance with honest love' in Act V:

[Martia]	Be good.
Fra.	Be honest.
[Martia]	Heav'n will not let you sin, and you'ld be carefull.
Fra.	What means it sends to help you, think and mend; You'r as much bound as we, to praise that frend.
Phil.	I am so, and I will so.[35]

In the opening scene of *The Widow*, Middleton makes two noteworthy uses of character *montage*. By juxtaposing the crude remarks of a clownish clerk with the passionate asides of the infatuated Francisco, who is intent upon catching a glimpse of Philippa at the outset of the play, he invests the illicit relationship which is in prospect with the atmosphere of depravity.[36] Philippa, like Eugenia in *The Old Law*, is a morally lax young woman married to an old man; but unlike Eugenia, and Violetta in *Blurt Master-Constable*, Philippa cannot be satisfied with pleasing outward appearances alone—compare the following speech, made by Philippa as she observes Francisco from the upper stage, with Violetta's remarks as she 'stands by marking Fontinell':[37]

---

[33] III. p. 32 (Bullen: V, 177–8).
[34] See above, p. 39.
[35] V. p. 65 (Bullen: V, 233–4).
[36] Middleton used substantially the same technique to set the prospective relationship of Fontinell and Violetta in a repellent atmosphere in Act I of *Blurt Master-Constable* (see above, pp. 11–12).
[37] See above, p. 11.

> He cannot see me now; ile mark him better
> Before I be too rash. Sweetly compos'd he is;
> Now as he stands, he's worth a womans love,
> That loves only for shape, as most on's doe.
> But I must have him wise as well as proper—
> He comes not in my Books else; and indeed
> I have thought upon a course to try his wit.[38]

To accentuate this feature of Philippa's character Middleton introduces a woman as promiscuous as Eugenia and Violetta into the play, in the person of Philippa's maid, and places her views side by side with Philippa's:

> Phil.   Yonders the Gentleman agen.
> [Maid] Oh sweet Mistrisse
>   Pray give me leave to see him!
> Phil.   Nay take heed—
>   Open not the window and you love me.
> [Maid] No, I've the view of whole body here, Mistrisse,
>   At this pore little slit—oh enough, enough!
>   In troth 'tis a fine out-side!
> Phil.   I see that.
> [Maid] Has curld his hair most judiciously well!
> Phil.   I ther's thy love now—it begins in barbarism. She buys a
>   Goose with feathers, that loves a Gentleman for's hair![39]

Philippa's unwillingness to love 'only for shape', and the disdain for a 'gaudy Goose' that she shares with Valeria,[40] are the saving graces that anticipate her sensible response to good advice at the end of the play.

The alliances that succeed at the end of *The Widow* are those of Ricardo and Valeria, and of Francisco and Martia. Neither contravenes moral law, and none of the four lovers is motivated by

---

[38] I. pp. 3–4 (Bullen: V, 129).   [39] I. p. 4 (Bullen: V, 129).

[40] The plots involving Philippa and Valeria have distinct main themes, one developing the idea that 'thers some providence | Which countermaunds libidinous appetites', and the other signalizing Valeria's ideal of a partner in matrimony. Moreover, Philippa and Valeria never converse in the play, and do not appear together until the final scene. Nevertheless, Valeria's reintroduction, at the beginning of Act II, of the general pattern of ideas introduced by Philippa in Act I—both women hold outward appearance to be an untrustworthy criterion of worth, both insist that a prospective mate should possess a certain quality, and both intend to use a test to discover the presence or absence of the desired quality—produces intuitable links between the two sisters, and brings a measure of thematic unity to their experiences.

expectation of material gain. The speeches in which Francisco expresses his feelings toward Martia echo the theme of the Valeria–Ricardo plot: when he is warned that Martia is a stranger, and advised not to commit himself 'till [he] hear[s] further of her Friends and portion', he replies, ' 'Tis only but her love that I desire; | She comes most rich in that'—'I lov'd her', he tells her father, '. . . for her self sir, and her own deservings.'

To discover which of her suitors 'loves [her] for [her] self . . ., not for [her] wealth' Valeria temporarily transfers all her property to her brother; when the 'great tryall' is over, she takes her property back. Valeria's 'great tryall' in *The Widow* operates in basically the same way as Evander's 'strange Edict' operates in *The Old Law*: each gives the individuals being tested an opportunity to display either humane feeling or greed for wealth— Valeria's avaricious suitors reveal themselves by abandoning their suits, and the 'weeds that grew about [Evander's] Court' expose themselves by denouncing aged parents and spouses for the sake of their inheritances. The ideal condition of love between the sexes to which Middleton draws his audience's attention in *The Widow* is thus concomitant with the ideal of filial devotion that Cleanthes stands for in *The Old Law*: Cleanthes cannot be tempted to betray his father to gain his inheritance, and Ricardo and Francisco prove that their affection is not motivated by hope of gaining wealth. Middleton approves of 'honest love' in *The Widow*, as opposed to illicit love, and he suggests that 'hand and faith' are the only benefits that individuals intent on marriage should seek from prospective partners; while doing so, however, he makes no attempt to attach glamour to love between the sexes, or to disguise the idea that its source is an appetite. In the epilogue, Ricardo restrains Francisco from deserting the company with the words,

> Stay, stay Sir! I'm as hungry of my Widdow
> As you can be upon your Maid, beleeve it;
> But we must come to our desires in order—
> There's duties to be paid, e'r we goe further.[41]

In *The Witch* Middleton again devotes most of his attention to love plots, and again emphasizes the distinction between 'honest love', love in which civilizing conditions are imposed on the

---

[41] V. p. [66] (Bullen: V, 235).

gratification of appetite, and what he called 'the hell of love' in an early poem,[42] 'untutred lust'. The Duke and Duchess of Ravenna plot, which Middleton adapted from Machiavelli's *Florentine History*, and the witch scenes, which owe their witch-lore to Reginald Scot's *Discoverie of Witchcraft*, are, like the Latrocinio scenes in *The Widow*, secondary sources of interest from the standpoint of theme. Almachildes, 'a fantasticall Gentleman' in the Duke and Duchess plot, serves, with Middleton's witches, as an example of the kind of idiotic depravity that Lazarillo represents in *Blurt Master-Constable*, and Amoretta, 'ye Duchess-woman', is an exemplar of virtue ('All I desire | is to preserve a Competent[43] honestie | both for mine owne, and his use that shall have me') who finds Almachildes's advances detestable;[44] but the words *'honest Love'* in the final lines of the play, *'And in all Times, may this daie ever prove | a daie of Triumph, Joie, and honest Love'*, are particularly relevant to the feelings that Sebastian, a young soldier, entertains towards Isabella, 'Neice to ye Governor [of Ravenna]'.

The situation that Sebastian faces in the play has been created by Antonio, 'the Devill, in a Sheepeskyn'. During Sebastian's absence at the wars his death 'i'th'feild' has been reported by Antonio and confirmed by Antonio's servant Gaspero, a man whose 'Condition ... weares ... about it a strong scent of Basenes'; on the day of his return Sebastian discovers that Isabella, his contracted wife, has that same day married Antonio, the wedding having been 'clap'd ... up sodainely'[45] by Isabella's uncle, who holds 'a good opinion of the Bride-groome | as he's faire-spoken ... and wondrous mild'.

The most important factor in Sebastian's love for Isabella is his consciousness of an inviolable spiritual bond that exists between them because of their mutual promises of faith before his

---

[42] See above, p. 8.   [43] Spelt 'Computent' in the MS.
[44] In 'The Problem of Middleton's *The Witch* and its Sources', *Notes and Queries*, CCXII (June 1967), 209–11, Mr. David George points out that the words of the love charm with which Almachildes attempts to seduce Amoretta in II. ii (see Bullen, V, 391–2) come from Virgil's *Eclogues*, VIII. Mr. George notes points of similarity between the Sebastian–Isabella–Antonio situation in *The Witch* and the Charlemont–Castabella–Rousard situation in *The Atheist's Tragedy*; his assumption that the latter served as inspiration for the former would tend to confirm Professor Bald's dating of the play.
[45] Spelt 'sodaniely' in the MS.

departure. 'She is my Wife', he tells his friend Fernando at the beginning of the play, 'by Contract before Heaven, and all the Angells.' The idea that a permanent bond of faith, witnessed by heaven, ennobles the union of man and woman is the key-note of the theme. Both Sebastian and Isabella defend this idea in the play, but during more than half of the action Sebastian places too great an emphasis on the superficial significance of his contract, and remains in the grip of his emotions:

> Wrongs don to Love
> strike the hart deepely. None can truely judge on't
> but the poore-sencible-Sufferer, whom it racks
> with un-beleived-Paines, which Men in health,
> that enjoy Love, not possibly can Act
> (nay not so much as thinck).[46]

The anguish that Vortiger and Horsus display in *The Mayor of Queenborough*, their 'yielding to Infirmity' when frustrated of their expectations, is a mockery of anguish, just as their wanton behaviour is a mockery of love; but Sebastian's love is 'honest'. His anguish does not proceed from the disappointment of a perverse lust, the disappointment that Horsus feels on learning that he is about to be supplanted as recipient of Roxena's favours by Vortiger, and which is allayed by an assurance that he will be allowed to share those favours; Sebastian's anguish proceeds from his fear that the rights of a husband[47] which he feels are his, by reason of his solemn engagement to Isabella, are in danger of being usurped by another, and Middleton does not treat his anguish scornfully.

The injustice of Sebastian's implicit criticism of Isabella, in the aside that precedes his interview with Hecate, is symptomatic of his morbid state of mind:

> I know what 'tis
> to pitty Mad-men now—they're wretched things
> that ever were created, if they be
> of womans-making, and her faithless vowes.[48]

---

[46] I. p. 2 (Bullen: V, 358).
[47] Those 'lawfull sweetes, unshamed mornings: Dangerlesse pleasures' to which Phoenix refers in his soliloquy on 'Reverend and honourable Matrimony' in *The Phoenix* (Bullen, I, 145–7).
[48] I. p. 13 (Bullen: V, 372).

His 'horrors [being] so strong and great already', he is able to overcome his aversion and enter the witches' den, where Hecate, although she realizes that 'he loves [her] not', gives him, 'for the Love of Mischeif', a charm that will prevent the consummation of the marriage of Antonio and Isabella; but she cannot 'part 'em utterly':

> We cannot dis-joyne *Wedlock*:
> 'tis of Heavens fastning. Well may we raise Jarrs,
> Jealouzies, Striffes, and hart-burning-Disagreements,
> like a thick Skurff ore life, as did our *Master* upon that patient Miracle;
> but the work it self our powre cannot dis-joynt.[49]

When Sebastian next expresses discontentment, in Act II, he is preoccupied with his 'losse of Joyes': 'Still She's not mine, that can be no Mans else till I be nothing . . .: holly Vowes witnes, that our Soules were married.' He is still distracted by the idea that his contract gives him a proprietary right to Isabella in IV. ii, when, having first disguised himself, like Andrugio in *More Dissemblers Besides Women*, and become Isabella's servant, and then decided to lure her to Fernando's house with the intention of taking his right by force, he appeals for Fernando's sympathy:

Seb. Yf ever you knew force of Love in life Sir, give to mine pitty.
Fer. You doe ill to doubt me.
Seb. I could make bold with no frend seemelier
  then with your self, because you were in presence
  at our Vow-making.
Fer. I'am a Witnes to't.
Seb. Then you best understand, of all men living
  this is no wrong I offer, no abuse
  either to faith, or frendship; for we'are registerd
  Husband, and wife in heaven . . .[50]

At this juncture Sebastian's pious words—'how more pretious the Soule is, then the Body'—are belying an ignominious purpose, much as the Cardinal's do in II. ii of *More Dissemblers Besides Women*.[51] The difference between the Cardinal and Sebastian in this particular is that for the Cardinal self-deception is a habit, whereas in Sebastian's case it is only a manifestation of

---

[49] I. p. 16 (Bullen: V, 375).
[50] IV. pp. 64–5 (Bullen: V, 423).
[51] See above, p. 70.

a temporarily unbalanced mind; and just as Sebastian's horror at the prospective consummation of the marriage of Antonio and Isabella has produced his unbalanced condition, so the shock of realizing that success in his enterprise in IV. ii is within reach restores him to his senses. He masters his passions with sound reason, and turns away from his ignoble course:

> I cannot so deceive her—'twer too sinful—
> there's more Religion in my Love, then soe.
> It is not treacherous Lust that gives Content
> t'an honest mind, and this could prove no better.
> Were it in Me a part of manly Justice,
> that have sought strange hard meanes to keep her Chast
> to her first vow, and I t'abuse her first?
> Better I never knew what Comfort were
> in womans love, then wickedly to know it.[52]

In the remainder of this soliloquy Sebastian does justice to Isabella's virtuous disposition and shows a better understanding of the bond that he has been on the point of profaning; he does not stress the aspects of the contract that have preoccupied him earlier, his observance of its outward form and the rights to which this observance entitles him, but rather the importance of an enduring faith between the individuals that it joins:

> What could the falcehood of one Night availe him
> that must enjoy for ever, or he's lost?
> . . . .
> No, he that would Soules sacred Comfort wyn,
> must burne in pure love, like a Seraphin.

The idea of a sacred contract that Sebastian habitually recurs to in the play recalls again Prince Phoenix's reference to 'Reverend and honourable Matrimony' as 'the onely and the greatest forme, | That put'st a difference beteene our desires | And the disordered appetites of Beastes', and the contrast between Sebastian's frenzied view of his contract, until the end of IV. ii, and his sane view of it thereafter brings out the idea that such a form should be interpreted conscientiously. Middleton emphasizes the theme of the Sebastian–Isabella plot by introducing a minor, contrasting, plot in Act II, and later skilfully combining it

---

[52] IV. pp. 69–70 (Bullen: V, 427–8).

with the action involving Sebastian and Isabella. The chief characters in this minor plot, Antonio's promiscuous sister Francisca, and Aberzanes, 'a Gent[leman] neither honest, wise, nor valiant', are lovers to whom the thought that 'a difference' should be put 'between [human] desires and the disordered appetites of Beastes' does not occur; and their very obliviousness to the ideas developed through Sebastian and Isabella lends prominence to those ideas.

PART FOUR

MIDDLETON'S LAST PLAYS

Anything for a Quiet Life
Women Beware Women
The Changeling
A Game at Chess

X
ANYTHING FOR A QUIET LIFE

Anything for a Quiet Life, described by A. W. Ward as 'one of Middleton's hastiest performances',[1] has the structural complexity and compression that characterize all Middleton's earlier and later dramatic writing, but it seems to lack the structural integrity and coherence which his other plays possess in spite of their complexity and compression. This appearance is mainly attributable to the fact that Middleton was intent upon entertaining his audience with surprises in *Anything for a Quiet Life*. Nevertheless, the dénouement is rather forced, and it seems to me that Ward was right in assuming that the play was written in haste. It also seems likely that *Anything for a Quiet Life* was the first play written by Middleton after a fairly long absence from play-writing,[2] probably spent writing masques and other relatively short entertainments, and it provides interesting indications of directions that his thought would take when writing *Women Beware Women*, *The Changeling*, and *A Game at Chess*.

Some of the surprises in *Anything for a Quiet Life* are rather obviously contrived. Old Franklin, who appears suddenly 'in mourning' at the beginning of Act V, is a *deus ex machina* for arranging the fate of his son, young Franklin, a former sea-captain and pirate. Young Franklin, who earlier in the play has been involved with his friend George Cressingham in cozening Water-Camlet the mercer and Sweetball the barber,[3] is not really dead; he accompanies his father in Act V 'disguis'd like an old Serving-man'. Appearing not to be much grieved at his son's

[1] *History of English Dramatic Literature*, 2nd edn., II, 523.
[2] R. C. Bald's suggestion of 1621 as the year of composition of *Anything for a Quiet Life* is supported by topical allusions pointed out by F. L. Lucas (see *The Works of John Webster* [London, 1927], IV, [65]).
[3] Middleton uses Sweetball's stolen brush as a mnemonic connection between the earlier action and the dénouement in much the same way that he uses stolen articles as consolidating threads in *Your Five Gallants* (see above, p. 55). Young Franklin steals the brush in II. iii, Sweetball bewails its loss in II. iv, and its return is promised in V. ii (see Bullen, V, 280, 283, 347, and 348).

death ('the perpetual fear of a worse end, had he continued his former dissolute course, makes me weigh his death the lighter'), Old Franklin proceeds to make young Franklin's creditors, 'in part, satisfaction' where he finds the debts 'conscionable'. He reveals the identity of the 'old Serving-man' at the end of the play:

> ... Nay, wonder not; I have not delt by fallacy with any: my son was dead: who e're out lives his vertues is a dead man. For when you hear of spirits that walk in real bodies, to the amaze and cold astonishment of such as meet 'em, and all would shun, those are men of vices, who nothing have but what is visible, and so by consequence they have no souls; but if the Soul return he lives agen, Created newly; such my Son appears
> By my blessing rooted, growing by his tears.[4]

Middleton's intention that his audience should be surprised by the revelation, in the final scene, of the real identity of the character called 'Selenger, Page to the Lord Beaufort' in the 1662 quarto's list of *dramatis personae* is clearer in the early edition than in the editions of Dyce and Bullen. In Dyce and Bullen the stage directions that precede Selenger's two appearances in the play, the first at the beginning of Act III and the second near the end of Act V, are *Enter* Mistress George Cressingham *disguised as a page, and* Mistress Knavesby' and '*Enter* Mistress Knavesby, *and* Mistress George Cressingham *in female attire.*'[5] In the 1662 edition the corresponding stage directions are simply '*Enter Selenger, Mris. Knaves-bee*' and '*Enter Selenger as a woman, and Mris. Knavesbee*':[6] there is no indication before the second stage direction that Selenger has been a woman in disguise; and there is no indication that George Cressingham is married, and that Selenger is his wife, until the end of the play.[7] Lord Beaufort's notable lasciviousness accounts for Selenger's disguise ('in her own [shape]', explains George Cressingham, 'I durst not place her so neer your Lordship'); but Middleton leaves it to his audience to infer that George Cressingham's wife has gone into service because of her husband's reduced circumstances.

---

[4] V. sig. [H2]–[H2]ᵛ (Bullen: V, 348).
[5] See *The Works of Thomas Middleton*, ed. Alexander Dyce (London, 1840), IV, 454 and 503, and Bullen, V, 284 and 341.
[6] See sigs. [D3] and [G4]ᵛ.
[7] See Bullen, V, 346–7, ll. 337–40.

The cozening scenes in *Anything for a Quiet Life* are reminiscent of those in *Michaelmas Term,* and Old Franklin's device and Selenger's disguise are variations respectively of the pretended-death deceptions in *A Chaste Maid in Cheapside* and *The Old Law,* and the male incogniti adopted by Mistress Low-water in *No Wit, No Help Like a Woman's,* Lactantio's 'page' in *More Dissemblers Besides Women,* and Martia in *The Widow.* Middleton produces the chief surprise in *Anything for a Quiet Life,* the alteration that Lady Cressingham evinces at the end of the play, with much the same technique as he uses in treating Sebastian in *The Witch.*

Lady Cressingham, 'a Girl of fifteen . . . bred up i'th Court', has recently married Sir Francis Cressingham, a widower, 'well sunk in years', whose imprudent schemes, among them 'certain dreams . . . in Alchimy to finde the Philosophers-Stone', promise to 'draw [him] to'th bottom'. It is again the situation of the young woman married to the old man, but Lady Cressingham's moral deficiency differs from those of Eugenia in *The Old Law* and Philippa in *The Widow.* The issue that is to remain in doubt until the end of Act V is established in the opening dialogue: Sir Francis is told that 'by all the consonancy of reason' his new wife 'is like to cross [his] estate'; Sir Francis disagrees, maintaining that Lady Cressingham has 'Discretion . . . beyond her years, . . . a Matrons sober staidness in her eye, and all the other grave demeanor fitting the Governess of a House'.

Young Lady Cressingham's reaction on realizing the powers of her new rôle as woman and wife is intemperate, like the reaction of Sebastian to the circumstances in which he finds himself at the beginning of *The Witch*; and, like Sebastian, she continues in an unbalanced condition of mind until Middleton introduces an experience that restores normality. In Lady Cressingham's case Middleton deliberately prolongs the unbalanced period—the period during which 'she does not know her self.' In her first appearance, at the end of Act I, Lady Cressingham's consciousness of her new authority as a wife is manifest in her proud self-assurance, and in her forward assumption of responsibility for her husband's affairs. When she next appears, in IV. ii, she has a more brutal consciousness of power, and she forces Sir Francis to comply with her wish that he should sell his land by swearing 'never [to] bed with [him] till [he has] seal'd'. The state of frenzy that the discovery of her power as a woman has induced in

Lady Cressingham's mind is indicated by the complete lack of
restraint in her speech to Saunder, Sir Francis's impudent
steward, at the end of the scene:

Lady. How likest thou my power over h[i]m?
Saun. Excellent.
Lady. This is the height of a great Ladies sway,
   When her night service makes her rule i'th day.[8]

Lady Cressingham continues to be 'full of business' in V. i. To
'settle [Sir Francis] in quiet, make [him] Master of a retir'd life',
she has taken over the control of his estate and limited him to 'a
hundred mark a year, t'one sute, and one man to attend [him]'.
Her officiousness has reduced Sir Francis to a 'dream' ('man is
never truly awake', he exclaims, 'till he be dead!'), and his son
George tries to remonstrate with her—"tis dangerous to a
woman, when her minde raises her to such height—it makes her
onely capable of her own merit; nothing of duty.' Lady Cressingham remains unmoved:

Yo[ung] Cress[ingham] ... the wealth you seem to command
   over is his, and he I hope will dispose of't to our use.
Lady. When he can command my will.[9]

This interview, which concludes with George's 'Oh! shee's lost
to any kinde of goodness!', serves to increase the audience's misgivings in regard to Lady Cressingham; but when Middleton
makes her tell George threateningly, 'So sir, you have been so
bold; by all can binde an oath, and Ile not break it, I will not be the
woman to you hereafter you expected', he provides a veiled hint
of the forthcoming surprise. In the last scene the surprise is
heralded by Sir Francis's unexpected appearance 'bravely'
attired, and George Cressingham's injunction that 'there must be
no remembrance, not the thought that ever youth in woman did
abuse you'. Then Lady Cressingham appears in *'civil habit'*, explains that George has 'ripen'd [her] pity with his dews of duty',
and assures Sir Francis that her 'harsh seeming usage' has been
motivated by good intentions. With characteristic compression,
Middleton forces his audience to conclude that the surprise has
been arranged at a second interview between Lady Cressingham
and George, Lady Cressingham presumably having sought out

    [8] IV. sig. F[1]ᵛ (Bullen: V, 309).
    [9] V. sig. G2 (Bullen: V, 331).

her son-in-law, after having reconsidered his remonstration and relented.

What George Cressingham calls 'a womans naughty pride' in V. i is one of the principal themes of the play. There is a natural jocularity in Middleton's mood when he treats the wilfulness of Lady Cressingham's parallel, Mistress Water-Camlet,[10] a recasting of Mistress Openwork, the jealous, scolding tradesman's wife in *The Roaring Girl*; but the temporary distraction of Lady Cressingham, with its brutal manifestations, is a more serious study. Lady Cressingham's background, which Sir Francis confidently describes in I. i, has been similar to that of the Duchess in *More Dissemblers Besides Women*; and having lived 'retiredly'—'her life did rectifie it self more by the Court Chappel, then by the Office of the Revells'—has been no more effective a safeguard against a headlong reaction to the world outside the cloister in her case than in the Duchess's. The theme that is dominant in *The Widow* and *The Witch*, that of human dignity versus sexual animality, is also a principal theme in *Anything for a Quiet Life*. Middleton treats it in the Lord Beaufort–Knaves-bee–Mistress Knaves-bee plot, and with Mistress Knaves-bee, whose mature self-determination and resourcefulness recall Mistress Low-water in *No Wit, No Help Like a Woman's*, he provides a contrast for the immaturity of Lady Cressingham.

Having been tempted with a promise of preferment, Knaves-bee, a materialist of the same order as Allwit in *A Chaste Maid in Cheapside*, tells his wife that he wishes her to enter into an illicit relationship with Lord Beaufort. In a soliloquy beginning 'Did I not know my Husband of so base contemptible nature, I should think 'twere but a trick to try me', Mistress Knaves-bee expresses her resentment, and she determines to visit Beaufort's house:

> ... and what Ile do there, a my troth yet I know not:
> Women though puzzel'd with the[s]e subtile deeds,
> May, as i'th Spring, pick Physick out of weeds.   *Exit Lady.*[11]

---

[10] In the opening scene Water-Camlet observes: 'When we were married first, I well remember, her railing did appear but a vision, till certain scratches, on my hand and face, assur'd me it was substantiall. She's a creature uses to way lay my faults, and more desires to finde them out, then to have them amended' (as in the Sir Francis–Lady Cressingham situation, so in the Water-Camlets situation, it is a youth named George, in the latter case one of Water-Camlet's apprentices, who is instrumental in restoring an harmonious relationship).

[11] II. sig. [C3] (Bullen: V, 268).

Mistress Knaves-bee devises her plan in the interval between this exit, at the end of II. i, and her next appearance, at Beaufort's house at the beginning of III. i. Her first action on being admitted is to pretend to be instantly infatuated with Selenger, whom she artfully manacles in a 'Skain of Gold'. After Lord Beaufort has entered the scene, witnessed the entanglement, and dismissed Selenger, Mistress Knaves-bee takes the second step in her plan, telling him, 'I love your Page, sir', and requesting his help as a go-between. In the dialogue in which Mistress Knaves-bee plays the voluptuary ('you may command him, sir—if not affection, yet his body, and I desire but that—do't and Ile command my self your prostitute'), and Lord Beaufort expostulates, Middleton characteristically employs eating imagery to emphasize the animality of lust:

Beau. You trifle sure—do you long for unripe fruit? 'Twill breed diseases in you.
Mris Kn. Nothing but worms in my belly, and there's a Seed to expel them; in mellow falling fruit I finde no rellish.
Beau. 'Tis true the youngest Vines yields the most Clusters, but the old ever the sweetest Grapes.
Mris Kna. I can taste of both sir; but with the old I am the soonest cloid: the green keep still an edge on appetite.
Beau. Sure you are a common creature!
Mris Kna. Did you doubt it? Wherefore came I hither else? Did you think that honesty onely had bin immur'd for you, and I should bring it as an Offertorie unto your shrine of Lust?[12]

Mistress Knaves-bee completes the discomfiture of Lord Beaufort by making him digest his own hypocrisy:

Beau. Y'are a bold Mischief—and to make me your Spokes-man! your procurer to my Servant!
Mris Kna. Do you shrink at that? Why, you have done worse without the sense of ill, with a full free conscience of a Libertine. Judge your own sin: was it not worse with a damn'd Broking-fee to a corrupt Husband, state him a Pandor to his own wife . . . : what a degree of baseness call you this?[13]

[12] III. sig. [D4] (Bullen: V, 289–90).
[13] III. sig. [D4]^v (Bullen: V, 290–1).

Throughout the play runs the theme stated in the title and in the prologue:

> How ere th'intents and appetites of men
> Are different as their faces, how and when
> T'employ their actions, yet all without strife
> Meet in this point, Any thing for a Quiet Life.[14]

With his customary concern to present a balanced, comprehensive view of life, Middleton brings a wide variety of 'intents and appetites' into *Anything for a Quiet Life*, ranging from the degenerate materialism of Knaves-bee, who 'takes the hardest course i'th world' to ingratiate himself with Lord Beaufort, to the humanity of Old Franklin, who answers George Cressingham's thanks with 'Sir, what I have done, looks to the end of the good deed it self, no other way i'th world.' Middleton gives a suggestion of this range in the prologue, by referring to the lawyer, who 'does not cease | To talk himself into a sweat with pain' and whose 'Fees buy Quiet', and to the 'poor man', who

> does endure the scorching Sun,
> And feels no weariness, his day-labor done,
> So his Wife entertain him with a smile
> And thank his travail, though she slept the while.[15]

Although the idea that pious observance and seclusion do not prepare an individual for life in the outside world has been frequently illustrated by Middleton in earlier plays, it is noteworthy that in *Anything for a Quiet Life* it is a mere girl who emerges from a retired life and temporarily loses her sense of proportion; for in his remaining three plays Middleton devotes a large part of his attention to refined young female characters, Bianca and Isabella in *Women Beware Women*, Beatrice-Joanna in *The Changeling*, and the White Queen's Pawn in *A Game at Chess*, all of whom, like Lady Cressingham, make the transition from girlhood to womanhood, and suffer for their inexperience in the process. A materialism similar to Knaves-bee's enters into the character of Leantio, the young husband in *Women Beware Women*; and the depravity and influence that Middleton combines in Lord Beaufort are the leading characteristics of the Duke of

---

[14] Sig. A2ᵛ (Bullen: V, [241]).
[15] Sig. A2ᵛ (Bullen: V, [241]).

Florence, who seduces Leantio's wife, and of the Black Bishop's Pawn, the would-be seducer in *A Game at Chess*.

Note: Several critics have held the view that John Webster collaborated with Middleton in *Anything for a Quiet Life*. In 'The Authorship of *Anything for a Quiet Life*', *PMLA*, XLIII (Sept. 1928), 793–9, W. D. Dunkel objects to this suggestion, but concedes that Webster might have revised the play. The pervasiveness of Middleton's characteristic themes and dramatic technique in *Anything for a Quiet Life* does not favour the idea of collaboration. Professor G. E. Bentley reviews the controversy on pp. 859–61 of Vol. IV of *The Jacobean and Caroline Stage* (Oxford, 1956), and concludes that 'No significant evidence has been presented that Webster had anything to do with *Anything for a Quiet Life*.'

XI
WOMEN BEWARE WOMEN AND THE CHANGELING

IN I. i of *Women Beware Women* Middleton establishes the issue that is to be resolved in the main plot,[1] in regard to Bianca,[2] the young bride of Leantio, in the same way as he presents the question about Lady Cressingham in the opening scene of *Anything for a Quiet Life*. Leantio, a man of small means, is admonished, as Sir Francis Cressingham is, for having chosen an unsuitable wife: 'What ableness have you', his mother asks him,

> to do her right then
> In maintenance fitting her birth and vertues?
> Which ev'ry woman of necessity looks for,
> And most to go above it, not confin'd
> By their conditions, vertues, bloods, or births,
> But flowing to affections, wills, and humors.[3]

Leantio, like Sir Francis, defends his choice; he maintains that Bianca is 'in a good way to obedience' and will remain that way if his mother does not 'mar all' by teaching her 'to rebel'. Leantio's mother does not 'mar all', although her dull-wittedness makes subsequent events possible: after Leantio's departure on business toward the end of Act I, the lecherous Duke of Florence catches

---

[1] 'The source of the main plot of the play is the notorious career of Bianca Capello, which seems to have been widely known at the end of the sixteenth and the beginning of the seventeenth centuries.... The second plot..., the Isabella–Hippolito story, is found in *Les Amours tragiques d'Hypolite et Isabelle*, published in Paris in 1610' (G. E. Bentley, *The Jacobean and Caroline Stage*, IV, 907).

[2] This character's name is spelled 'Brancha' throughout the text of the 1657 edition. Modern editors, after Dyce, alter the spelling to 'Bianca', as the latter is the character's name in the source. Roma Gill may be correct in assuming that 'O's Brancha ... probably represents a misreading of MS's *i* as *r*' (*Women Beware Women* (London, 1968), p. 5). It is worth noting, however, that Middleton had a certain fondness for allegorical names (e.g. Sordido in this play, which is the Italian for 'filthy'), and he may have had in mind the Italian *branca*, with its figurative meaning of a clutching or grasping hand (see *Garzanti*) in reference to his character's dormant love of luxury, successfully awakened by the Duke in II, ii.

[3] I. p. 89 (Bullen: VI, 240).

a glimpse of Bianca, and he seduces her in II. ii, with the contrivance of Livia, a twice-married widow who recalls Frank Gullman (the courtesan who procures Mistress Harebrain for Penitent Brothel in *A Mad World, My Masters*), and Guardiano ('I have had a lucky hand these fifteen year | At such Court Passage'). The Duke seduces Bianca with veiled threats—'I should be sorry the least force should lay | An unkinde touch upon thee . . . I can command, | Think upon that'—and, finally, with the appeal that Hellgill uses to corrupt the country wench in *Michaelmas Term*,[4] the appeal to love of easy living:

> . . . can you be so much your Beauties enemy,
> To kiss away a moneth or two in wedlock,
> And weep whole year in wants for ever after?[5]

In III. i Bianca is 'strangely alter'd'—as Mistress Knaves-bee pretends to be ('I have kist Ambition, and I love it . . . I will forget all that I ever was, and nourish new sirrah, I am a Lady') to disconcert her degenerate husband in IV. ii of *Anything for a Quiet Life*: Bianca makes the awakening of her 'womans naughty pride' manifest in her dissatisfaction with Leantio's mother's house:

> This is the strangest house
> For all defects, as ever Gentlewoman
> Made shift withal . . .[6]

But Bianca is not merely awakened to her powers as a woman, as Lady Cressingham is, and she is not, like the latter, merely temporarily distracted. Bianca is permanently brutalized by her experience; the signs of the death of her human spirit become clear as the play progresses. Toward the end she furtively plans the downfall of a reprover, as the unhappy Francisca does in III. ii of *The Witch*.

The lines that explain the experience of the hero of *Michaelmas Term*[7] are also applicable to Bianca's: it is not through 'lack of Sence' that Bianca becomes a victim of the Duke, but through lack of experience of the world—a lack of such knowledge of 'worldly craft' as that which enables Mistress Knaves-bee to oppose corruption with its own weapons:

[4] See above, p. 36. [5] II. p. 130 (Bullen: VI, 288).
[6] III. pp. 134–5 (Bullen: VI, 294). [7] See above, p. 34

This trick hath kept mine honesty secure.
Best Soldiers use policy: the Lions skin
Becomes not the body when 'tis too great,
But then the Foxes may sit close, and neat.[8]

The relationship between a cloistered upbringing and incompetence for life in the outside world is implicit in *Anything for a Quiet Life*; in *Women Beware Women*, Middleton makes the relationship explicit: Bianca observes, in a soliloquy in IV. i,

> This was the farthest way to come to me,
> All would have judg'd, that knew me born in Venice,
> And there with many jealous eyes brought up,
> That never thought they had me sure enough,
> But when they were upon me; yet my hap
> To meet it here, so far off from my birthplace,
> My friends, or kinred. 'Tis not good in sadness,
> To keep a maid so strict in her yong days.[9]

Bianca's sense militates against her ignorance, and Middleton takes a special interest in her individual tragedy. As Miss Una Ellis-Fermor says, 'Middleton seems to have grasped the principle (as did few of his contemporaries) that the more generously a nature is endowed, especially perhaps a woman's, the more bitter is its corruption if it is thwarted or maimed....'[10]

Particularly notable in Middleton's skilful study of Bianca's psychological experience is the way in which he shows that the Duke takes control of her will. She makes no reply to the Duke's last seduction speech, and it is clear, when she re-emerges, that she has been in a semi-mesmeric or dream-like state while submitting to his embraces:

> I saw that now,
> Fearful for any womans eye to look on:
> Infectious mists, and mill-dews hang at's eyes;
> The weather of a doomsday dwells upon him.[11]

With the exception of the Duke's brother, the Lord Cardinal, whose docility[12] suggests an ultimate inability, analogous to

---

[8] *Anything for a Quiet Life*, III. sig. [D4]ᵛ (Bullen: V, 291).
[9] p. 166 (Bullen: VI, 333).   [10] *The Jacobean Drama*, p. 142.
[11] II. pp. 131–2 (Bullen: VI, 290).   [12] See below, pp. 171, n. 28.

Bianca's, to cope with evil, the rest of the principals in *Women Beware Women* take part in a more general tragedy, one that interested Middleton continually, the tragedy of human hypocrisy.

The dramatic experience of young Isabella roughly parallels Bianca's, but a 'lack of Sence' makes her vulnerable to corruption as well as lack of experience, and she recalls the self-indulgent Violetta in *Blurt Master-Constable*, Maria in *The Family of Love*, Aurelia in *More Dissemblers Besides Women*, and Roxena in *The Mayor of Queenborough*. When her uncle, Hippolito, tells her, 'As a man loves his wife, so love I thee', in I. ii, Isabella is startled, but when Livia deludes her into believing that Hippolito is not her uncle, in II. i, and hints at how she may both marry the wealthy, oafish Ward whom her father proffers, and carry on an adulterous relationship with Hippolito (the same situation that Roxena maintains with Vortiger and Horsus), she leaps at the plan. Isabella's irate

> Was ever Maid so cruelly beguil'd
> To the confusion of life, soul, and honor,
> All of one womans murd'ring![13]

when she learns, in IV. ii, that Livia has lied about her consanguinity with Hippolito, brings out the kind of moral dimsightedness that fascinated Middleton. 'Oh shame and horror!' Isabella cries at the idea of incest, but she does not see that 'In that small distance from yon man to [her]' there has already lain, if not 'sin enough to make a whole world perish', yet sin enough, quite apart from incest. Her defective conceptions of 'honor' and 'shame' correspond to a defective understanding of herself: she blames Livia, but her 'All of one womans murd'ring!' outburst refers, ironically, to herself. The surface meaning of Middleton's warning, *Women Beware Women*, might be stated as follows: 'young and inexperienced women, beware of vicious women such as Livia, vicious women who may, like Simonides in *The Old Law*, "corrupt a thousand by example"'; but beneath the veil of irony in the play there is a warning about man's treacherous capacity for self-deception: *Women Beware Women* also means 'women beware yourselves'. As regards Isabella's preparation for life, 'She

---

[13] p. 181 (Bullen: VI, 350).

has the full qualities of a Gentlewoman', her father says in III. ii, 'I have brought her up to Musick, Dancing, what not | That may commend her Sex . . . ?'; after the revelation of her adultery in IV. ii Middleton points the moral in a characteristic way. He emphasizes the superficiality of Isabella's refinement by giving it to Sordido, the Ward's boorish servant, to comment, 'Well, give me a wench but with one good quality, to lye with none but her husband, and that's bringing up enough for any woman breathing.'

A defective conception of love—which corresponds to the obviously insensate attitude toward relationships between the sexes evinced by the Duke, Fabritio (Isabella's father), Guardiano, Sordido, and the Ward—is a tragic deficiency shared, in various forms, by Hippolito, Isabella, Leantio, and Bianca. Livia, whose character has a symbolic function similar to that of Imperia's character in *Blurt Master-Constable* and Hecate's in *The Witch*, stands both at the centres of these two groups, to accentuate the moral derelictions of each, and between them, as a unifying link. As the degenerate master-mind of the allegorical chess game in II. ii ('my black King makes all the haste he can'), she epitomizes the moral callousness of the first group; and in Act V she is the central figure, the grotesque marriage-goddess, of the richly ironic masque that aptly represents the moral superficiality of the second.

Middleton produces a continuous consciousness of the love delusions of Hippolito, Isabella, Leantio, and Bianca through his diction,[14] and the use of his distinctive derisory vein; he introduces his comments, as in the speech of Sordido quoted above, without regard to conventional propriety. The word 'love' is used mockingly throughout the play, for none of the characters knows what love is; 'love' usually carries with it the suggestion of lust, and 'comfort' and 'joy', the suggestion of the gratification of lust.

Hippolito and Isabella have been posing as Platonic lovers for some time: 'Oh affinity,' Guardiano observes on their first appearance, 'What peece of excellent workmanship art thou? | 'Tis work clean wrought, for there's no lust, but love in't.'

[14] For useful discussions of Middleton's diction in *Women Beware Women* and *The Changeling* see Mr. Christopher Ricks's 'Word-Play in *Women Beware Women*', *Review of English Studies*, XII (Aug. 1961), 238–50, and 'The Moral and Poetical Structure of *The Changeling*', *Essays in Criticism*, X (July 1960), 290–306.

Isabella, knowing herself no better than she knows Hippolito, has been naïvely infatuated with her uncle, and the latter's revelation of the 'grief that will not leave [him]' is all that is required to transform that juvenile posture into curiosity about lust. When she considers the 'means', suggested by Livia, by which that curiosity may be satisfied, she points, with unconscious irony, to her own tragedy, for while she never has had, neither does she now have, the means to know her 'self', but only lust:

> Have I past so much time in ignorance,
> And never had the means to know my self
> Till this blest hour?[15]

Hippolito, whose display of Platonic love for his niece has been a grotesque imposture from the outset, shows signs of stupidity that recall several of Middleton's earlier libertines. 'I would 'twere fit', says he (who has been lusting after Isabella 'since [he] first saw [her]') in an aside in I. ii,

> I would 'twere fit to speak to her what I would; but
> 'Twas not a thing ordain'd, Heaven has forbid it,
> And 'tis more meet, that I should rather perish
> Then the Decree Divine receive least blemish.
> Feed inward you my sorrows, make no noise,
> Consume me silent, let me be stark dead
> Ere the world know I'm sick. You see my honesty,
> If you befriend me, so.[16]

In the same scene, this profession (and 'blushes') notwithstanding, Hippolito is brought, with very little persuasion, 'to speak to [Isabella] what [he] would'; after receiving her impulsive rejection he again repines and shows a disposition to die, recalling the ludicrous languishments of Fontinell in *Blurt Master-Constable* and Philip Twilight in *No Wit, No Help Like a Woman's*, and the tantrums of Vortiger and Horsus in *The Mayor of Queenborough*. He continues to repine at the beginning of II. i, but Livia's sisterly 'love' induces her to go about to 'bring forth | As pleasant Fruits as Sensualitie wishes',[17] and he finds Isabella fully prepared at their next meeting to 'Gallop down hill [to

---

[15] II. p. 113 (Bullen: VI, 268).
[16] I. p. 99 (Bullen: VI, 251).
[17] See above, p. 164.

borrow Horsus's phrase[18]] as fearless as a Drunkard'. At first he misinterprets her frenzied appearance ('There seems to me now | More anger and distraction in her looks'); but she soon makes her intentions clear, whereupon Hippolito shows himself quite ready, not only to overlook what 'Heaven has forbid' as regards incest, but to share Isabella's favours with the oafish Ward, as Horsus—whose barbarian behaviour is at least matched by a barbarian exterior—shares Roxena with Vortiger: 'This marriage [Isabella's to the Ward]', he says to himself, 'now must of necessity forward; | It is the onely vail Wit can devise | To keep our acts hid from sin-peircing eyes.'

The line 'There is no love at all, but what lust brings' has application to the connubial relationship of Leantio and Bianca, as well as to the illicit relationship of Hippolito and Isabella. There is an innocent sincerity in Bianca's speeches until the moment of her wordless exit with the Duke in Act II—Middleton modifies his derisive treatment markedly in these speeches, and in so doing reveals his special sympathy with Bianca; at the same time it is quite clear that Bianca's attachment to Leantio is voluptuous rather than regardful: Leantio has not inspired her respect, but merely introduced her to sensual pleasure. Leantio's interest in Bianca is less simple in character, and there are aspects of his accommodation to life which Middleton does not condone.

Leantio is affected with a materialism of the same general order as that which makes Knaves-bee willing to play the pander to his own wife for the sake of preferment in *Anything for a Quiet Life*. It is clear enough in Act I that he cherishes Bianca; he does not cherish her for any fine human qualities, however, but rather as a materially precious object, which he gloats over having stolen from a rich environment—'the most unvaluedst purchase, | That youth of man had ever knowledge of'. 'Look on her well', he tells his mother, '. . . say if 't be not the best peece of theft | That ever was committed.' The action in III. iii, the Ward's and Sordido's examination of Isabella's lip, face, hair, eyes, nose, and feet, and their attempt to examine her teeth, corresponds symbolically to Leantio's appreciation of Bianca, which apart from his satisfaction with her naïve tractability, is confined to her 'hidden vertues', that is, to her bodily qualifications: 'View but her face', says Leantio,

[18] See *The Mayor of Queenborough*, p. 26 (Bullen: II, 37).

> you may see all her dowry,
> Save that which lies lockt up in hidden vertues,
> Like Jewels kept in Cabinets.[19]

In III. ii Leantio fulsomely accepts a petty office which the Duke offers by way of compensation ('The service of whole life give your Grace thanks!'), but he remains petulant:

> ... I'm rewarded
> With Captainship o'th'Fort; a place of credit
> I must confess, but poor; my Factorship
> Shall not exchange means with't. He that di'd last in't,
> He was no drunkard, yet he di'd a begger
> For all his thrift.[20]

After Bianca's departure with the Duke in this scene, Leantio indulges in long impassioned speeches that recall Fontinell in *Blurt Master-Constable*—'Oh hast thou left me then Bianca, utterly! | Bianca! now I miss thee ...'; these are rendered ludicrous by Livia's vain attempts to gain his attention, and by the fact that the 'affliction' he finds 'so insupportable' is merely the loss of a highly favoured means of gratifying his lust, the loss that causes Vortiger and Horsus to yield to 'Infirmity' in *The Mayor of Queenborough*. During a break in Leantio's outpourings Livia tells him that Bianca is 'most assuredly ... a strumpet'; he has come to this obvious conclusion for himself early in the scene, but he shows the same absurd reluctance to give up the illusion of security to be found in ignorance shown by Vortiger, and by Antonio in *The Witch*:[21]

> Ha: most assuredly! Speak not a thing
> So vilde so certainly, leave it more doubtful.[22]

---

[19] I. p. 89 (Bullen: VI, 239). There are, as Mr. Ricks writes, 'innumerable references to treasure, precious stones, silver: all the familiar bric-à-brac of romantic love takes on a disconcertingly materialist tone' ('Word-Play in *Women Beware Women*', p. 239). When Middleton treats the theme of materialism versus philanthropy in *The Old Law*, he uses the treasure image to stress the preferability of natural human sympathy to an inordinate, dehumanizing love of wealth (see above, pp. 125 and 129). In Leantio's speeches in Act I of *Women Beware Women* treasure imagery signalizes not only Leantio's general devotion to material desires, but also the fact that his interest in Bianca is limited to her externals.
[20] III. p. 159 (Bullen: VI, 323).
[21] See Bullen, II, 46, and V, 432, and compare VII, 11, ll. 38-9.
[22] III. p. 156 (Bullen: VI, 320).

When Leantio has spent his passion and feels a 'better ease', Livia at last succeeds in making him understand her offer not only of the cure for the 'disease' from which they are both suffering, but of that which makes him think he is hearing 'the flattery of some dream', wealth:

> Liv. Do but you love enough, I'll give enough.
> Lean. Troth then, I'll love enough, and take enough.
> Liv. Then we are both pleas'd enough.[23]

A noteworthy feature of Middleton's development of the character of Leantio is his reintroduction of the theme that occupied his attention when treating the temporary madness of Sebastian in *The Witch*, the idea that it is not the outward observance that dignifies marriage, but rather conscientious maintenance of faith. Leantio's view of marriage recalls the chief focus in Sebastian's when Sebastian is not himself—his preoccupation with his rights in the woman who is his 'Wife by Contract before Heaven'. Leantio has a smug, absurdly pharisaical conception of himself: 'beauty able to content a Conqueror,' he says near the beginning of the play, 'Whom Earth could scarce content, keeps me in compass; | . . . Now when I go to Church, I can pray handsomely; | Not come like Gallants onely to see faces.' He assumes a posture of moral superiority again in III. i— 'Honest Wedlock | Is like a Banquetting house built in a Garden, | . . . when base Lust | . . . Is but a fair house built by a Ditch side'; when he notices the change in Bianca, later in the same scene, he reveals his superficiality by yearning, in his 'O thou the ripe time of mans misery, wedlock,' soliloquy, for the life that the discontented husband in *The Phoenix* craves,[24] the life of a debauchee. When he is apostrophizing Bianca in III. ii ('As long as mine eye saw thee, | I half enjoy'd thee'), he reflects that marriage should have given him the right to possess Bianca for life; since she is no longer his, he asks, 'then what's marriage good for?', and proceeds with a fatuous lamentation:

> What a happiness
> Had I been made of, had I never seen her;
> For nothing makes mans loss grievous to him,

[23] III. p. 160 (Bullen: VI, 324).
[24] See Bullen, I, 111–13.

But knowledge of the worth of what he loses;
For what he never had he never misses.[25]

Leantio views marriage as a ceremony the merely perfunctory observance of which automatically places a person in a class apart from those who indulge their sexual appetite outside of wedlock; beyond this he thinks only, as distracted Sebastian does, of the right of possession that his observance entails; finally, there is neither trust nor respect in his feeling for Bianca: in I. i he thinks of his mother as one who can provide 'assurance of [Bianca's] restraint' during his absence, and when he speaks of his 'knowledge of [Bianca's] worth', in the lines quoted immediately above, he alludes to his knowledge of her externals. Middleton conveys all these ideas of Leantio's derisively, and it seems to me that he meant it to be understood that Leantio speaks truer than he knows when he boasts that his theft of Bianca is 'seal'd from Heaven by marriage': that a love such as Leantio's, devoid of trust, respect, and sympathy and having no other object than 'a fair womans body', is a mockery of love; that a marriage such as his, lacking a bond of faith and conceived of as nothing more than a 'Banquetting house', is a mockery of marriage; and that the form of marriage itself has no automatic power, and no value as a civilizing institution—no capacity to produce the 'difference' that Middleton's hero in *The Phoenix* speaks of, 'betweene our desires | And the disordered appetites of Beastes, | [that make, like Hippolito,] their mates those that stand next their lusts'—when it is given an entirely self-interested, brutishly materialistic interpretation.

In Acts IV and V Middleton completes his process of dissuading his audience from feeling any sense of 'magnificence in sin' in characteristic manner. Leantio's absurd display of vindictiveness before Bianca in IV. i provokes the Duke to inform Hippolito that Livia has become Leantio's mistress. 'The reputation of his Sisters honor's | As dear to him as life-blood to his heart', observes the Duke; but Hippolito listens to the Duke's 'How does that lusty Widow, thy kinde Sister?', 'her ignorant pleasures | Onely by lust instructed, have receiv'd | Into their services, an impudent Boaster', and other insulting references to Livia with oafish insensibility. Hippolito continues to present a romanti-

[25] p. 158 (Bullen: VI, 322).

cally unappealing figure to the end: he condemns Leantio, as Sir Walter Whorehound first condemns Allwit in *A Chaste Maid in Cheapside*,[26] not for his inquiity but for his failure to hide it ('there's a blinde time made for't; | . . . there's no pity | To be bestow'd on an apparent sinner'); he then kills Leantio, grotesquely visualizing himself, like Antonio his crapulous predecessor in *The Witch*,[27] guardian of 'the perpetual honor of [his] house'; finally, he offers to kill himself in a fit of anguish, like Philip Twilight in *No Wit, No Help Like a Woman's* and Vortiger in *The Mayor of Queenborough*, and, there being no Savourwit or Horsus at hand to prevent him, he runs on a sword. The other principals come to their inglorious ends through the success or miscarriage of 'mischiefs' planned by Livia, Guardiano, Isabella, and Bianca, and 'acted | Under the privilege of a marriage triumph | At the Duke's hasty Nuptials.'[28] Guardiano's fall through the stage trap-door, because of the miscarriage of his primary device for killing Hippolito, recalls the trick played upon Lazarillo by Imperia and Simperina in *Blurt Master-Constable*.[29] In the final scene Middleton follows his procedure in *The Mayor of Queenborough* by bringing his anti-romantic treatment to an emphatic climax: the laughable Guardiano incident; the bizarre 'mischiefs' of the other schemers; derisive bombast, such as the Duke's dying 'My heart swells bigger yet! help here, break't ope, | My brest flies open next'; and the ironies of the nuptial masque ('Juno Nuptial-Goddess, thou that rul'st o'r coupled bodies . . .'), are all part of Middleton's concluding comment on human attraction to a world of appearances and the espousal of abject values in *Women Beware Women*.

[26] See above, p. 95.
[27] See Bullen, V, 435–7.
[28] The Duke's plan to make his relationship with Bianca acceptable to the Cardinal by marrying her comments indirectly on Leantio's misunderstanding of the meaning of marriage. 'Must marriage,' asks the Cardinal, 'that immaculate robe of honor, | That renders Vertue glorious, fair, and fruitful | To her great Master, be now made the Garment | Of Leprousie and Foulness?' Although the Cardinal points out the speciousness of the plan, he has a weakness of character that renders him incompetent to deal with the Duke's hardened corruption: earlier, he displays an other-worldly credulity reminiscent of the Cardinal in *More Dissemblers Besides Women* and Constantius in *The Mayor of Queenborough* (Bullen, VI, 343–4); later, a tractable shallowness, by making 'peace' and expressing 'content' with the debauchees (ibid., 361); and he continues to call the Duke his 'noble' brother.
[29] See above, p. 21.

In *The Changeling*,[30] in which Middleton treats the themes of *Women Beware Women* again, all the action has reference, directly or indirectly, to a relationship formed in the opening scene between Alsemero, a soldier-traveller, and Beatrice-Joanna, the young heroine.

Like the relationships between the sexes in *Women Beware Women*, that of Alsemero and Beatrice is one of mutual infatuation. Alsemero, hitherto ostensibly immune from the attractions of women but secretly in search of a virgin, has been attracted by Beatrice's externals in church, and has concluded, rightly, that she meets his requirement. He begins the opening soliloquy as follows:

> Twas in the Temple where I first beheld her,
> And now agen the same—what Omen yet
> Follows of that?[31]

That he fears that the 'Omen' may not be good is suggested by his reply to his own question: 'None but imaginary— | Why should my hopes or fate be timerous?'; but he goes on, recalling distracted Sebastian in *The Witch* and Leantio in *Women Beware Women*, to reassure himself that his superficial attraction to Beatrice is somehow sanctified by its association with the church: 'The place is holy, so is my intent: | I love her beauties to the holy purpose.'[32] Middleton gives the church a kind of *persona* in the play; its first manifestation, an ill-boding hint, is only dimly perceived by Alsemero in the context of a discussion of the wind with his companion Jasperino:

> Als. Even now I observ'd
> The temples Vane to turn full in my face,
> I know 'tis against me.

[30] 'The main plot of [*The Changeling*] is derived from the first volume of John Reynolds's *Triumphs of God's Revenge against . . . Murder*, 1621 . . . a minor source [was] Leonard Digges's translation, *Gerardo, the Unfortunate Spaniard* [1622]' (G. E. Bentley, *The Jacobean and Caroline Stage*, IV, 863). For notes on the latter source, which relates to the heroine's use of her waiting-woman as a substitute bride on her wedding night, to conceal the loss of her virginity, and the subsequent murder of the waiting-woman (IV. i, V), see Bertram Lloyd's 'A Minor Source of 'The Changeling''', *Modern Language Review*, XIX (Jan. 1924), 101–2, and E. G. Mathews's 'The Murdered Substitute Tale', *Modern Language Quarterly*, VI (June 1945), 187–95.

[31] I. sig. B[1] (Bullen: VI, [5]).

[32] Middleton's play on the word 'holy' here emphasizes the weakly self-deceptive aspect of Alsemero's hypocrisy.

Jas. Against you?
    Then you know not where you are.
Als. Not well indeed.
Jas. Are you not well sir?
Als. Yes, Jasperino.
    Unless there be some hidden malady
    Within me, that I understand not.[33]

On the appearance of Beatrice, Alsemero, although he has never spoken to her before, immediately kisses her and announces that he 'loves [her] dearly'. Beatrice cautions him—'Our eyes . . . are rash sometimes, and tell us wonders . . . which when our judgements find, | They can then check the eyes, and cal them blind'.[34] —but Beatrice's judgement is as untrustworthy as that precocious 'discretion' that Sir Francis Cressingham claims for Lady Cressingham in the first scene of *Anything for a Quiet Life*; like Lady Cressingham again, Beatrice is morally unprepared for life in spite of attendance at church. She soon begins to turn against Alonzo, whom she has promised to marry five days earlier[35]— 'sure, mine eyes were mistaken, | This [Alsemero] was the man was meant me'; her father, who has welcomed Alonzo because of his 'fair and noble ornaments', appears shortly afterwards and observes, with unconscious significance, 'your devotion's ended'. 'For this time, Sir', Beatrice replies, and adds aside,

    I shall change my Saint, I fear me, I find
    A giddy turning in me.[36]

In the course of Acts II, III, and IV, Beatrice procures the murder of Alonzo, is forced to yield herself in payment, and marries Alsemero. At the beginning of Act V she waits outside her husband's chamber, on the night of her marriage, for the emergence of her servant Diaphanta, whom she has bribed with a

[33] I. sig. B[1]ᵛ (Bullen: VI, 6–7).
[34] I. sig. B2 (Bullen: VI, 9).
[35] The idea that Beatrice breaks an agreement with Alonzo, an idea that receives special emphasis in the play (see below, pp. 177–78) is Middleton's. Reynolds's Beatrice has made no commitment to Alonzo before seeing Alsemero; rather she has received him 'coldly': 'although shee were not yet acquainted with Alsemero, yet shee made it the thirteenth article of her Creede, that the supreme power had ordained her another husband, and not [Alonzo] Piracquo' (*The Triumphs of Gods Revenege* [*sic*], *Against . . . Murther* (London, 1621), Bodleian Art 4º G. 29, p. 116).
[36] I. sig. [B3] (Bullen: VI, 12).

sum of money to supply her place secretly in the nuptial bed to conceal her loss of virginity. '*A clock strikes one*': 'One struck, and yet she lies by't—' Beatrice begins the opening soliloquy; at the end of it appears the stage direction '*Strike two*', and the words 'Heark by my horrors, | Another clock strikes two.' While Deflores, her other collaborator, takes hasty steps to avert the discovery which may result from Diaphanta's procrastination, the stage direction '*Struck 3 a clock*' appears, and Beatrice cries, 'List oh my terrors, | Three struck by St. Sebastians!' The chimings of the clocks, and Beatrice's references to them, strengthen the tension of the scene by accentuating Beatrice's fearful impatience. Middleton may well have intended that 'Three struck by St. Sebastians!' should also signalize the presence of the 'temple', working out appropriate punishments for the sins of Alsemero, Beatrice, and Diaphanta. Later, when Beatrice confesses the murder of Alonzo, Alsemero thinks back to his merely lustful attraction to Beatrice in the church:

> Oh the place it self ere since
> Has crying been for vengeance, the Temple
> Where blood and beauty first unlawfully
> Fir'd their devotion, and quencht the right one—
> 'Twas in my fears at first, 'twill have it now.[37]

Alsemero, whose 'frailty' is a pharisaical distaste for 'toucht' women,[38] and who possesses an absurd physician's closet and a 'pretty secret' to 'know whether a woman be maid, or not', is punished with poetic justice: 'I a suppos'd husband chang'd embraces | With wantonness', he says at the end of the play; the fact that he has been taken in by the substitution of Diaphanta, not hitherto 'toucht' by man but readily corruptible, and has derived with complete satisfaction from 'wantonness' all that he

---

[37] V. sig. I[1] (Bullen: VI, 106). In regard to the fact that Alsemero is attracted to Beatrice in church Reynolds writes, 'It is both a griefe and a scandall to any true Christians heart, that the Church ordained for thankes-giving and Prayer unto God, should be made a Stewes, or at least, a place for men to meet and court Ladies' (*The Triumphs*, p. 114). Alsemero has been conscious of an omen in IV. ii: after quarrelling with Alonzo's suspicious brother Tomazo, he says, "Tis somewhat ominous this, a quarrel entred | Upon this [my wedding] day—my innocence relieves me, | I should be wondrous sad else' (Middleton plays on 'innocence' in *The Changeling* as he does on 'innocent' in *Micro-cynicon* (see above, p. 6, n. 7), suggesting here the moral dimsightedness of Alsemero).

[38] See Bullen, VI, 11, ll. 118–28; and 80, l. 106–8.

THE CHANGELING 175

looked for from Beatrice, has given a final emphasis to his original superficiality. Diaphanta and Beatrice both meet their ends at the hands of Deflores: he shoots Diaphanta and then burns her in a fire that he has set earlier ('Oh poor virginity! thou hast paid dearly for't... Diaphanta's burnt'); later he completes Beatrice's confession for her ('she's a Whore'), and stabs her. Last to die is Deflores himself: he dispatches himself, absurdly, with his penknife.

Through his characterization of Beatrice, Middleton redevelops the closely related tragic themes of a young woman's ignorance of the world, ignorance of herself, self-delusion, and moral incompetence; and he had to make departures from his primary source to do so. The original Beatrice is notably self-possessed throughout: she remains in confident control of the situation until the end, when Alsemero finds her 'in the act of adultery' with Deflores 'and shoots and stabs them both'; it is after her marriage to Alsemero, when the latter's jealousy has made her tire of him, and willingly, that she enters an illicit relationship with Deflores,[39] not before her marriage, and under constraint, as in *The Changeling*. Self-possession is what Middleton's Beatrice most conspicuously lacks. Like Lady Cressingham in *Anything for a Quiet Life*, and the young women in *Women Beware Women*, 'she does not know her self.' The interjection 'I fear me' in her 'I shall change my Saint' speech[40] has significance that is hidden from her (just as her father's commonplace, 'your devotion's ended',[41] and Jasperino's way of insisting that the wind favours a voyage to Malta, 'you know not where you are',[42] have meanings that are hidden from them): Beatrice has reason to 'fear' herself. Alsemero makes his impulsive onset in I. i, and she is powerless to withstand it and meet her previous commitment to Alonzo. She experiences her 'giddy turning', lies to her father about the nature of her 'discourse' with Alsemero, and is thereafter until her death in a distracted state of mind that corresponds to the unbalanced condition of Lady Cressingham, and of Isabella in *Women Beware Women*. By II. ii, where the idea of using Deflores to eliminate Alonzo dawns upon her ('Blood-guiltiness becomes a fouler visage, | And now I think on one'),

[39] See *The Triumphs*, pp. 132–4.   [40] See above, p. 173.
[41] See above, p. 173.   [42] See above, p. 173.

she is fully in the grip of what George Cressingham terms 'a womans naughty pride', and, consequently, 'as fearless as a Drunkard'. She takes the initiative from Alsemero impetuously, recalling Lady Cressingham's arbitrary treatment of Sir Francis until the last scene of *Anything for a Quiet Life,* and Isabella's domination of degenerate Hippolito at the end of II. i of *Women Beware Women.* Alsemero accepts Beatrice's ascendancy and his abrupt dismissal tamely, remarking fatuously in a parting aside, 'My love's as firm as love e're built upon.' Middleton makes one of his most effective uses of contrast by immediately juxtaposing the scene in which Beatrice procures the murder of Alonzo: Beatrice's attempts to dominate the interview with Deflores are rendered at once laughable and pathetic by the wide-awake asides and rejoinders of that 'wondrous necessary man', whose interest in Beatrice is the same as Alsemero's, but undisguised. She begins with patronage: 'What ha' you done to your face a-late? Y'ave met with some good Physitian— | Y'have prun'd your self me thinks—you were not wont | To look so amorously'; 'Not I,' observes Deflores aside, 'tis the same Phisnomy to a hair and pimple, | Which she call'd scurvy scarce an hour agoe.' Later she makes a pitiably clumsy attempt to play on Deflores's sympathy:

Bea. [*aside*] We shall try you—Oh my Deflores!
Def. [*aside*] How's that? She calls me hers already, my Deflores—
You were about to sigh out somwhat, Madam?
Bea. No, was I?—I forgot—Oh!
Def. There 'tis agen—the very fellow on't.
Bea. You are too quick, sir.
Def. There's no excuse for't—now I heard it twice, Madam:
That sigh would fain have utterance. Take pitty on't
And lend it a free word—'las how it labours
For liberty—I hear the murmure yet beat at your bosome.[43]

Beatrice's failure to understand the nature of the interest that makes Deflores 'Some twenty times a day, no not so little, | ... force errands, frame wayes and excuses | To come into her sight' is another symptom of her inexperience; and her failure to understand Deflores comments on her insensitivity to the shallowness of Alsemero. When Deflores comes, in III. iv, to claim 'the sweet recompence that [he] set down', in his own mind, for

[43] II. sig. D2^v (Bullen: VI, 39).

murdering Alonzo, she continues to evince an ignorance similar to that shown by Maria in *The Family of Love*, when Gerardine asks that she should allow him to 'give more scope to true desire', and she replies, 'What wouldst thou more then our minds firm contract?'⁴⁴ After she does realize what Deflores wants, she shows that she has the same kind of defective moral vision that makes Isabella scruple about incest in *Women Beware Women*, but permits her to accept eagerly the financially advantageous marriage with the Ward while premeditating adultery; and the same unbalanced disinclination to accept responsibility for her actions :⁴⁵

> Why 'tis impossible thou canst be so wicked,
> Or shelter such a cunning cruelty,
> To make his death the murderer of my honor.
> Thy language is so bold and vitious,
> I can not see which way I can forgive it with any modesty.⁴⁶

As in II. ii, so in III. iv, Deflores is master of the situation, and he replies, 'Push, you forget your self—a woman dipt in blood, and talk of modesty!' Middleton reintroduces his theme of 'honest love' in *The Changeling*,⁴⁷ and he emphasizes Beatrice's tragic ignorance of the meaning of that kind of love in III. iv, where Deflores presents her with Alonzo's amputated finger, bearing the diamond ring symbolic of her promise to Alonzo,⁴⁸ at the beginning of their interview, and tells her, toward the end of it,

---

⁴⁴ See Bullen, III, 48–50.   ⁴⁵ See above, pp. 164–5.
⁴⁶ III. sig. F[1] (Bullen: VI, 65).   ⁴⁷ See above, p. 173, n. 35.
⁴⁸ Beatrice can pronounce the price of the diamond with authority, but she is unaware that it signifies the brightness and permanence of genuine human faith—'the true value, |' she tells Deflores, 'Tak't of my truth, is neer three hundred Duckets.' Deflores's insensate cutting off of Alonzo's ring finger to 'approve the work' underlines the enormity of the murder for the audience, and the extent of Beatrice's derangement ('Bea. Bless me! What hast thou done?... Def. Why is that more then killing the whole man?') But Middleton also makes the amputation of the ring finger refer back indirectly to Beatrice's original 'giddy turning', the failure of the spirit to which the physical murder is by way of anticlimax. Deflores's sudden notice of the ring, 'Ha! What's that | Threw sparkles in my eye?—Oh 'tis a Diamond | He wears upon his finger'; his futile attempt to remove it, 'What, so fast on? Not part in death?'; his return of Beatrice's 'token' with its symbolism emphatically manifest, 'it was sent somewhat unwillingly, | I could not get the Ring without the Finger. . . . He was loath to part with't, for it stuck, | As if the flesh and it were both one substance'—all of this action alludes to Middleton's theme that a bond of faith between human beings should be inviolable and permanent, and to the fact that Alonzo, foolish though he was (like Sir Francis Cressingham) not to perceive the juvenile instability of his prospective mate, accepted her 'token' in the spirit of that idea.

>   . . . peace and innocency has turn'd you out,
>   And made you one with me.
> Bea. With thee, foul villain?
> Def. Yes, my fair murdress—do you urge me?
>   Though thou writ'st maid, thou whore in thy affection:
>   'Twas chang'd from thy first love, and that's a kind
>   Of whoredome in thy heart.[49]

By combining the tragic and comic aspects of her behaviour, and skilfully varying the proportions of tragic and comic elements in each scene, Middleton imparts a poignant realism to his characterization of Beatrice.

The two essential features of the character of Deflores, which is no less fully realized than that of Beatrice, are pointed out by Alonzo's vengeful brother Tomazo: 'that Deflores has a wondrous honest heart', he observes in IV. ii; and in V. ii he says, 'But me thinks honesty was hard bested | To come there for a lodging —as if a Queen | Should make her Palace of a Pest-house.' By representing Deflores as a physically repulsive and 'wondrous honest' man, Middleton makes him a foil to the outwardly attractive, hypocritical Alsemero. The latter, with his private collection of nostrums for testing women's virtue, has been posing as a 'stoic' in regard to women; when he finds Beatrice a second time in a pious attitude in church he can ask himself, 'Why should my hopes [i.e. his hopes that Beatrice is a virgin] . . . be timerous?', and he eagerly accosts her; but he does not make it clear in words that in his 'Twas in the Temple' soliloquy, at the beginning of the play, he was attempting to impose a veil of propriety on his merely lustful appreciation of Beatrice, until he anticipates, in V. iii, the church's 'vengeance' for his profanity[50] and admits, ''Twas in my fears at first'. Deflores is lustfully infatuated with Beatrice too, and he makes no secret of the fact: while Beatrice makes her superfluous attempts to ingratiate herself with him in II. ii, he tells the audience, ''Tis half an act of pleasure to hear her talk thus to me.' He also has the same 'hopes' as Alsemero:

>   And were I not resolv'd in my belief
>   That thy virginity were perfect in thee,

---

[49] III. sig. F[1]ᵛ (Bullen: VI, 65).

[50] See above, p. 174. In *Women Beware Women* Leantio reveals that he has been given to the same kind of impiousness as Alsemero (see above, p. 169). See also Bullen, VII, 20, ll. 129–32.

THE CHANGELING 179

I should but take my recompence with grudging,
As if I had but halfe my hopes I agreed for.[51]

But while Beatrice's maidenhood contributes to his lustful appreciation of her, Deflores does not equate the physical condition of virginity with virtue. He deprives Beatrice of her physical virginity, 'her honors prize', but his conviction that she has already forfeited her honour itself, her honesty—that, in other words, from a spiritual standpoint she is a whore beforehand—is plainly stated, first after he witnesses her secret interview with Alsemero in II. ii—'I have watcht this meeting, and doe wonder much | What shall become of t'other [i.e., Alonzo] ... if a woman | Fly from one point, from him she makes a husband, | She spreads and mounts then like Arithmetick'—and again in his 'Though thou writ'st maid' speech toward the end of III. iv.[52] In these observations of Deflores, Middleton was providing a datum from which the superficiality of Alsemero's character might be judged. Preoccupied with Beatrice's physical chastity, Alsemero reacts to Jasperino's two reports that she has been discovered in suspicious circumstances with Deflores; to the first by applying his nostrums, of which unbeknown to him Beatrice has informed herself of the secret and can therefore deceive him; and to the second by questioning her, 'Are you honest?', and accusing her, 'You are a Whore', whereupon he hears a confession of murder but a denial of the specific charge. Still troubled by doubts as to whether or not Beatrice has been 'toucht', Alsemero resorts to drawing out Deflores; when Deflores responds with his unequivocal 'she's a Whore., Alsemero cries,

I could not chuse but follow [*aside*:]—oh cunning Divels!
How should blind men know you from fair fac'd saints.[53]

In his aside, 'I could not chuse but follow', Alsemero explains, before proceeding with his impassioned outburst, that he has been under an overpowering necessity to seek from Deflores the resolution of his doubts on the question of Beatrice's virginity; but Middleton has chosen his words to make the phrase comment

[51] III. sig. F[1] (Bullen: VI, 64.)
[52] See above, p. 178.
[53] V. sig. I[1]ᵛ (Bullen: VI, 107).

archly[54] on the bluntness of Deflores's revelation, and derisively on the fact that Alsemero now has no choice but to understand at last what anyone less obtuse would have understood from the information he received in IV. ii:

Jas.   Then fell we both to listen [i.e., he and Diaphanta fell to eavesdropping], and words past [from Deflores to Beatrice] Like those that challenge interest in a woman.
Als.   Peace, quench thy zeal, tis dangerous to thy bosom.
Jas.   Then truth is full of perill.
Als.   Such truths are.[55]

Beneath the superficial irony that Alsemero has remained 'blind' to Beatrice's liaison with Deflores in spite of palpable evidence is the profound irony that while he has finally managed to have his doubts dispelled on that point, he has never had any doubts whatever in respect of Beatrice's breach of faith with Alonzo—that he has never seen, as Deflores has, and never does see, the significance of her 'giddy turning'. The ugliness of Deflores[56] has a symbolic quality: it is the apparent mark of the lustfulness which he shares with Alsemero, but which is masked in the latter by a fair-seeming exterior; it is a symbol of his 'wondrous' honesty, his badge of authority as a moral spokesman.

As Professor William Empson has noted, there is a 'striking parallel between De Flores and the subordinate keeper Lollio'[57] in the madhouse scenes[58] of the underplot (where two gallants,

---

[54] For other examples of archness arising from Middleton's consciousness of his position as manager of the behaviour of a character, note that Deflores is 'resolv'd' from the outset on the question that perplexes Alsemero (see above, pp. 178–9); and that Tomazo is in Middleton's confidence to the extent that he can predict with assurance in IV. ii that Deflores will eventually explain to him, as he does in the last scene (see Bullen, VI, 110, ll. 167–70), what has happened to Alonzo: 'He'l bring it out in time, I'me assur'd on't.' Compare Middleton's arch prediction in *Anything for a Quiet Life* (above, p. 156), and see above, p. 50, n. 29.

[55] IV. sig. G[1] (Bullen: VI, 79–80).

[56] Reynolds's Deflores is described simply as 'a Gallant young Gentleman'.

[57] *Some Versions of Pastoral* (London, 1950), p. 50.

[58] In *The Story of Bethlehem Hospital from its Foundation in 1247* (London, 1923), p. 158, Mr. E. G. O'Donoghue writes, 'a comic scene was transferred [into *The Changeling*] from such a ward as ours; and one of the characters is the keeper of the house—possibly Dr. [Hilkiah] Crooke.' In 'A Factual Interpretation of *The Changeling's* Madhouse Scenes', *Notes and Queries*, CXCV (June 1950), 247–8, Mr. R. Reed points out similarities between Bethlehem Hospital and the scene suggested in *The Changeling*, and between the circumstances of Dr. Crooke and his steward and incidental circumstances of Dr. Alibius and Lollio in the play.

Antonio and Franciscus, impersonate madmen to find acceptance in a madhouse and attempt to seduce Isabella, wife of Alibius, the doctor in charge):

> [Lollio] demands 'his share' from Isabella as a price for keeping his mouth shut about Antonio, just as De Flores does from Beatrice. This is not irony but preparation ('device prior to irony'); coming in the scene after De Flores commits the murder and before he demands his reward it acts as a proof of Isabella's wisdom and a hint of the future of Beatrice.[59]

Lollio's assumption that Isabella will agree to a liaison is the same assumption as Knaves-bee makes about his wife in *Anything for a Quiet Life*, and like Knaves-bee he is wrong. Middleton makes Isabella stand in relation to Beatrice as Mistress Knavesbee does to Lady Cressingham: as the self-possessed and competent woman to the unstable and erratic. In III. iii Isabella scorns Antonio's advances (which parallel Alsemero's in I. i), telling him that he is a 'fool indeed': 'I'le not discover you— | That's all the favour you must expect.' Antonio continues to play the fool, however, and Middleton makes Isabella discomfit him in a way that recalls Mistress Knaves-bee's discomfiture of Lord Beaufort in *Anything for a Quiet Life*.[60] As Mistress Knavesbee plays the part of a voluptuary to show Lord Beaufort the ugly reality of his own position, so in IV. iii Isabella counterfeits a madwoman and provokes Antonio's 'I'le kick thee if again thou touch me, | Thou wild unshapen Antick!'[61] Then, following Lollio's prescription, 'Abuse 'um, that's the way to mad the fool, and make a fool of the madman', she reveals her identity, pretending that she has adopted her disguise 'to beguile | The nimble eye of watchful jealousie' and feigning indignation at his rudeness; recurs to her earlier assessment of him, 'Keep your Caparisons, y'are aptly clad'; and leaves him to torment himself with the thought that he had almost achieved his object, and

[59] *Some Versions*, pp. 50–1.   [60] See above, pp. 268–70.
[61] In *Anything for a Quiet Life* the Mistress Knaves-bee–Lord Beaufort scene (III. i) in the underplot is balanced in the main plot by the interview at the end of V. i, where George Cressingham tells Lady Cressingham that 'she does not know her self'; there is a similar balance in *The Changeling* between the Isabella–Antonio passage in IV. iii, where Isabella, in the underplot, corresponds to Mistress Knavesbee, and III. iv in the main plot, where Deflores, in so far as it is his function to tell Beatrice the truth about herself, corresponds to George Cressingham.

spoiled his chance by his own stupidity. Isabella's part is to exemplify the woman who, knowing the world and herself, is proof against 'a giddy turning' and capable of keeping faith with 'him she makes a husband'.

Employing a technique that appears for the first time in his earliest extant play and often afterwards,[62] Middleton shows his audience individuals, in Deflores and Lollio, whose animality, though gross, has at least the merit of being undisguised, and forces pharisaical Alsemero and posturing Antonio and Franciscus to suffer by contrast. Lollio mocks the affectations of Antonio in III. iii;[63] and in IV. iii he defrauds Franciscus, who shares Antonio's disposition to represent lust as poetry:[64] Lollio accepts money from Franciscus for 'past pains', and, claiming that he will 'deserve more', tells him, 'My mistress loves you, but must have some proof of your love to her . . . you must meet your enemy and hers.' Lollio's lies reproduce basically the same situation as Alsemero faces in II. ii, and the dialogue that follows reflects derisively on Alsemero's ready offer in that scene, with no regard for Alonzo's previous claim to Isabella, to pick a fight with him whom Beatrice has come to regard as 'an enemy, a hatefull one':

Lol.   . . . you must meet her enemy and yours.
Fran. He's dead already.
Lol.   Will you tell me that and I parted but now with him?
Fran. Shew me the man.
Lol.   I that's a right course now—see him before you kill him in any case. . . .[65]

What Professor Empson calls 'the chorus of imbeciles', comprising the regular inmates of Dr. Alibius's madhouse, has a part to play analogous to that of Deflores and Lollio: 'the madhouse dominates every scene; every irony refers back to it.'[66] The lunacy of the lunatics is manifest, like the animality of Deflores and Lollio. The moon is the symbol of the changeling, and Middleton uses it to establish a parallel between the derangement of the lunatics and the condition of mind of those who bring

---

[62] See above, p. 22, and below, pp. 198–199.
[63] See Bullen, VI, 54 and 56.
[64] Ibid., 48–50.
[65] IV. sig. G[4]ᵛ (Bullen: VI, 90).
[66] *Some Versions*, p. 49.

THE CHANGELING

no more than 'giddy' infatuation to relationships between the sexes.[67] Professor Empson writes: 'the effect of the vulgar asylum scenes is to surround the characters with a herd of lunatics, howling outside in the night, one step into whose company is irretrievable.'[68] The affinity is between the animal-like disposition of most of the characters to make 'their mates those that stand next their lusts', as Prince Phoenix puts it, and the disposition of lunatics, described by Isabella in *The Changeling*, to 'act their fantasies in any shapes | Suiting their present thoughts'—

> Sometimes they imitate the beasts and birds,
> Singing, or howling, braying, barking; all
> As their wilde fansies prompt 'um.[69]

At the end of the play Deflores proclaims, 'her honors prize | Was my reward, I thank life for nothing | But that pleasure': that announcement is brutal and tragic because it signalizes a failure of the human spirit to realize its human potential, just as the howling of a lunatic is brutal and tragic because it signalizes an inability of the human spirit to realize itself.

But one is made conscious in Middleton's work that the 'brutish reluctations' of a hypocrite place him in a class apart from, and below, the individual whose brutishness is manifest as such. In *The Changeling* Middleton gives it to Isabella and Lollio to deal with the minor hypocrites; for Alsemero he reserves the substitute bride device—'the assumption', as Professor Empson says, '... that Alsemero will take [Diaphanta's] virginity without discovering she is not his wife is more really brutal than anything in the asylum scenes.'[70] In the opening scene, fitting his style to his subject, Middleton conveys the impression of Alsemero's secret lustfulness by implication: Jasperino expresses surprise at the practised competence with which the 'stoic'[71] kisses Beatrice; then, using a characteristic technique, he makes Jasperino follow Alsemero's move by accosting Diaphanta in the same manner

---

[67] See Bullen, VI, 49, ll. 83; 82, ll. 1–4; and 111, ll. 199–212.
[68] *Some Versions*, p. 52.
[69] III. sig. E2ᵛ (Bullen: VI, 54–5).
[70] *Some Versions*, p. 51.
[71] Jasperino is deluded about Alsemero as the Cardinal is about Lactantio in *More Dissemblers Besides Women* (see p. 64, above), Alsemero being a subtle extension of his chaste-seeming but emphatically depraved predecessor. Middleton also makes Alsemero, like Antonio in *The Witch*, deceptively 'faire-spoken ... and wondrous mild' (see above, p. 146).

('Yonder's another Vessell; I'le board her if she be lawfull prize; down goes her top-sail!'), and the juxtaposition of the parallel actions permits the audience to intuit the fact that despite Alsemero's refined exterior his interest in Beatrice is of the same merely lustful nature as Jasperino's in Diaphanta. Middleton also intimates Alsemero's dissimulation in the opening dialogue by writing in a secretive and subtly derisive vein, using equivocal and suggestive words and phrases to produce the atmosphere of deception.[72] In the last scene Alsemero[73] becomes a grotesque moralizer, recalling Vortiger in *The Mayor of Queenborough*, Antonio in *The Witch*, and Hippolito in *Women Beware Women*.[74] When he says, near the end of the play, 'I a suppos'd husband chang'd embraces | With wantonness', he means that while embracing Diaphanta he supposed himself to be embracing his wife; but Alsemero, who has entered into what Tomazo calls a 'snatcht marriage' and used it, like Leantio in *Women Beware Women*, merely to give lust the cloak of propriety, is also 'a suppos'd husband' in the sense that he is a fraud in the capacity of husband: he would have exchanged embraces 'with wantonness', that is, in a spirit of wantonness, even if it had been Beatrice with her virginity intact whom he had embraced.

With a similar irony, distracted Beatrice criticizes Diaphanta at the beginning of Act V because she 'cannot rule her blood, to keep her promise'. The pathos of Beatrice's experience arises from the fact that she is vulnerable from the outset because of ignorance. Her commitment to Alonzo has been made under the influence of her parent, but she is conscious that her sudden attraction to Alsemero is a 'turning', and it is a 'giddy' turning. Having no judgement, Beatrice is quite incapable of the self-possession displayed by her foil in the underplot: like Lady Cressingham in *Anything for a Quiet Life*, and Bianca and Isabella in *Women Beware Women*, she is tragically unprepared for life.

[72] For example, see Bullen, VI, 8, ll. 52–8.
[73] Reynolds's Alsemero, like Middleton's, never questions Alonzo's sudden mysterious disappearance.
[74] See Bullen, II, 112, and above, pp. 170–71.

XII

A GAME AT CHESS

OF the work that was probably Middleton's last contribution to the theatre, Miss M. C. Bradbrook writes: 'His *Game at Chess* is the most famous example of a comment on contemporary affairs of state: although allegorical in form, its references were so exclusively directed towards the Spanish Marriage proposed for Prince Charles that its staging was an unbelievable audacity.'[1] Professor R. C. Bald's important edition of *A Game at Chess*[2] provides an account of the historical background of the play (including a discussion of Middleton's indebtedness to contemporary pamphlets and identification of the individuals and groups represented allegorically), descriptions of its stage history and texts, and a list of documents relating to the play.[3]

As regards the characters in the part of the play that is not directly concerned with the Spanish marriage, Professor Bald follows Fleay in identifying the White Queen as the Church of England, and points out that 'the Black Bishop's Pawn is simply intended to be a representative of the [Jesuit] order, bent on corrupting the members of the Church of England, who are typified in the White Queen's Pawn.'[4] The validity of these inferences is borne out by the opening speech of the induction. A character representing the spirit of Ignatius Loyola finds himself

---

[1] *The Growth and Structure of Elizabethan Comedy* (London, 1955), p. 228.
[2] (London, 1929).
[3] See also the articles listed by Professor Bentley in *The Jacobean and Caroline Stage*, IV, 870–1, and L. B. Wright's 'Propaganda Against James I's "Appeasement" of Spain', *Huntington Library Quarterly*, VI (Feb. 1943), 149–72; G. R. Price's 'The Latin Oration in *A Game at Chesse*', ibid., XXIII (Aug. 1960), 389–93; P. G. Phialas's 'An Unpublished Letter About *A Game at Chess*', *Modern Language Notes*, LXIX (June 1954), 398–9; R. Southall's 'A Missing Source-Book for Middleton's "A Game at Chesse"', *Notes and Queries*, CCVII (Apr. 1962), 145–6; R. Pineas's comments on the preceding article, ibid., CCX (Sept. 1965), 353–4; E. M. Wilson's and O. Turner's 'The Spanish Protest Against "A Game at Chesse"', *Modern Language Review*, LXIV (Oct. 1949), 476–82; and G. Bullough's '"The Game at Chesse": How It Struck a Contemporary', ibid., XLIX (Apr. 1954), 156–63.
[4] See Introduction to *A Game at Chesse*, pp. 11 and 13.

in England ('Hah! where? what Angle of the world is this...?'), and, by using the phrase 'never yet deflowr'd' in reference to the inhabitants, announces the seduction motif that is to involve the White Queen and her pawn, and links it directly to the missionary zeal of the Jesuits:

> Heer's too much light appeares, shot from the Eyes
> Of Truth and Goodnesse never yet deflowr'd:
> Sure they [Loyola's 'sonnes and Heires'] were never here;
>   then is their Monarchie
> Unperfect yet...[5]

The attempted seduction of the White Queen's Pawn is the predominant plot of the play, and in the induction Middleton ensures that the audience will recognize its two chief characters from the Black House. He mentions them first in the initial dialogue between Loyola and Error:

> Ig. Were any of my Sonnes plac'd for the Game?
> Er. Yes and a Daughter too (a Secular Daughter)
>   That playes the Black Queenes Pawne—
>   He the Blacke Bishops.[6]

Using a version of his procedure at the beginning of *Your Five Gallants* ('hactenus quasi inductio, *a little glimpse giving*'), Middleton then brings all the characters onto the stage, and he distinguishes from among the various black-costumed actors the two who will figure in the opening action of Act I:

> Ig. ... I see my Son and Daughter.[7]
> Er. Those are two Pawnes,
>   The Black Queenes and the Bishops.[8]

Middleton's imputation of sexual depravity within the Jesuit organization, through the persons of the Black Bishop's Pawn and the Black Queen's Pawn, begins in the opening scene and continues throughout the play. It takes its authority from contemporary attacks against alleged abuses of Roman Catholic

---

[5] p. 1 (Bullen: VII, [9]).   [6] p. 2 (Bullen: VII, 12).
[7] Spelt 'Daughters' in the quarto of which Mal. 247(1) is an example, but the word is singular in another of the early quartos (see Bullen, VII, 13, n. 1) and in Professor Bald's edition of the Trinity holograph (see p. 52, l. 65).
[8] p. 3 (Bullen: VII, 13).

clergy,[9] and the plot involving these two characters and the White Queen's Pawn may be viewed at one level as another attack such as Middleton makes against a Protestant sect in *The Family of Love*, and the chess game as a re-employment of the allegorical device he first used in *Women Beware Women*,[10] the pieces mentioned corresponding in part to the Duke, Livia, and Bianca. But the allegorical dimension of the 'Dreame, a Vision' indicated by Professor Bald, the representation of the members of the Church of England in the White Queen's Pawn, is no less important than the attack on the Jesuits, and for many features of his last essay in social criticism Middleton drew on the materials of his own previous work.

Middleton portrays the White Queen's Pawn in the image of a young woman who presents the outward appearance of moral competence, but who is in fact vulnerable because of inexperience. It is the image that he first presented in this last group of plays in Lady Cressingham in *Anything for a Quiet Life*; that he first treated at length, in a somewhat older woman, in the Duchess in *More Dissemblers Besides Women*; and that is partly prefigured in several less fully realized characters in his earliest plays.

At the beginning of I. i the Black Queen's Pawn marks her white counterpart, and her 'Soule bleedes at [her] Eies' because she is 'not ours, but the Daughter of Heresie'. The White Queen's Pawn is affected by the tears as virtuous Hippolita is by dissembling Eugenia's in *The Old Law*, and like Hippolita, that 'Easie fool' as Eugenia calls her, she concludes that the weeper is trustworthy. 'If ever goodnes made a gracious promise, |' remarks the Black Queen's Pawn, 'It is in yonder looke: what little paines | Would build a fort for Vertue to all Memorie | In that sweet Creature, were the Ground-worke firme'; and the White Queen's Pawn replies, 'It hath ben all my glory to be firme | In what I have profess'd.' The Black Queen's Pawn begins the course of conversion by saying that 'firmnes that way [that is, in the Anglican faith] makes[11] [the White Queen's Pawn] more infirme | For the right Christian Conflict', preparing the way for her co-worker, the Black Bishop's Pawn, who will 'cherish | All his young-tractable, sweet obedient Daughters | Even in his

[9] See for example Professor Bald's quotation from T. Robinson's *Anatomie of the English Nunnerie at Lisbon* (1622) in the notes to his edition of the play, p. 140.
[10] See above, p. 165.   [11] Spelt 'maks' in Mal. 247(1).

bosome'. On the appearance of the latter, the White Queen's Pawn reveals her proneness to make surface appearance the basis of judgement again by exclaiming, 'By my penitence | A comely presentation! and the habit | To Admiration, reverend.'

Middleton begins his characterization of the Black Bishop's Pawn by letting him utter his appraisal of the White Queen's Pawn in a poetic idiom: it recalls the disposition of many of Middleton's earlier voluptuous dissemblers to disguise their lustful intentions in poetry:

> Let me contemplate
> With holy wonder, season my accesse,
> And by degrees, approach the Sanctuary
> Of unmatch'd Beauty, set in Grace, and Goodnesse.
> Amongst the Daughters of Men, I have not found
> A more Catholicall Aspect. That Eie
> Doth promise single life, and meeke obedience;
> Upon those Lipes (the sweete fresh buds of youth)
> The holy dewe of Prayer, lyes like Pearle
> (Dropt from the opening Eye-lids of the Morne
> Upon the bashfull Rose)— . . .
> . . . .
> . . . how delightfully
> The curteous Phisicke of a tender Penance
> Whose utmost cruelty should not exceed
> The first feare of a Bride, to beat downe frailetie,
> Would work to sound health your long festerd judgeme[n]t.[12]

The polished poetic idiom makes the Black Bishop's Pawn eminently plausible, and eminently dangerous. The insinuation of fleshly allusions into a sacred context, reminiscent of the secretive, subtly derisive vein that Middleton uses in the opening scene of *The Changeling*, looks forward to the attempted rape that the Black Bishop's Pawn resorts to in II. i, when his 'sanctimonious breath' and the perusal of a 'Tract of Obedience' fail to prepare the White Queen's Pawn to yield him her honour.

The White Queen's Pawn's 'Ground-worke' is sufficiently firm to enable her to remain 'impregnable' to the wiles of the Black Bishop's Pawn; and the attempted rape is thwarted—'Heaven was pleas'd' to send an 'unlook'd for accident'—through

[12] I. p. 6 (Bullen: VII, 17–18).

the private scheming of the Black Queen's Pawn, who serves Middleton as *deus ex machina*, and explains in IV. i, recalling Deflores in *The Changeling*, 'My Bloods game is the wages I have work't for.'

In II. ii the White Queen's Pawn fulfils her promise, 'I will discover thee (Arch-Hypocrite)', but the Black Bishop has had 'Letters (Ante-dated)' prepared, and the Black Knight uses them in an attempt to show that the accused pawn has been absent for the past ten days. The White King seems to be persuaded by this evidence, however the White Knight hints at a 'faire policie' that will save the White Queen's Pawn from being lost. In III. i the White Knight can show proof that the letters are forgeries, but the Black Knight is not silenced until the Black Queen's Pawn testifies to the truth of the White Queen's Pawn's charge. In giving her testimony the Black Queen's Pawn is still serving her 'owne turne', and Middleton's. She assures the surprised Black House that her action will facilitate 'A new Trap | For [the White Queen's Pawn's] more sure confusion'; in effect, her pretending to have been 'an Agent—on Vertues part' allows her to take a surer hold on the confidence of the White Queen's Pawn, and leads to the production of another situation in which Middleton can carry on his indirect social commentary.

The Black Queen's Pawn announces that she has foreseen the White Queen's Pawn's marriage and her prospective husband in a 'Magicall glasse [she] bought of an Egyptian'.[13] The marriage I take to symbolize the conversion of Anglicans to Roman Catholicism desired by the Jesuits, and the White Queen's Pawn's 'I have promis'd single life to all my affections' the spirit of Anglican Protestantism. In spite of her promise, the White Queen's Pawn re-evinces the dangerous tractability that she has shown in I. i and at the beginning of II. i: having been assured that 'the Man' is 'An absolute honest[14] Gentleman, a compleat one | . . . heire to three red Hatts, | Besides his generall hopes in the Black House', she says, 'I long to see this man.'

From the co-operation of the Black Queen's Pawn and the Black Bishop's Pawn in III. iii[15] and IV. i the audience must

---

[13] Professor Bald notes William Rowley's use of this device in *A Shoemaker a Gentleman* ('Notes', pp. 150–1).
[14] The Trinity MS. reads 'handsome' (see also Bullen, VII, 77, n. 5).
[15] In Bullen's edition, III. ii.

conclude that at some time previously the former has led the latter to believe that by following her plan he will be able to seduce the White Queen's Pawn.[16] In III. iii the Black Queen's Pawn has brought the White Queen's Pawn to 'the Roome he did appear to [her] in'. After some prearranged preliminary deception she can conclude, 'My truth reflects the clearer'; she then proceeds with the mock-invocation that concludes as follows:

> By the meekenesse of her Minde,
> By the softnes of her Kinde,
> By the lustre of her grace,
> By all these, thou art summond to this Place.[17]

There follow the stage directions '*Musique, Enter Bl. Bs. P. as in apparition richly attired.*' Although the White Queen's Pawn has been as fearful at first as Bianca is when left alone with the Duke in II. ii of *Women Beware Women*,[18] she is fascinated by the spectacle, and when the 'apparition' departs she pleads, 'Oh let him stay a while, a little longer.' Soon afterwards, she suffers qualms:

> Oh I did ill to give consent to see it!
> What certainety is in our blood or State?
> What we still write is blot[t]ed out by Fate,[19]
> Our wils is like a Cause that is Law-tost—
> What one Court orders is by another crost.[20]

The Black Queen's Pawn meets these remarks as Shortyard meets the misgivings of Easy in *Michaelmas Term*,[21] with summary rejection: 'I finde no fit place for this passion here, | 'Tis meerely an Intruder'; at the end of the scene she observes aside, 'She's caught and (which is strange) by her most wronger.' In IV. i she brings the White Queen's Pawn and the Black Bishop's Pawn,

---

[16] Compare the inference Middleton requires his audience to make in *More Dissemblers Besides Women* noted above, p. 76, n. 41.

[17] p. 44 (Bullen: VII, 83–4).

[18] Compare Bullen, VII, 82, ll. 4–7, and VI, 285, ll. 328–31.

[19] For other examples, of which there are many in Middleton's drama, of the use of the word 'fate' by characters inclined to self-indulgence, see Bullen, I, 53, ll. 88–9, and IV, 390, ll. 271–5. By making the White Queen's Pawn adopt the first person plural in this speech, Middleton makes her remarks point to man's frequent tendency to vacillate, regard himself as the slave of circumstance, and relinquish responsibility for his own actions.

[20] III. p. 44 (Bullen: VII, 84).

[21] See above, p. 32.

still *'richly attired'*, together. As regards the former, the action recalls, as in III. iii, the 'giddy turning' of Beatrice in *The Changeling*: 'How is my soules growth alter'd! That single life | (The fittest garment that Peace ever made for't) | Is grown too streight, too stubborne on the sodaine.' The Black Bishop's Pawn makes a further display of his hypocrisy: he protests, 'I cannot be married by mine Order', but accepts that he may 'venture | Upon a Contract' to gain 'the relish of this night' with no 'staine to [his] vowe'.

When the White Queen's Pawn reappears in IV. iii, she has been formally contracted and brought to fulfil the Black Queen's Pawn's prediction, 'She shall doe reason then.' In dumb show the audience sees the White Queen's Pawn, a 'wife, all but Church Ceremony', saved by another 'unlook'd for accident'; the Black Queen's Pawn about to win the 'wages' of her 'Bloods game'; and the Black Bishop's Pawn about to 'couple' unwittingly, like Almachildes in *The Witch* and Alsemero in *The Changeling*, with the wrong woman:

Scena tertia. Enter as in a dumbe shew, Black-Queenes Pawn with a Taper, conducts the W. P. to one Chamber, then convaies the Blacke Bish. Pawne into another Chamber, and putting out the light, followes him.[22]

Middleton brings the White Queen's Pawn plot to its conclusion in V. ii. As regards her contracted husband's failure to meet her in IV. iii, the White Queen's Pawn assumes that the proposal of an appointment was 'but a Triall of [her] Dutie'.[23] When she sees the Black Bishop's Pawn in the *'reverend habit'* in which she has seen him in I. i and II. i, she is able to recognize 'her most wronger'. The latter exults in his imagined conquest in IV. iii, but is soon made to understand that he is 'lost of all hands'.

In the White Queen's Pawn plot we have a clear expression both of Middleton's personal alliance with the Church of England and of his concern for its security. At each crisis the White Queen's Pawn has only been saved from corruption by 'Heaven'; otherwise, she has been, as the Black Bishop's Pawn observes, 'prepar'd for't'. In pursuance of a theme that is evident in his earliest writing,[24] Middleton has been at pains to indicate the

[22] p. 53 (Bullen: VII, 103).
[23] The Trinity MS. reads 'love' (Professor Bald's edition, p. 109, l. 1).
[24] See above, p. 6.

dangers that lurk in a world of appearances; and he has shown his heroine's vulnerability to them. He makes his warning more direct, inviting the audience to identify themselves with the White Queen's Pawn, in the speech in which she tells her would-be corrupter that he 'should never speake | The language of unchastnes in that [reverend] habit':

> If you'l persist still, in your Devills part,
> Present him as you should do. And let one
> That carries up the goodnes of the play
> Come in that habit, and Ile speake with him:
> Then will the parts be fitted, and the Spectators
> Know which is which. They must have cunning Judgement
> To finde it else; for such a one as you
> Is able to deceive a mightie Audience.
> Nay those you have seduc'd (if there be any
> In the Assembly) if they see what manner
> You play your Game with me, they cannot love you.[25]

In the thwarting of the plot to overthrow the White Queen herself, the *'attempt upon the White Queenes person, whose fall or prostitution* [the Black King's] *lust most violently rages for'*, Middleton makes the nobility of the White House show a wise policy that recalls such earlier heroic figures as Prince Phoenix in *The Phoenix* and Duke Evander in *The Old Law*. A rumour is circulated that the White King has been taken: 'oh he's gone! |' cries the White Queen—who is as much taken in by the rumour as the Fat Bishop, the black conspirator—'Ensnar'd, entrapt, surpriz'd amongst the black ones!' At the end of the scene, after the black conspiracy has been exposed, the White King (James) calls for the same kind of trust from the White Queen (the Church) that Sebastian has inspired in Isabella in *The Witch*:

> W.Q.   My fear's past then.
> W.K.   Feare? You never were guilty of an injury
>   To Goodnes but in that.
> W.Q.   It staid not with me (Sir).
> Wh.K. It was too much if it usurp'd a thought.
>   Place a Good Guard there.
> Wh.Q. Confidence is set (Sir).[26]

[25] V. p. 59 (Bullen: VII, 114–15).
[26] IV. p. 57 (Bullen: VII, 108–9).

A GAME AT CHESS

The censure which the White King addresses to the treacherous Fat Bishop in this scene—and to the White King's Pawn, whose 'heart's in the Blacke House', in III. i—conveys the same spirit of disappointment at outraged trust as Mistress Openwork's rebuke of Goshawk in IV. ii of *The Roaring Girl*.[27]

As Professor Bald points out, 'the visit to Madrid [in connection with the proposed Spanish marriage] is allegorically portrayed in IV, iv, V, i, V, iii.'[28] As 'an arch-dissembler' in V. iii, the White Knight draws out the confession 'What we [the Black House] have done | Hath bin dissemblance ever', and thereby obtains 'Check Mate by discoverie'. He accomplishes this overthrow as Mistress Knaves-bee accomplishes the discomfiture of Lord Beaufort in III. i of *Anything for a Quiet Life*, and Isabella that of Antonio in IV. iii of *The Changeling*, by pretending to be as inclined to his opponent's lustfulness as is his opponent. The two latter scenes may take some of their inspiration, as Professor Bald is strongly of the opinion that the first does, from 'the test imposed by Malcolm on Macduff in IV, iii of *Macbeth*'.[29] As the deceptions practised by Mistress Knaves-bee, Isabella, and the White Knight are not very different from those of Prince Phoenix and Fitsgrave in *The Phoenix* (1602) and *Your Five Gallants* (1605), I am inclined to agree with Professor Bentley, who writes, 'the *Macbeth* indebtedness seems dubious to me' (*The Jacobean and Caroline Stage*, IV, 878).

[27] See Bullen, VIII, 108, ll. 83–6; 74, ll. 265–'271' [=273]; and IV, 111, ll. 207–'212' [=213].
[28] Introduction to *A Game at Chesse*, p. 10.
[29] Ibid., p. 16.

CONCLUSION

From his early poetry we learn that Middleton began his literary career with the attitude of a critic, and a conviction that the uses of literature are serious. His progress beyond the adolescent sententiousness of *The Wisdom of Solomon Paraphrased*, and observations such as 'were it number'd well, | There are more devils on earth than are in hell' in his early work, to concern with the nature of the problems that lie in the way of moral progress, and with the formulation of mature ideals of human behaviour, becomes increasingly evident. Middleton's artistic point of view was conditioned by his humanity and tempered by experience, but it remained fundamentally critical and didactic.

In *The Phoenix* and *Your Five Gallants*, and later in *A Fair Quarrel* and *The Old Law*, Middleton makes his position relatively obvious, through Phoenix and Fidelio, Fitsgrave, Captain Agar, and Evander and Cleanthes. Usually, however, he employs more indirect and intimative modes of thematic expression; and these, together with the distinctive economy and compression of his dramatic technique, place the reader very much under the necessity of visualizing his plays in performance, a point which is suggested in regard to *The Changeling* by Miss M. C. Bradbrook's observation that 'the unity of its plot and subplot ... is immediately seen in the acting.'[1] Middleton carries his critical and didactic point of view into all his plays, irrespective of genre, and several of his latest themes and other dramatic materials find their origins in his early writing.

The conflict of the human and the animal in man, and the presence of a universal power, 'resisting vice, assisting righteousness',[2] are themes that Middleton introduces in *The Wisdom of Solomon Paraphrased*; he introduces the theme of appearance versus reality in *Micro-cynicon*; chastity, represented by Lucrece

---

[1] *The Growth and Structure of Elizabethan Comedy*, p. 155.

[2] God is referred to as the source of this force in nature only in *The Wisdom of Solomon Paraphrased*, which Middleton concludes with the lines "Twas God, his people's aid, their wisdom's friend, | In whom I did begin, with whom I end.'

CONCLUSION

('She was as chaste as fair, as fair as chaste'), and brutality, represented by Tarquin, are his subjects in *The Ghost of Lucrece*. All these themes continued to influence his work.

The human and the animal in man, and appearance versus reality, receive their first treatment in dramatic form in *Blurt Master-Constable*, where Violetta and Fontinell appear initially to be people of refinement, but soon reveal their superficiality— to the chorus of Lazarillo's 'I burne ... I pine away with the desire of flesh' and the overt voluptuousness of Imperia, 'the freckle cheeke Madona'. *Blurt Master-Constable* also shows us Middleton's first experiment with plot and character *montage*, the technique with which he was often again to obtain the intimative concentration of his themes, either, as in *Blurt Master-Constable*, in a play's over-all structure—*The Mayor of Queenborough* and *The Changeling* being outstanding examples —or on a smaller scale, as in the nexus of minor plots in *The Roaring Girl*.

In *Blurt Master-Constable* and the Gerardine–Maria plot of *The Family of Love* Middleton makes his first travesties of romantic love, and the plays being written for the Children of Paul's and the Children of the Revels respectively, he may well have taken encouragement in these early ventures from the realization that boys, in the rôles of Fontinell and Violetta, and Gerardine and Maria, would enter into the spirit of burlesque with special enthusiasm. *The Mayor of Queenborough* is also a travesty: if the 'tragic interest' of this later play is 'insufficiently concentrated',[3] it is not because Middleton failed to understand the correct ingredients of the conventional, awe-inspiring tragedy of ambition. His derisory vein, and his use of his sources— deliberately omitting details that might inspire admiration for Vortiger's audacity, and substituting others of his own invention that would emphasize the meanness of, and awaken contempt for, self-seeking brutality—show that Middleton was intent upon projecting the image of a tyrant in his own unromantic way, and the symbolic underplot is part of the design of that projection.

Notable variations on the Tarquin–Lucrece motif are the situations involving Falso and his niece in II. iii of *The Phoenix*, the physician and Jane in III. ii of *A Fair Quarrel*, the Duke and

---

[3] *Hengist, King of Kent*, ed. R. C. Bald, xlvi.

Bianca in II. ii of *Women Beware Women*, Deflores and Beatrice in III. iv of *The Changeling*, and the Black Bishop's Pawn and the White Queen's Pawn in II. i of *A Game at Chess*; and there are others, such as the Sir Gilbert Lambtone–Mistress Low-water situation in *No Wit, No Help Like a Woman's*, that do not involve a direct seduction confrontation. Falso's neice and Fidelio's mother in *The Phoenix*, and the 'suspectlesse virgin', Katherine, in *Your Five Gallants*, reflect the image of Lucrece; but the virtue of Middleton's later heroines has either been strengthened by experience, or, as in the case of the Duchess in *More Dissemblers Besides Women*, is in the process of being so strengthened. Mistress Knaves-bee in *Anything for a Quiet Life*, and Isabella in *The Changeling*, carry this quality of independent moral competence into Middleton's latest plays, and the lack of it leads to the tragedies of Isabella and Bianca in *Women Beware Women* and Beatrice in *The Changeling*, and to the near-tragedies of Lady Cressingham in *Anything for a Quiet Life* and the White Queen's Pawn in *A Game at Chess*. Middleton's departures from his principal source for *The Changeling* in portraying Beatrice show his determination to redevelop in his last plays the theme of 'apprenticeship to life', introduced in *The Phoenix* and *Michaelmas Term*. The abruptly revealed veneer of Violetta in *Blurt Master-Constable* and the inexperience of Maria in *The Family of Love* look forward to the maturely conceived and fully realized characterization of 'giddy' Beatrice, and to the other unprepared and vulnerable young women of the last plays.

Middleton reserved poetic modes of expression for distinct purposes. In *The Wisdom of Solomon Paraphrased* and *The Ghost of Lucrece*, and such passages as the apostrophes to 'Reverend and honourable Matrimony' and 'sober Law' in *The Phoenix* and Cleanthes's apostrophe to 'nature' in *The Old Law*, he was clearly striving to convey the seriousness of his subject with impressive diction. His use of imagery, particularly the eye imagery with which he alludes to moral vision and the food imagery with which he alludes to sexual appetite, is extensive throughout the canon. From the travesty of romantic attitudes, especially towards love between the sexes, that recurs continually in the plays, I infer that Middleton never ceased to be suspicious of the glamour-producing tendencies of 'unprofitable sweetness and delicious false conceits'. His derisory vein sometimes takes a burlesque

CONCLUSION 197

form which mocks high-sounding utterances of pseudo-refined sentiments and anguished or impassioned but empty protestations, accentuating at once the distorted condition of the speaker's sense of values and the crudeness of his pose. But Middleton also understood the subtler methods of the arch dissembler, and could adjust his style to suit more polished forms of deceitfulness. It is worth noting, in this regard, that the lines[4] which Professor Bald uses to illustrate his observation that 'occasionally there leaps out a passage that none but a true poet could have written',[5] and from which Mr. Dyce suggests that Milton adopted a phrase for *Lycidas*,[6] are part of a speech which Middleton wrote to be spoken by one of the most insidious of his consummate hypocrites.

The qualities of character to which Middleton gives his approval are those symptomatic of the viability of the human spirit. In *The Old Law* and *The Widow* he invents tests that point the contrast between fellow feeling and degenerate materialism. In *The Witch* he makes the Sebastian–Isabella plot focus on the nature of the spiritual union of man and woman through trust,[7] skilfully dovetailing the action involving Aberzanes and Francisca, who are conspicuously unconscious of such a consideration. In *A Fair Quarrel*, where Middleton was adapting an idea that caught his interest in *The Charge of Sir Francis Bacon Knight*,[8] he creates a situation that contrasts devotion to truth with devotion to vainglorious pride. Devotion to 'truth's refin'd purity' is the human ideal to which Middleton gives the greatest stress from first to last. In *The Phoenix, Michaelmas Term*, and *Your Five Gallants*, he lays the stress on knowledge of the world. In later plays experience becomes the key to self-knowledge, and stress falls on the critical introspection that the Duchess calls for at the conclusion of *More Dissemblers Besides Women*, 'We all have

---

[4] 'That Eie . . . Rose' in the passage quoted above, p. 188.
[5] Introduction to *A Game at Chesse*, p. 18.
[6] *The Works of Thomas Middleton*, IV, 316, n. c.
[7] Since Isabella is Sebastian's by precontract, Sebastian could intercede in the marriage of Antonio and Isabella at the beginning and state his previous claim; but Middleton disregards this possibility in order to be able to represent Sebastian's temporary distraction—a period during which Sebastian is preoccupied with his rights in, rather than his responsibilities to, Isabella, and which he terminates by coming to his senses and justifying Isabella's 'Had my first Love liv'd and return'd saffe, he would have been a light to all Mens Actions, his faith shinde so bright.'
[8] See Appendix E.

faults; look not so much on his. | Who lives i'th'world that never did amiss?' Middleton develops his theme of self-development through creditable response to experience in characters as various as Prince Phoenix in *The Phoenix*, Witgood in *A Trick to Catch the Old One*, the Duchess in *More Dissemblers Besides Women*, and the Colonel in *A Fair Quarrel*.

Middleton was able to combine idealism with realism, and to maintain a sympathy that is devoid of sentimentality. In *A Chaste Maid in Cheapside* and *Women Beware Women* he examines the thought processes of the professional wittol, Allwit, and the degenerately materialistic Leantio with the same fidelity as that with which he enters into the nobility of purpose of Captain Agar in *A Fair Quarrel* and Cleanthes in *The Old Law*. His conception of 'honest love' is a realistic rather than a romantic theme, which he contrasts with the emulation of 'Beastes, | Making their mates those that stand next their lusts'. Its essential characteristics are a regard that goes beyond material self-interest, such as the judicious Valeria seeks from a prospective mate in *The Widow*, and a faith like that which exists between Fitzallen and Jane in *A Fair Quarrel*. Middleton characterizes individuals whose approach to love and other human relationships falls below these simple human standards in a variety of ways.

Lazarillo, who takes a 'Night-walke' in the fetid cellar of Imperia's brothel, and Curvetto, in *Blurt Master-Constable*, are the first representatives of a class of boorish clowns whose animality is extenuated by its sheer obviousness; Lipsalve and Gudgeon in *The Family of Love*, Chaugh and Trimtram in *A Fair Quarrel*, the Ward and Sordido in *Women Beware Women*, and Lollio in *The Changeling* are among its members. These individuals whose motives are unconcealed, and the squalid details that attend their characterization, reflect derisively on characters who share their motives but disguise them with fair seeming. By their instrumentality Middleton tacitly directs his audience to the conclusion that if anything is more abject than simple 'untutred lust', it is 'untutred lust' that is hidden, or sophisticated, with the 'sweet honey-poison' of poetry, or affected religious zeal. The distinction is conveyed explicitly by the hero of *The Phoenix* when he denounces the jeweller's wife, 'Thou worse then common: private, subtill harlot', and by the Cardinal in *More Dissemblers Besides Women* when he tells Lactantio, 'Th'open

CONCLUSION 199

villain | Goes before thee to mercy, and his Penitency | Is blest with a more sweet and quick return.' Middleton's tendency was to give thematic pertinence to all elements of his drama. The function of Lazarillo and his descendants of indirectly accentuating truths about other characters is shared to a large extent by Deflores, with his 'wondrous honest heart', in *The Changeling*. The combination of antithetical features in his character is foreshadowed in Lipsalve in *The Family of Love*, who is aware that 'outward apparance is no authentick instance of the inward desires'; and the patent barbarism of the Saxon warrior Horsus that lends impressiveness to his denunciation of Vortiger in *The Mayor of Queenborough*—

Vor. This was your Counsel now.
Hor. Mine? 'twas the Counsel
 Of your own lust and bloud; your appetite knows it.[9]

—looks forward to the physical ugliness which is Deflores's badge of authority as a moral spokesman. Having the disposition to conceal the real nature of their motives from themselves, or others, or both, in common, the hypocrites in Middleton's plays are otherwise variously characterized by 'brutish reluctations'; indifference to the welfare, or disregard of the previous claims, of others; being affectedly 'faire spoken . . . and wondrous mild', and grotesquely ready to condemn the shortcomings of others; and a resentment, such as Antonio expresses in *The Witch*, for any disturbance of a blissfully deluded condition of mind:

What's all this now?
I feele no ease; the Burthens not yet off
so long as th'Abuse sticks in my knowledge—
oh, 'tis a paine of hell to know ones shame!—
had it byn hid, & don, it'had ben don happy,
for he that's Ignorant lives long, and merry.[10]

It can confidently be said of Middleton that he had little inclination to be one of those writers of whom the Duke warns his son in *The Phoenix*, writers whom 'love or feare, make . . . partiall'. His choice and treatment of his materials from life and of his sources in literature, his use of language, the breadth and depth of his

[9] V. p. 72 (Bullen: II, 108).
[10] IV. pp. 73–4 (Bullen: V, 431).

interest in character, the continuity of his themes, and the concentrated thematic relevance of the various components of his dramatic structures, reveal his individuality and independent strength of purpose. From the evidence of characterization, structure, themes, and mode of thematic expression, it is clear that Middleton dominated the production of *The Roaring Girl*, and—whether they were collaborations, or plays written by Middleton that were later revised—of *A Fair Quarrel*, *The Old Law*, *The Widow*, and *The Changeling*; the 'seamless unity' which Miss M. C. Bradbrook finds in these plays[11] would be a natural result of the strong controlling influence of one mind.

The intimative character of Middleton's dramatic technique, harmonizing with the latency and complexity of human thought, contrasts with the simplicity of the moral design in his plays. 'To beguile goodnes', says Thomasine in *Michaelmas Term*, 'is the coare of sins.' In later plays 'goodnes' is a quality that is acquired through experience, self-knowledge, and learning to 'resist, and conquer'; it becomes the attribute of individuals who cannot be beguiled. In Middleton's dramatic microcosm success as a human being develops from some achievement, no matter how rudimentary, of self-knowledge, from some unsentimentalized subordination of the demands of animal nature to those of human nature, some victory, great or small, of reason over 'the irrational passions and appetites'; and tragedy lies in ignorance of self and the world, moral incompetence, and the perversion of the human spirit.

[11] Miss Bradbrook writes: 'Middleton's power to work with other men and produce a play of apparently seamless unity is one of the most astonishing features of the Jacobean drama' (*The Growth and Structure of Elizabethan Comedy*, p. 164).

APPENDIX A

The Canon and Chronology of Middleton's Plays

The following list presents the canon of Middleton's plays as represented in Mr. Bullen's *The Works of Thomas Middleton*.[1]

Blurt Master-Constable or The Spaniard's Night-walke
(a) 1602. (b) 1601–2.
(c) Mal. 245 (2).

The Phoenix
(a) 1607. (b) 1602.
(c) Mal. 225 (5).

The Famelie of Love
(a) 1608. (b) 1602.
(c) Mal. 245 (5).

Michaelmas Terme
(a) 1607. (b) 1604.
(c) Mal. 224 (6).

A Mad World, my Masters
(a) 1608. (b) 1604.
(c) Mal. 245 (6).

Your five Gallants
(a) n.d. (licensed for printing in March 1608). (b) 1605.
(c) Mal. 245 (1).

A Trick to catch the Old-one
(a) 1608. (b) 1606.
(c) Mal. 797.

The Roaring Girle or Moll Cut-Purse
(a) 1611. (b) 1607–8.
(c) Mal. 246 (1).

A Chast Mayd in Cheap-side
(a) 1630. (b) 1613.
(c) Mal. 245 (8).

[1] The list is arranged chronologically according to the years of composition assigned by Professor R. C. Bald (see above, p. xvi, n. 5). The information presented is: (a) date of first printing [in the case of *The Witch* MS., the date of transcription]; (b) conjectural date of composition; and (c) Bodleian Library shelf-mark of the copy used in this study.

APPENDIX A

No $\begin{Bmatrix} Wit \\ Help \end{Bmatrix}$ Like a Womans

(a) 1657.   (b) c. 1615.[2]
(c) Mal. 247 (3).

More Dissemblers besides Women
(a) 1657.   (b) c. 1615.
(c) Mal. 247 (4).

A Faire Quarrell[3]
(a) 1. 1617.   (b) 1615–16.
    2. 1622 ('With new Additions').
(c) 1. Mal. 233 (8).
    2. Mal. 246 (2).

The Mayor of Quinborough[4]
(a) 1661.   (b) 1615–20.
(c) Mal. 198 (6).

The Old Law: or A new way to please you
(a) 1656.   (b) c. 1616.
(c) Mal. 246 (6).

The Widdow
(a) 1652.   (b) 1616.
(c) Mal. 246 (5).

The Witch
(a) Between 1619 and 1627.[5]   (b) 1616.
(c) MS. Malone 12.

[2] From interpretation of the almanac references in this play, Mr. David George infers that it was written in 1611 (see 'Weather-wise's Almanac and the Date of Middleton's "No Wit No Help Like a Woman's"', *Notes and Queries*, CCXI (Aug. 1966), 297–301.

[3] Quotations from this play were taken from the 1622 quarto (Mal. 246[2]); readings were compared with the edition of 1617.

[4] For a description of the Lambarde and Portland MSS. of this play see 'The Texts' (pp. xxxi–xxxvi) in Professor R. C. Bald's edition (noted above, p. 130, n. 1). Professor Bald uses the Lambarde MS. as copy text, noting that the MSS. contain 175 lines not in the quarto, which he suggests may be a censored version, whereas the quarto contains 'about 25 lines not in the manuscripts'; and that 'corrections from [the quarto] have been frequently incorporated in the text'. The conclusion of the MSS. goes beyond that of the quarto to represent Aurelius's vindication of Castiza's virtue and his hailing her as his future wife.

I do not find Bald's arguments for the antecedence of the MSS. convincing. It seems much more likely that the quarto represents the play as it was written by Middleton, and that the MSS. are copies of a subsequent version to which the reviser's principal contributions were two songs, what apparently seemed to him a more agreeable conclusion, and an epilogue.

[5] See the Introduction of F. P. Wilson's and W. W. Greg's edition of *The Witch* (Oxford, 1948 [1950]), pp. vii–viii.

APPENDIX A

Any Thing for a Quiet Life
(a) 1662. (b) 1621.
(c) Mal. 246 (7).

Women Beware Women
(a) 1657. (b) *c.* 1621.
(c) Mal. 247 (5).

The Changeling
(a) 1653. (b) 1622.
(c) Mal. 246 (9).

The Spanish Gipsie[6]

A Game at Chesse
(a) n.d. (b) 1624.
(c) Mal. 247 (1).

[6] See above, p. xvi, and Appendix C (b).

APPENDIX B

An excerpt from 'The Epistle to the Reader; or, The True Character of this Book' in Thomas Middleton's *The Black Book* (printed 1604)

To all those that are truly virtuous, and can touch pitch and yet never defile themselves; read the mischievous lives and pernicious practices of villains, and yet be never the worse at the end of the book, but rather confirmed the more in their honest estates and the uprightness of their virtues;—to such I dedicate myself, the wholesome intent of my labours . . . [to] unmask the world's shadowed villanies: and I account him as a traitor to virtue, who, diving into the deep of this cunning age, and finding there such monsters of nature . . . as panders, harlots, and ruffians do figure, if he rise up silent again, and neither discover or publish them to the civil rank of sober and continent livers, who thereby may shun those two devouring gulfs, to wit, of deceit and luxury, which swallow up more mortals than Scylla and Charybdis. . . . Wherefore I freely persuade myself, no virtuous spirit . . . but will approve my politic moral, where, under the shadow of the devil's legacies, or his bequeathing to villains, I strip their villanies naked, and bare the infectious bulks of craft, cozenage, and panderism, the three bloodhounds of a commonwealth. And thus far I presume that none will or can except at this—which I call the Black Book, because it doubly damns the devil—but some tainted harlot, noseless bawd, obscene ruffian, and such of the same black nature and filthy condition, that poison the towardly spring of gentility, and corrupt with the mud of mischiefs the pure and clear springs of a kingdom. And to spurgall such, who reads me shall know I dare; for I fear neither the ratsbane of a harlot nor the poniard of a villain.[1]

The soliloquy on 'impudence' in *Your Five Gallants*

The Divill scarce knew what a portion hee gave his children, when he allowde 'em large impudence to live upon, & so turnd em into th'world. Surely he gave away the third part of the riches of his kingdome. Revenues are but fooles too't; the filed tongue and the undaunted fore-head
Are mighty patrimonies wealthier then those
The Citty-Sire, or the Court-father leaves.

[1] *Works*, VIII, [5]-6.

In these behold it. Riches oft like slaves
Revolt; they beare their fore-heads to their graves.
What soonest grasps advancement, mens great suites,
Trips downe rich widowes, gaines repute and name,
Makes way where ere it comes, bewitches all.
Thou impudence, the minion of our dayes
On whose pale cheekes favor and fortune playes!
Call you these your five Gallants? Trust me they'r rare fellowes.
They live on nothing; many cannot live on something!
Heere they may take example;—Suspectlesse virgin!
How easie had thy Goodnesse bene beguilde;
Now onely rests, that as to me they'r knowne,
So to the world their base Arts may be showne.[2]

The Letter to the Reader in *The World Tost at Tennis*

After most harty commendations (my kinde and unknowne friends) trusting in *Phoebus*, your understandings are all in as good health as *Simplicitie's* was at the writing hereof: This is to certifie you further, that this short and small Treatise that followes, call'd *A Masque, The Device*, further Intituled, *The World tost at Tennis*: How it will be now toss'd in the World, I know not, a toy brought to the Presse rather by the Printer, then the Poet; who requested an Epistle for his passe, to satisfie his perusers how hitherto he hath behav'd himselfe. First, for his Conception; he was begot in *Braine-ford*, borne on the Bankeside of *Hellicon*, brought up amongst Noble, Gentle, Commons, and good Schollers of all sorts, where (for his time) he did good and honest service beyond the small Seas; hee was faire-spoken, never accus'd of scurrilous or obsceane language, (a vertue not ever found in Sceanes of the like condition) of as honest meaning reputed, as his words reported; neither too bitterly taxing, nor too soothingly telling the Worlds broad abuses, moderately merry, as sententiously serious, never condemn'd but for his brevitie in speech, ever wishing his Tale longer, to be assur'd he would co[n]tinue to so good a purpose: Having all these hansome qualities simply and no other compounded with knaverie, there is great hope he shall passe still by the faire way of good report, persevering in those honest courses which may become the sonne of *Simplicitie*: who, though he be now in a Masque, yet is his face apparant inough: and so (loving Cousins) having no Newes to send you at this time, but that Deceit is

[2] IV. sig. G[1]–G[1]ᵛ (Bullen: III, 208).

entring upon you, (whom I pray you have a care to avoid) and this notice I can give you of him, there are some sixe or eight Pages before him; the Lawyer and the Divell behinde him; in this care I leave you, not leaving to be

Your kinde and loving Kinsman,
Simplicitie.
—Mal. 246 (4), sig. A4–A4^v.

APPENDIX C

(a) Thomas Middleton and William Rowley

William Rowley's name appears below Thomas Middleton's on the title-pages of the earliest known editions of four plays and a masque: *A Fair Quarrel* (Rowley's name is affixed to the dedicatory epistle of this play), *The Changeling, The Old Law*,[1] *The Spanish Gipsy*, and *The World Tost at Tennis*. Two of these, the first- and last-mentioned, were published while both men were living.[2] *The Changeling* and *The Spanish Gipsy* came into print twenty-six years, and *The Old Law* twenty-nine years, after Middleton's death in 1627 (Rowley appears to have predeceased him by just over a year).

On the basis of this evidence it was concluded by certain nineteenth-century students of Jacobean drama that Middleton, at the height of his career and with some twenty years of writing and many single-handed successes behind him, accepted Rowley, heretofore known only as a comic actor and occasional hack-writer, as an equal partner in collaborative play-writing. Collaboration was common in the period, of course, and since Middleton, like most, if not all, his fellows had done some of it by way of apprenticeship during his early days in London about the turn of the century, and had obtained the assistance of his old associate, Thomas Dekker, for the production of a special scene in *The Roaring Girl* in 1607 or 1608,[3] no one seems to have questioned the reasonableness of the assumption.

In 1953 Mr. Edward Engelberg observed that 'the most complete study of the Middleton–Rowley collaboration is over fifty years old, and essentially it has remained unchallenged.'[4] By 'the most complete study' he meant Miss P. G. Wiggin's 'An Inquiry into the Authorship of the Middleton–Rowley Plays',[5] and when he used the word 'essentially' to modify 'it has remained unchallenged', he alluded to Professor W. D. Dunkel's essay, 'Did Not Rowley Merely Revise Middleton?'[6]

Miss Wiggin's 'Inquiry', which makes a statement about 'the individual shares of Thomas Middleton and William Rowley in writing *A*

---

[1] It is generally agreed that the appearance of Philip Massinger's name on the title-page of *The Old Law* indicates that Massinger may have revised the play.
[2] *A Fair Quarrel* was issued twice in 1617. The second issue contained 'new Additions' which were also included in the edition of 1622.
[3] See above, pp. 100–101 and 109–10.
[4] 'A Middleton–Rowley Dispute', *Notes and Queries*, CXCVIII (Aug. 1953), 330.
[5] *Radcliffe College Monographs*, IX (1897).
[6] *PMLA*, XLVIII (Sept. 1933), 799–805.

Fair Quarrel, *The Changeling*, and *The Spanish Gipsy*', has been instrumental in perpetuating the idea of Middleton and Rowley as equal collaborators. It is based on metrical evidence, which I shall refer to later, and an interpretation of the two men's views of life.

Mr. Engelberg suggests that Miss Wiggin's use of 'higher tests' to support a division of *The Changeling* is unreliable:

Her argument . . . ignores the context of the dramatic situations, and sidesteps the difference in dramatic necessity between Beatrice and Jane. [Miss Wiggin draws a parallel between III. ii of *A Fair Quarrel*, which she ascribes to Rowley, and III. iv of *The Changeling*, in order to argue that he also had a hand in the latter] . . . it overlooks the meaning of two other 'temptation scenes,' and dismisses unjustly some striking parallel passages.[7]

Later he writes: '. . . the two additional examples reviewed here serve to confirm that Middleton's position on women and the temptations of sin is not, as Miss Wiggin would have us believe, mere cynicism. . . . He has been consistently praised for his understanding of women. . . .'[8] For his last remark Mr. Engelberg might have availed himself of the authority of Professor Ellis-Fermor: '. . . his discernment of the minds of women; in this no dramatist of the period except Shakespeare is his equal at once for variety and for penetration.'[9]

Miss Wiggin appears to be torn between admiration for Middleton's ability 'to hold . . . the mirror up to Nature', and revulsion at what the mirror seems to her to reveal:

He showed a far closer study of life than Rowley, and a keener insight into motives. . . . With many excellences, however, we see that owing to his low view of human nature, he was inferior to Rowley in power to win sympathy for his characters, to hold the reader's interest in them to the last. We find that his serious plays decrease in interest towards the end,—this is as true of 'More Dissemblers Besides Women,' whose characters, though they are not, with the exception of Lantantio [*sic*], wicked, are wholly devoid of dignity, as it is of 'Women Beware Women,'—and that no one of them has that romantic charm that distinguishes Rowley's best work.[10]

As is indicated in the last clause, Miss Wiggin prefers the romantic view of man she finds in Rowley's plays. Earlier she has written: 'In "All's Lost by Lust," on the contrary, the *dramatis personae* inspire intense sympathy in the reader, and merely by reason of this one characteristic, Rowley's tragedy would probably make a more popular acting play than "Women Beware Women". . . .'[11] In her later re-

---

[7] 'A Middleton–Rowley Dispute', p. 330.
[8] Ibid., p. 332.
[9] *The Jacobean Drama*, p. 149.
[10] 'An Inquiry', p. 24.
[11] 'An Inquiry', p. 23.

marks Miss Wiggin again proffers her view of Middleton as a misanthropist, and, attributing to Rowley as a distinguishing mark a 'respect for human nature, especially for women. . . . [a quality] so noticeably lacking in the plays of Middleton', she suggests that Rowley exerted a tempering influence on Middleton.

While it is very likely true that a romantic play would appeal to a wider audience than a play that offers a criticism of society, it seems to me that Miss Wiggin's inference from the fact that Middleton sometimes presents an unattractive picture of life that he had no 'respect for human nature, especially for women' is a decidedly hasty generalization. Evidently Miss Wiggin was not aware of the 'variety' that Professor Ellis-Fermor refers to in regard to Middleton's characterizations of women, for creditable character in women, such as Miss Wiggin admires in Jane in III. ii of *A Fair Quarrel* and ascribes to Rowley's production, is in fact part of a strong recurrent theme that takes its origin in Middleton's earliest writing. Miss Wiggin's statement that the characters in *More Dissemblers Besides Women* and *Women Beware Women* are 'wholly devoid of dignity' overlooks, among other things, the behaviour of Andrugio and the meaning of the dramatic experience of the Duchess in the former play, and Middleton's sympathy with the unhappy circumstances of the young women in the latter. In my opinion, no writer has ever been more genuinely in sympathy with the problems of his fellow men, or more conscious of his custodianship; and it was precisely because he placed a very high value indeed upon 'human' nature that he so often represented the ugliness of uncontrolled animal nature on the stage.

We know of the widespread acceptance of the idea that Middleton and Rowley were equal collaborators by the reception which countersuggestions have been given. That Mr. Engelberg's suggestion that Middleton wrote both III. iv of *The Changeling* and III. ii of *A Fair Quarrel* without Rowley's influence was not popular is indicated by the fact that it receives no mention in two books on Middleton[12] published subsequently to his essay.

Professor Dunkel's study is more comprehensive than Mr. Engelberg's: it demonstrates that underplots and characterizations traditionally held to have been Rowley's are substantially the same as plots and characterizations that Middleton had produced years before. Professor Dunkel nowhere departs from readily demonstrable facts, nowhere deals in fallacies of disputation, and is nowhere arbitrary (his theme and the undogmatic form in which it is submitted are explicit in the title, 'Did Not Rowley Merely Revise Middleton?'); but Mr. Schoenbaum

[12] Samuel Schoenbaum, *Middleton's Tragedies* (New York, 1955) and R. H. Barker, *Thomas Middleton* (New York, 1958).

gives his work summary rejection as follows: 'Since Dunkel offers no stylistic data to indicate the presence of Middleton's hand in the scenes usually ascribed to Rowley, his theory may be dismissed as unfounded.'[13]

Elsewhere, Mr. Schoenbaum describes Miss Wiggin's essay, which contains a kind of stylistic analysis that he finds acceptable, as 'excellent'; and while referring to the 'untrustworthy texts' of Rowley's plays and observing that 'under such circumstances statements about metrics may well have an insecure foundation', he nevertheless quotes profusely from Miss Wiggin, having reassured himself as follows: 'It would seem, indeed, that in almost every respect Rowley's style is individual enough to make possible a reasonably precise estimate of his share in the collaborations with Middleton.'[14] Mr. R. H. Barker, to whom Mr. Schoenbaum is largely indebted,[15] follows Miss Wiggin's division of *The Changeling* and *A Fair Quarrel*, but there is a rather tenuous transition from 'is, or seems to be' to 'almost certainly' in his reference to the latter play: 'In *A Fair Quarrel* it is, or seems to be, fairly easy to separate the work of the collaborators. The comic scenes, the underplot, and the first scene of the main plot are almost certainly Rowley's; the main plot after the first scene is almost certainly Middleton's.'[16] As to their subscription to the traditional view of the association of Middleton and Rowley, and their endorsements of Miss Wiggin's essay, the one explicit, the other tacit, it is difficult to say to what extent the tradition inspires confidence in Miss Wiggin and vice versa.[17]

In a note appended to his commendation of Miss Wiggin's essay Mr. Schoenbaum writes, 'Fleay's division of *The Changeling* is identical with Wiggin's and appeared earlier; yet it is to Wiggin that we must turn, for Fleay gives no evidence to back up his findings.'[18] In an edition of *The Changeling*[19] Mr. N. W. Bawcutt also follows the Fleay-Wiggin division of the play, and, in dismissing Mr. Engelberg and Professor Dunkel, implies a like preference for Miss Wiggin's evidence:

> This part of the play [III. ii of *A Fair Quarrel*] is usually assigned to Rowley, and the corresponding part of *The Changeling* to Middleton [Mr. Bawcutt seems to be unaware that Miss Wiggin would have Rowley 'powerful in determining' the 'character' of the corresponding part of *The*

---

[13] *Middleton's Tragedies*, p. 214.
[14] Ibid., p. 208.
[15] See Preface to *Thomas Middleton*, p. [vii].
[16] *Thomas Middleton*, p. 105.
[17] An early essay which relies on Miss Wiggin's is C. W. Stork's 'Life of Rowley' in *William Rowley: His 'All's Lost by Lust', and 'A Shoemaker, a Gentleman'* (Philadelphia, 1910). Another modern example is D. M. Robb's 'The Canon of William Rowley's Plays', *Modern Language Review*, XLV (Apr. 1950), 129–41.
[18] *Middleton's Tragedies*, p. 247, n. 3.
[19] (London, 1958).

APPENDIX C 211

Changeling as well]; E. Engelberg, however, has argued not very convincingly that both are by Middleton.[20]
W. D. Dunkel's argument that Rowley merely revised a work originally written solely by Middleton has virtually nothing to support it.[21]

In regard to the method Miss Wiggin used, apparently she was unaware that Mr. F. G. Fleay was one of its most strenuous pioneers and resolute advocates:[22]

> It is true that Mr. Fleay has attempted to make a division. Indeed, he has assigned every scene of these plays to either one dramatist or the other. Unfortunately, however, misprints have in some instances made his division uncertain. Moreover, as he has allowed himself on several occasions to fall into downright contradictions in his Middleton–Rowley work that cannot be accounted for as misprints, and has in no case given reasons for his statements, we cannot regard these as anything more authoritative than mere expressions of opinion, and cannot yield them unquestioning belief.[23]

This was an ironic denunciation of Mr. Fleay, who had written, twenty-three years earlier,

> This . . . is the great step we have to take; our analysis, which has hitherto been qualitative, must become quantitative; we must cease to be empirical, and become scientific: in criticism as in other matters, the test that decides between science and empiricism is this: 'Can you say, not of what kind, but how much? If you cannot weigh, measure, number your results, however you may be convinced yourself, you must not hope to convince others, or claim the position of an investigator; you are merely a guesser, a propounder of hypotheses.'[24]

Despite Miss Wiggin's castigation of Mr. Fleay for not having 'given reasons for his statements', an examination of her evidence derived from the application of versification tests does not reveal reasons that would carry her own statements outside the realm of 'mere expressions of opinion', conduce to the yielding of 'unquestioning belief', or warrant a confidence that would preclude consideration of another kind of evidence and the possibilities that it suggests.

Miss Wiggin bases her entire study on nineteenth-century editions of the plays, rather than on the early texts, and gives the following explanation in a footnote:

[20] Introduction to *The Changeling*, p. xxxv, n. 3.
[21] Ibid., p. xliii, n. 1.
[22] See 'On Metrical Tests as applied to Dramatic Poetry: Part I. Shakspere', and '. . . Part II. Beaumont, Fletcher, Massinger', *Transactions of the New Shakspere Society*, 1st. Ser., Part I (1874), 1–15 and 51–72.
[23] 'An Inquiry', p. 3.
[24] 'On Metrical Tests as applied to . . . Shakspere', p. 2.

APPENDIX C

In speaking of 'prose' and 'verse' in connection with these early plays, it should be remembered that the division is incontestable only where it is evident to every ear. The quartos are so wretchedly printed that they are not to be depended upon; for instance, *A Woman Never Vext*, is printed throughout as verse, the lines, it need hardly be said, being divided upon no principle that can be discovered. Whenever possible it is probably safest to follow the reading of Dyce, whose ear for rhythm is invariably correct. He has altered the arrangement of the text rather freely; but his edition of the Middleton–Rowley plays is, on the whole, reliable and it furnishes the basis for the following examination of their verse.[25]

Miss Wiggin speaks of 'wretchedly printed' quartos, cites Rowley's *A New Wonder, A Woman Never Vext* as an example, and goes on to say that 'it is probably safest to follow the reading of Dyce.' Opposite this play in her 'Bibliography', however, we find 'Dilke, 1814; Dodsley, edited by Hazlitt, 1875',[26] and, in fact, Mr. Dyce did not edit *A New Wonder, A Woman Never Vext*. Miss Wiggin may have considered that Mr. Dilke's 'ear for rhythm' was, like Mr. Dyce's, 'invariably correct'. However that may be, she quotes lines which represent, in substance,[27] Mr. Dilke's treatment of the quarto of 1632, and her observation 'he has altered the arrangement of the text rather freely' in regard to Mr. Dyce[28] is also applicable to Mr. Dilke in his editing of *A New Wonder, A Woman Never Vext*.

The validity of Miss Wiggin's pretext for using nineteenth-century editions may be assessed by examining the example she chose to illustrate her condemnation of the quartos. On Plates I and II[29] is reproduced, as typical, the third opening of a copy[30] of the earliest known edi-

[25] 'An Inquiry', p. 29 f., n. 3.
[26] *A New Wonder, A Woman Never Vext* appears for the first time in *Dodsley's Old English Plays*, in the edition of 1875. Hazlitt follows the Dilke edition of 1814.
[27] There are a number of transcription errors. For example, taking the quarto as basic text, and representing 'Dodsley, edited by Hazlitt' by *H* and Wiggin by *W*, there are the following in the ten lines from *A New Wonder, A Woman Never Vext* quoted on p. 26:
raysde] rais'd *Dilke, H*; raised *W*,
Pigeon-holes] pigeon-holes *Dilke, H*; pigeon-holds *W*,
more] *Dilke, H*; worse *W*
(see Plate I, last line; and Plate II, ll. 7 and 8).
[28] See below, Appendix D. It may be noted that Mr. W. R. Arrowsmith, Mr. Dyce's scholar-contemporary, maintained that in Mr. Dyce's edition of Middleton, Middleton's 'language and the language of his times, is not truly represented'. Mr. Arrowsmith based this criticism on Mr. Dyce's inconsistent practice of altering Middleton's syntax (see 'Note on Some Peculiarities in Mr. Dyce's Edition of Middleton's Works', *Notes and Queries*, XII (8 and 15 Dec. 1855), 443–4 and 464–6.
[29] See below, between pp. 218 and 219.
[30] Bodleian Mal. 167(4).

APPENDIX C 213

tion of *A New Wonder, A Woman Never Vext*, the quarto of 1632. The description 'wretchedly printed' is plainly not applicable: there are no apparent errors of substitution, transposition, omission, or insertion; no signs of defective type or 'foul case'; no turned or omitted letters; and no errors in presswork. As to the general set-up of the pages, there is no evidence of either the 'padding out' or 'compression' that Mr. Charlton Hinman describes[31] in connection with misjudgements in casting-off copy. On the contrary, the wide range of the compositor's line length (1.7 to 9.3 cm on p. 2, and 4.3 to 8.9 cm on p. 3) suggests that the lines, far from 'being divided upon no principle that can be discovered', were set exactly according to manuscript copy, perhaps a holograph, and exemplify the 'vaguely blank verse groupings' that Mr. Bonamy Dobrée mentions when referring to the decline of blank verse as a poetic form.[32] The hyphenated word 'quicke- | Sands' (p. 3, ll. 6–7), on a page that reveals patent unconcern for justification, strengthens this impression.

But if it is questionable whether the quartos may be taken to represent the *ipsissima verba* of Middleton and Rowley, ideas about their verse styles derived from the nineteenth-century texts are at least equally questionable; and I submit that the absence of this kind of data from Professor Dunkel's essay, decried directly by Mr. Schoenbaum, and indirectly in the phrase 'virtually nothing to support it' by Mr. Bawcutt, does not justify their summary dismissal of evidence that places the traditional view of the relationship of Middleton and Rowley in doubt.

Before turning to Professor Dunkel's essay, it will be useful to consider some details of the careers of Middleton and Rowley previous to the appearance of their names on the title-page of *A Fair Quarrel* in 1617.

---

[31] See 'Cast-off Copy for the First Folio of Shakespeare', *Shakespeare Quarterly*, VI (Summer 1955), 261–9.

[32] While it is true that Middleton occasionally wrote with 'great prosodic beauty', usually, as Mr. Dobrée puts it, 'he used blank verse as a household drudge.' Mr. Dobrée continues, 'But if this medium became worse and worse as a poetic form, it did not for that reason turn out a less happy dramatic vehicle. What happened was that it became more and more the rule for the playwrights to make sentences in vaguely blank verse groupings and string them loosely together' (*Histriophone: A Dialogue on Dramatic Diction* (London, 1925), p. 34). Miss M. St. C. Byrne's opinion tends to place in doubt the whole question whether the application of versification tests to the work of any but a very few Elizabethan dramatists is likely to yield meaningful results: 'Very few writers are capable of anything so distinguished as a recognizable style, and the minor Elizabethan dramatists are definitely not among that happy band. Men like Munday and Chettle used blank verse as quickly, as slickly, and in as unremarkable a manner as the modern journalist uses his so-called prose' ('Bibliographical Clues in Collaborate Plays', *The Library*, 4th Ser. XIII (June 1932), 22–3).

APPENDIX C

Middleton subscribed at Queen's College in April 1598. How long he spent there and whether he took a degree is not known, but the testimony of a witness in a family lawsuit shows that he was in London and associating with actors by early 1601.[33] In 1602, the year of publication of his *Blurt Master-Constable*, his name was entered five times in Henslowe's diary.[34] In 1603 he was associated with the already well-established dramatist, Thomas Dekker.

Middleton no doubt profited from his association with Dekker in several ways, and it would seem that Middleton's inventiveness and versatility won him the esteem of his older colleague. In his *The Magnificent Entertainment: Given to King James ... upon the day* [15th Mar. 1603] *of his Majesties Trvumphant* [sic] *Passage ... through ... London*, Dekker, who is remembered as 'a man of happy and lovable temperament', appended the following remarkable acknowledgement to the speech of Zeale:

> If there be any glorie to be won by writing these lynes, I do freelie bestow it (as his due) on Tho. Middleton, in whose braine they were begotten, though they were delivered heere: *Quae nos non fecimus ipsi, vix ea nostra voco.*[35]

It has been suggested that Middleton's influence helped to move Dekker in the direction of realism; that in *The Honest Whore* Dekker 'has assimilated Middleton's influence and used it ... for his own purposes'.[36] Be that as it may, in regard to humanity at least, Middleton had 'a mind congenial' with Dekker's, and it is noteworthy that when they collaborated for the last time, in *The Roaring Girl* in 1607–8, Middleton's was the dominant hand.

Rowley's name appears for the first time affixed with those of John Day and George Wilkins to an epistle that was added to the second issue of the 1607 quarto of *The Travels of Three English Brothers*.[37] By that year Middleton had written at least seven plays for which he is given undivided credit; before the appearance in print of *A Fair Quarrel* Middleton had been a writer for twenty years, had had some sixteen years' experience as a playwright, and had written at least fifteen plays and several other entertainments without assistance.

Little is known of Rowley except that he was an actor of comic parts who essayed to write plays both independently and in collaboration. He was acting as 'one of the responsible leaders' of the Duke of York's

---

[33] See above, p. xvii, n. 14.
[34] See above, p. xviii.
[35] Bodleian Mal. 602(1), sig. I1.
[36] T. M. Parrott and R. H. Ball, *A Short View of Elizabethan Drama* (New York, 1958), p. 110.
[37] See Bentley, *The Jacobean and Caroline Stage*, V, 1015.

APPENDIX C 215

(later Prince Charles's) company in 1609,[38] and is named among the actors in a patent that was issued to that company in 1610.[39] In his unassisted tragedy, *All's Lost by Lust*, under 'Pedro an old fellow Father to Margaretta' in the *dramatis personae*, we find 'Jacques, a simple clownish Gentleman, his sonne, personated by the Poet'. Gerard Langbaine credits him with a winning personality: '... as to ... his intimate Acquaintance with the prime Poets of that Age, I can speak at large. He was not only beloved by those Great Men, *Shakspear*, *Fletcher*, and *Johnson*; but likewise writ with the former, *The Birth of Merlin*.[40] Langbaine is indebted to a 1622 title-page ascription for his connection of Rowley with Shakespeare in *The Birth of Merlin*, but there is no reason to doubt that Rowley possessed an agreeable disposition or that he was on friendly terms with the outstanding playwrights of the day, including Middleton, in whose *The Inner-Temple Masque*[41] his name is listed among 'The Speakers' opposite the rôle of Plumporridge. Apparently Rowley was associated with Prince Charles's company to the end of his life, but he also occasionally acted with the King's Men between 1623 and 1625.[42]

As Professor Bentley says, 'there is little evidence that Rowley received any literary recognition as a dramatist in his own day.'[43] Nine of Middleton's plays, by contrast, and probably the undated *Your Five Gallants*[44] as well, were published during Middleton's lifetime; and although the introductory remarks of seventeenth-century publishers may be unreliable guides to the literary reputations of their near contemporaries, it may be noted that in a Letter to the Reader attached to the joint first editions of *More Dissemblers Besides Women* and *Women Beware Women* in 1657, Humphrey Moseley wrote as follows: 'When these amongst others of Mr. *Thomas Middleton*'s Excellent Poems, came to my hands, I was not a little confident but that his name would prove as great an Inducement for thee to Read, as me to Print them: Since those Issues of his Brain that have already seen the Sun, have by their worth gained themselves a free entertainment....'[45]

Since *A Fair Quarrel* was printed in 1617, and the masque bearing the

[38] See Bentley, *The Jacobean and Caroline Stage*, V, 1015.
[39] See Sir E. K. Chambers, *The Elizabethan Stage* (Oxford, 1923), II, 242; and J. T. Murray, *English Dramatic Companies, 1558–1642* (London, 1910), I, 230–1.
[40] *An Account of the English Dramatick Poets* (Oxford, 1691), II, 428.
[41] Entered in the Stationers' Register on 10 July 1619, as *The Temple Maske Anno 1618'*.
[42] See Murray, *English Dramatic Companies*, I, 162, and table opposite 172, n. 14; and Bentley, *The Jacobean and Caroline Stage*, II, 556.
[43] *The Jacobean and Caroline Stage*, V, 1017.
[44] Entered in the Stationers' Register, under the title 'the ffyve Wittie Gallantes', on 22 Mar. 1608. See Chambers, *The Elizabethan Stage*, III, 440.
[45] Bodleian Mal. 247(4), sig. A3.

names of Middleton and Rowley was published while both men were still living, it is reasonable to assume that an understanding or some kind of an arrangement existed between them beginning in or not long before 1617. As to the nature of that arrangement, the idea of a partnership characterized by mutual consultation seems to me to be the least likely of several possibilities. Judging from his letters to the reader in *The World Tost at Tennis*[46] and *The Family of Love,* Middleton as a literary artist had little personal vanity or Jonsonian *jalousie de métier*; yet there is a noteworthy expression of contempt for poor workmanship in the preamble to *The Triumphs of Truth,* which he 'redeem'd into Forme, from the Ignorance of some former times, and their Common Writer [Anthony Munday]'. After a preliminary observation that 'there is no subject upon earth received into the place of his gouvernement with the like State & Magnificence as is the Lord Mayor of . . . London', he goes on to say:

This being then infallible (like the Mistresse of our Triumphs) and not to be denied of any, how carefull ought those Gentlemen to be, to whose discretion and Judgement the weight and charge of such a businesse is entirely referred and committed by the whole Society, to have all things correspondent to that Generous and Noble freenesse of cost and liberality, the streames of Art, to aequall those of Bounty, a Knowledge that may take the true height of such an Honorable Solemnity; the miserable want of both which in the *impudent common Writer,* hath often forc'd from me much pitty and sorrow; and it would heartily grieve any understanding spirit to behold many times so glorious a fire in bounty and goodnesse offering to match it selfe with freezing Art, sitting in darknesse, with the candle out, looking like the picture of *Black Monday.*[47]

The facetious context of this rather pointed innuendo keeps it outside the realm of spleen; but if Middleton could entertain such sentiments about Munday in 1613, it hardly seems likely that three or four years later he would feel inclined to seek the assistance of a man of Rowley's patently modest gifts. It has been conjectured that Middleton needed Rowley the comedian to write 'comic underplots', but this idea overlooks the fact that in the preceding sixteen years Middleton had written plays that contain comic action of the same kind as that which is found in the plays involved in the tradition.

In 'Did Not Rowley Merely Revise Middleton?' Professor Dunkel writes, 'In each of the plays Miss Wiggin assigns the opening and closing scenes to both authors, the main plot to Middleton, and the minor action to Rowley. Curiously enough, however, the minor action of each play seems to me to present striking similarities to Middleton's

---

[46] See Appendix B.
[47] Bodleian London Gough 122(5), sig. A3–A3ᵛ.

dramatic method in his comedies of London life.'[48] Being aware of Middleton's 'habit of repeating characters, incidents, and devices',[49] he was able to support his thesis by showing that many details of characterization and situation in Middleton's earlier plays make their reappearance in work that has been ascribed to Rowley's invention by critics who have assumed an equal collaboration. Professor Dunkel's first conclusions are those that would immediately suggest themselves: '... these similarities cannot be dismissed as a curious coincidence.... If [they] are acknowledged, why should the comic scenes be assigned to Rowley ... rather than to Middleton?'[50] But his suggestion that Rowley revised Middleton is a questionable one. Highly skilled and experienced writers such as Shakespeare and Middleton may have been resorted to for *rifacimento* work, but it seems doubtful that Rowley would have been a 'play-doctor'. I think that Mr. C. Barber, who finds a clue to Middleton's authorship in a scene (IV. iii of *The Changeling*) commonly ascribed to Rowley,[51] comes closer to deducing the real nature of the relationship between Middleton and Rowley when he writes, '... Dunkel's resemblances do not necessarily seem to me to support his thesis that Rowley was merely a reviser: they rather suggest that Middleton had a hand in the planning of the whole play, even of the scenes mainly written by Rowley.'[52] It seems to me that the only person who had something important to gain from the association was Rowley, in the capacity of pupil-assistant to Middleton.

Rowley's prologue to *All's Lost by Lust* contains some suggestions as to his outlook. It is a prologue that shares with Elizabethan prologues and epilogues, generally, the consciousness of an audience prone to criticize, but it is unusual in its artless candour and in being undisguisedly aggressive, albeit somewhat patronizing, from beginning to end, rather than apologetic:

> Thus from the Poet am I bid to say,
> He knowes what Judges sit to doome each Play,
> (The over-curious Criticke, or the wise)
> The one with squint, t'other with sunne-like eyes,
> Shootes through each Scaene: the one cryes all things downe,
> T'other hides strangers faults close as his owne,
> Las! Those who out of custome come to geere,
> (Sung the full quire of the nine Muses here)
> So carping, not from wit, but apish spite,
> And fetherd ignorance, thus our Poet does slight.

[48] p. 799.   [49] See above, p. xv.   [50] 'Did Not Rowley', p. 800.
[51] See 'A Rare Use of the Word "Honour" as a Criterion of Middleton's Authorship', *English Studies*, XXXVIII (Aug. 1957), 162–3.
[52] 'A Rare Use', pp. 163–4.

> T'is not a gay sute, or distorted face,
> Can beate his merit off, which has wonne grace
> In the full Theater, nor can now feare
> The teeth of any snakie whisperer:
> But to the white, and sweet unclouded brow,
> (The heaven where true worth moves) our Poet does bow;
> Patrons of Arts, and Pilots of the Stage,
> Who guide it (through all tempests) from the rage
> Of envious whirle-windes. O doe you but steere
> His Muse this day, and bring her tot'h wish'd shore,
> You are those Delphicke powers, whom shee'le adore.[53]

This is a fairly clear indication that Rowley was not content with being a clown and a hack-writer. The lines suggest that he aspired to the reputation of an independent playwright, and that his initial attempts in that direction had met with small success. There are indications that he had known the awful disapprobation which that most democratic of institutions, the Elizabethan theatre, could afford—where 'your carman and tinker claim as strong a voice in their suffrage and sit to give judgment on the play's life and death as well as the proudest Momus among the tribe of critic'; but there is also the suggestion that having somehow 'wonne grace | In the full Theater', he felt that such humiliations should no longer be his due: 'nor can [his merit] now feare | The teeth of any snakie whisperer'. Rowley may have thought that he should be proof against the fangs of the 'snakie whisperer', because his name had been connected with Middleton's in *A Fair Quarrel* some short time before.[54]

There may be an allusion to Rowley in the Letter to the Reader in *The World Tost at Tennis*.[55] Middleton's authorship of this letter is signified by the whimsical signature 'Simplicitie', which recalls 'Wise Innocent', his persona in *Micro-cynicon*, and by the tone and archly secretive vein of the writing itself.[56] After producing a list of his personal 'qualities' to serve the printer's 'passe', he says that he hopes they are such as 'may become the sonne of *Simplicitie*: who, though he be now in a Masque, yet is his face apparant inough'. The 'sonne of *Simplicitie*' could well be a humorous allusion to Rowley, who may have had the rôle of Simplicity in the masque.

But to know whether Rowley was a reviser or whether he wrote very

---

[53] Bodleian Mal. 187(2), sig. A3ᵛ.

[54] The composition of *All's Lost by Lust* has been assigned conjecturally to *c.* 1619 ('The Canon of William Rowley's Plays', p. 138).

[55] See Appendix B.

[56] Middleton uses a phrase similar to 'trusting in *Phoebus*, your understandings are all in as good health as *Simplicitie's* was at the writing hereof' in the facetious context of the letter signed 'Thomasine Tweedles' in *The Family of Love* (see Bullen, III, 114, ll. 324–5).

PLATE I

2 *A new Wonder,*

Read the grosse summe of your broade cloathes.
   Geor. 68. peices at B, ss, and 1; 57. at 1, ss, and o.
   Ric. Iust; leade, xix tunne.
   O. Fost. As evenly we will lay our bosomes as our bottomes
With love as merchandise, and may they both increase
To infinites.
   Br. Especially at home; that golden traffique love
Is scantier far than gold; and one myne of that
More worth than twenty Argoseyes
Of the worlds richest treasure.
   O. Fost. Here you shall dig, and finde your lading.
   Br. Here's your exchange; and as in love
So wee'le participate in merchandize.
   O. Fost. The merchants casualty:
We alwayes venture on uncertaine ods,
Altho we beare hopes Embleme the anchor with us.
The winde brought it, let the wind blow't away agen;
Should not the Sea sometimes be partner with us
Our wealth would swallow us.
   Br. A good resolve: but now I must be bold
To touch you with somewhat that concernes you.
   O. Fost. I could prevent you; is't not my unthrifty brother?
   Br. Nay, leave out the adjective (unthrifty,)
Your brother Sir, tis he that I would speake of.
   O. Fost. He cannot be nam'd without unthrifty Sir,
Tis his proper Epithite, would you conceite
But what my love has done for him
So oft, so chargeable, and so expensive,
You would not urge another addition.
   Br. Nay Sir, you must not stay at quantity
Till he forfeit the name of brother
Which is inseparable, hee's now in Ludgate Sir,
And part of your treasure lyes buryed with him.
   O. Fost. I, by vulgar blemish; but not by any good account;
There let him howle, tis the best stay he hath;
For nothing but a prison can containe him
So boundlesse is his ryot; twice have I raysde

His

Appendix C(a)

A Woman never Vext.

His decayed fortunes to a faire estate
But with as fruitlesse charity, as if I had throwne
My safe landed substance backe into the Sea,
Or dresse in pitty some corrupted Iade,
And he should kick me for my courtesie.
I am sure you cannot but heare, what quicke-
Sands he findes out, as Dice, Cards, Pigeon-holes,
And which is more, should I not restraine it,
Hee'd make my state his prodigality.
  Br. All this may be Sir, yet examples dayly shew
To our eyes, that Prodigalls returne at last
And the lowdest roarer, (as our Citty phrase is)
Will speake calme and smooth ; you must helpe with hope Sir,
Had I such a brother, I should thinke that heaven had
Made him as an instrument for my best charity
To worke upon ; This is a Maxime sure, Some
Are made poore, that rich men by giving may
Encrease their store. Nor thinke Sir, that I doe
Tax your labors and meane my selfe for to stand
Idlely by, for I have vowd if heaven but blesse
This voyage now abroad, to leave some
Memorable relique after me, that shall
Preserve my name alive till Doomesday.
  O.Fost. I Sir, that worke is good, and therein could I
Ioyne with your good intents, but to releeve
A wast-good, a spendthrift.———
  Br. O no more, no more good Sir.
  O.Fost. Sirra, when saw you my son *Robert* ?
  Ric. This morning Sir, he said he would goe visit his Vncle.
  O.Fost. I pay for their meetings I'me sure ; that boy
Makes prize of all his fingers light on
To releeve his unthrifty Vncle.
  Br. Does he rob, introth I commend him.
  O.Fost. Tis partly your fault, Sirra you see't, and suffer it.
  Ric. Sir, mine's a servants duty, his a sonnes,
Nor know I better how to expresse my love
Vnto your selfe, than by loving your son,
          A 3   *O.Fost.*

Appendix C(a)

APPENDIX C   219

closely under Middleton's direction is less important than to recognize, as Professor Dunkel did, that Middleton's characteristic dramatic method pervades *A Fair Quarrel* and *The Changeling*; and in my discussion of these plays, and *The Old Law*, I have attempted to supplement his evidence by showing the pervasiveness in them of the idiom of Middleton's thought. *The Spanish Gipsy* presents, as Professor Dunkel says, 'an entirely different problem', and requires separate consideration.

(b) *The Spanish Gipsy*

In his *Sidelights on Elizabethan Drama* (Oxford, 1924), Mr. H. D. Sykes wrote:

... I have long doubted whether Middleton had any hand in [*The Spanish Gipsy*], finding it utterly dissimilar in style from his other dramatic work, whether assigned to him alone or to Middleton and Rowley.... It is, I am convinced, substantially, if not wholly, from the pen of John Ford. That the main part of the play is his I feel no doubt whatever, and as clear traces of his hand are also to be found in the Sancho and Soto and gipsy scenes (usually attributed to Rowley) I am strongly disposed to believe that Ford wrote the whole play.... The internal evidence is at least sufficient to show that *The Spanish Gipsy* is substantially Ford's play, that henceforth it should be included among his dramatic works and excluded from Middleton's.[57]

By referring to the questionable professional ethics of Richard Marriot, the publisher, Mr. Sykes brings in doubt the authenticity of the 1653 title-page ascription;[58] he then proceeds to support his thesis by showing evidence of Ford's style in the play. Miss M. J. Sargeaunt agrees with Mr. Sykes's attribution of *The Spanish Gipsy* to Ford, with the exception of the gipsy scenes:

But the whole tone and atmosphere of the Gipsy scenes are completely unlike anything of Ford's.... parts of these scenes have a quality of gaiety and cheerful mirth, with some outbursts of real lyric beauty full of the charm and freshness of the countryside and the joyousness of the free gipsy life. Such qualities are entirely alien to the temper of Ford's writing.[59]

Mr. Clifford Leech is conscious of 'the accent of Ford' in the main plot.[60]
Mr. H. J. Oliver is circumspect: 'it ... seems necessary to say that although there are language clues, there is nothing in the characterization or plotting that seems particularly characteristic of Ford.... I

[57] pp. 183–4.   [58] *Sidelights*, pp. 184–5.
[59] *John Ford* (Oxford, 1935), p. 50.
[60] *John Ford and the Drama of his Time* (London, 1957), p. 33.

question very much whether you can do more than say that Ford at some stage of the play's history probably "had something to do" with it.'[61] In Mr. Engelberg's opinion, 'the opening scenes bear Middleton's stamp',[62] and Professor Ellis-Fermor is conscious of Middleton's influence in the characterization of the heroine of the main plot: 'In spite of a growing conviction that Ford learnt much from Middleton, I am not yet prepared to see in this study [Clara] more than Ford's hand alongside Middleton's. I find it hard as yet to resign this character entire to Ford.'[63] Professor Dunkel writes, 'In the comic action of *The Spanish Gipsy*, we ... have less tangible evidence of Middleton's writing, it would seem, than in *A Fair Quarrel* and *The Changeling*', but he sees several 'similarities of dramatic method' between the minor plot of *The Spanish Gipsy* and Middleton's early plays,[64] and refers to Mr. E. C. Morris, who accounts for a greater 'rapidity' of action that he finds in *The Spanish Gipsy*, as compared with other Middleton plays, by suggesting that Rowley revised it.[65]

In 1815 Mr. C. W. Dilke opposed attribution of the greater share of *The Spanish Gipsy* to Middleton: 'The characters of Clara and Constanza [the heroine of the minor plot] are drawn with extreme delicacy; perhaps they are above Rowley's powers; yet I must confess myself inclined to believe ... that he had the greater hand in it.'[66] Similarly, Mr. C. W. Stork, who held Rowley largely responsible for a quality of 'wildness and romance' that he found in the play 'at every turn', felt that Rowley's share was sometimes underestimated.[67]

There is an over-all frivolous quality about *The Spanish Gipsy* which makes it differ markedly from the other twenty plays that Mr. Bullen included in *The Works of Thomas Middleton*, and which makes it seem doubtful that Middleton had a hand in the actual writing of it. Yet as regards some of the general situations and characters, I think it would be too much to say that it is 'utterly dissimilar in style from [Middleton's] other dramatic work'. Sancho and Soto, for example, do resemble some of Middleton's characters, as Professor Dunkel says, 'in the broad outlines'; and the explanation of the resemblances which Professor Dunkel and other writers have seen in *The Spanish Gipsy* to features of Middleton's plays may be that the play was written in

[61] *The Problem of John Ford* (Carlton, Australia, 1955), pp. 33 and 34.
[62] 'A Middleton–Rowley Dispute', p. 331.
[63] *The Jacobean Drama*, p. 151, n. 1.
[64] See 'Did Not Rowley', pp. 803–5.
[65] See Introduction to *The Spanish Gipsie and All's Lost by Lust* (Boston, U.S.A., 1908), pp. xxviii–xxix.
[66] *Old English Plays* (London, 1815), IV, [117].
[67] See *William Rowley: His 'All's Lost by Lust', and 'A Shoemaker, a Gentleman'*, p. 42.

APPENDIX C

imitation of Middleton. Ford, attempting to imitate Middleton, may have written the main plot, and been assisted by Rowley with the gipsy scenes, which Miss Sargeaunt finds 'alien to the temper of Ford's writing'; moreover, if Ford, whom Professor Ellis-Fermor refers to as Middleton's 'successor and pupil',[68] was Middleton's pupil in fact, Middleton may have been involved directly with *The Spanish Gipsy* by providing him, and Rowley, with some general suggestions.

[68] *The Jacobean Drama*, p. 151.

APPENDIX D

Some readings from Alexander Dyce's edition of *A Fair Quarrel* in *The Works of Thomas Middleton*, Vol. III, compared with the quartos of 1622 and 1617[1]

	1617 quarto
p. [449] Dyce	A3 Mal. 246 (2)	Mal. 233 (8)

We cannot be too careful o'her, too tender!
'Tis such
A brittle niceness, a mere cupboard of glasses,

We cannot be to carefull ore, to tender,
Tis fuch a brittle niceneffe a meere cubbord of glaffes, nicenes;]

p. 450 | A3ᵛ

Cap.'s Fr. Young? why, do you
Make youth stand for an imputation?
That which you now produce for his disgrace

Cap. Fri. Yong? why, do you make youth ftand for   doe]
an imputation: that which you now produce for his
difgrace,

p. 451 | A3ᵛ

Rus. Here's noble youths! belike some wench has
   cross'd 'em,
And now they know not what to do with their
   blood.

Ruff. Heres noble youths, belike fome wench has
crost 'm, and now they know not what to doe with
their blood.

p. 451 | A4

Col.'s Fr. Words did pass
Which I was bound to answer, as my opinion
And love instructed me;

[1] Examination of the quartos of 1617 and 1622 reveals that the pages of the latter were composed from a copy of the former. Minor variations in punctuation and orthography are occasionally to be found. For the passages reproduced, these are indicated to the right of the line in which they occur. Regarding the general condition of the quartos, and how they were dealt with by nineteenth-century editors, see Margery Fisher's 'Notes on Metre' in her editions of *Women Beware Women*, pp. 47–9, and *A Chast Mayd in Cheap-side*, pp. 31–4 (Oxford, 1937).

APPENDIX D

And should I take in general fame into 'em,
I think I should commit no error in't.

Col. fri. Words did paſſe
Which I was bound to anſwer, as my opinion
And loue inſtructed me, and ſhould I take in
    generall fame,
Into 'em, I thinke I ſhoud commit no error in't.   in't,]

p. 452 | A4

You're a captain, sir; I give you all your due.
You are a Captaine ſir, I giue you all your due.   captaine]

p. 452 | A4ᵛ

Cap. Ager. I shrink not; he that goes the foremost may
    Be overtaken.
Capt. I ſhrinke not, he that goes the formoſt,   Cap.]
May be oretaken.

p. 453 | A4ᵛ

Col. My fame,
Life of the life my reputation.
Death! I am squar'd and measur'd out;
My heights, depths, breadth, all my dimensions
    taken!
Colo. My fame,
Life of the life, my reputation,
Death? I am ſquar'd and meaſur'd out, my heights
Depths, breadth, all my demenſions taken,

APPENDIX E

A Fair Quarrel, *The Peace-Maker*, and *The Charge of Sir Francis Bacon Knight*

Middleton's pamphlet *The Peace-Maker* was published in 1618. It purports to have been written by the King,[1] and James was sufficiently flattered to approve of its publication.

It has been noted by Rhodes Dunlap that, when Middleton treated the subject of duelling in *The Peace-Maker*, he 'cheerfully helped himself to some choice passages' from *The Charge of Sir Francis Bacon Knight*, a pamphlet on duelling published four years earlier.[2] Dunlap remarks that where Bacon speaks of 'noble and gentle blood . . . adventured in the field in service of the king & realme' in one of the borrowed passages, Middleton substitutes 'adventured in honorable service', to make the statement 'less bellicose-sounding'. Another borrowed passage in *The Peace-Maker*, however, briefer than its original, and somewhat more refined in tone, reiterates the 'bellicose-sounding' idea noted by Dunlap, and it is significant that this passage is suggestive of the theme of Middleton's play *A Fair Quarrel*, published in 1617. The passage in *The Peace-Maker* reads:

For hereby have Gentlemen lost the true knowledge and understanding of Fortitude and Valour. For true Fortitude distinguisheth of the grounds of Quarrels, whether they be just; and not onely so, but whether they be worthie; and sets a better value upon mens lives, then to bestow them idly; which are not so to be trifled away, but offered up and sacrificed to honourable Services, publike Merits, good Causes, and Noble Adventures.[3]

The corresponding passage in *The Charge of Sir Francis Bacon Knight* is as follows:

---

[1] Middleton's name does not appear on *The Peace-Maker*. The introductory remarks are addressed to 'all Our true-loving, and Peace-embracing Subjects'. Middleton's authorship of the pamphlet was discovered by Bullen in an entry, dated 19 July 1618, in the *Calendar of Domestic State Papers*, which records the issue of the licence for publication (see Bullen, I, xliv–xlv).

[2] 'James I, Bacon, Middleton, and the Making of *The Peace-Maker*', in *Studies in the English Renaissance Drama*, ed. J. W. Bennett, O. Cargill, and V. Hall (New York, 1959), p. 92.

[3] Bodleian 4° L. 66. Art. (8), sigs. D2ᵛ–D3 (Bullen: VIII, 339).

APPENDIX E

... men have almost lost the true notion and understanding of Fortitude and Valour. For Fortitude distinguisheth of the grounds of quarrels, whether they bee just; and not onely so, but whether they be worthy; and setteth a better price upon mens lives then to bestow them idly. Nay it is weakenesse, and disesteeme of a mans selfe, to put a mans life upon such ledgier performances. A mans life is not to be tryfled away; it is to bee offered up and sacrificed to honorable services, publike merites, good causes, and noble adventures. It is in expence of blood as it is in expence of mony: it is no liberality to make a profusion of mony upon every vaine occasion, nor noe more it is fortitude to make effusion of bloud except the cause bee of worth. And thus much for the causes of this evill.[4]

Bacon denounces the inane quarrels of vain-glorious men in his *Charge*, and Middleton does the same in *The Peace-Maker*. In the passage from the *Charge* quoted above, however, Bacon turns to the man of fortitude, and speaks of him as one who 'distinguisheth of the grounds of quarrels, whether they bee just; and . . . whether they be worthy', and his 'noe more it is fortitude to make effusion of bloud except the cause bee of worth' includes a warrant for his man of fortitude to make 'effusion of bloud' when he does find 'the cause bee of worth'. Bacon concludes his pamphlet with '. . . a petition to the noblesse and gentlemen of England, that they would learne to esteeme themselves at a just price. . . . their blood is not to be spilt like water or a vile thing, therefore that they would rest perswaded there cannot be a forme of honor, except it be upon a worthy matter.'[5]

Middleton intended Captain Agar, the hero of *A Fair Quarrel*, to be an exemplar of the kind of fortitude Bacon defines. In Act I a friend of Agar's points the contrast between Agar and a vain-glorious colonel:

Yong? . . . That which you now produce for his [Agar's] disgrace,
Infers his noblenes, that being yong
Should have an anger more inclind to courage
And moderation then the Colonell:
. . . .
And let the cause be good ([there is a] conscience in him
Which ever crownes his acts, and is indeed,
Valours prosperity), he dares then as much,
As . . . [the colonel].[6]

Eventually the colonel provokes a quarrel with Agar, and Agar's soliloquy at the beginning of Act II again suggests the idea that 'Fortitude distinguisheth of the grounds of quarrels, whether they bee just':

---

[4] Bodleian Wood 616(9), pp. 13–14.
[5] Ibid., pp. 34–5.
[6] Bodleian Mal. 246(2), sig. A3ᵛ.

> And is't not miserable valour then,
> That man should hazard all upon things doubtfull?
> . . . .
> Could but my soule resolve my cause were just,
> Earth's mountaine, nor seas surge should hide him from mee.[7]

The causes that Captain Agar considers just in a private quarrel may not have been among those that Bacon had in mind when he spoke of 'honorable services, publike merites, good causes, and noble adventures' as being the ends for which 'a mans life' might properly be sacrificed. It is noteworthy too that when Middleton's hero expresses a loathness to 'hazard all' in what may not be a worthy cause, he is not concerned about the jeopardizing of his life, but of his 'Eternity'. Still Middleton's use of Bacon's 'men have almost lost the true notion . . . of Fortitude' passage in the part of *The Peace-Maker* that deals with duelling shows that he had more than a transient interest in that passage,[8] and he clearly took the basic idea, 'Fortitude distinguisheth of the grounds of quarrels, whether they bee just; and . . . whether they be worthy', and applied it to a situation of his own invention.

[7] Bodleian Mal. 246(2), sigs. C3^v–C4.

[8] *The Charge of Sir Francis Bacon Knight* was published in 1614, the year which R. C. Bald gives as *terminus a quo* for the composition of *A Fair Quarrel* on the basis of external evidence (see 'The Chronology of Middleton's Plays', p. 40).

BIBLIOGRAPHY

BOOKS

ANONYMOUS. *A Supplication of the Family of Love . . . for grace and favour Examined.* . . . Cambridge, 1606. Bodleian 4° F 14 Th.

ANONYMOUS. *The Womans Champion . . . Mrs. Mary Frith . . . from her Cradle to her Winding-Sheet.* London, 1662. Bodleian Wood 654ª 22.

ARBER, EDWARD, ed. *A Transcript of the Registers of the Company of Stationers of London; 1554–1660.* 5 vols., privately printed, London, 1875–94.

BACON, SIR FRANCIS. *The Charge of Sir Francis Bacon Knight.* London, 1614. Bodleian Wood 616 (9).

BARKER, R. H. *Thomas Middleton.* New York: Columbia University Press, 1958.

BENTLEY, G. E. *The Jacobean and Caroline Stage.* 5 vols., Oxford: Clarendon Press, 1941–56.

BRADBROOK, M. C. *The Growth and Structure of Elizabethan Comedy.* London: Chatto and Windus, 1955.

BUSH, DOUGLAS. *The Renaissance and English Humanism.* Toronto: University of Toronto Press, (1939) 1962.

CHAMBERS, SIR E. K. *The Elizabethan Stage.* 4 vols., Oxford: Clarendon Press, 1923.

CHEYNEY, E. P. *A History of England from the Defeat of the Armada to the Death of Elizabeth,* Vol. II. New York: Longmans, Green, and Company, 1926.

DEKKER, THOMAS. *The Magnificent Entertainment.* London, 1604. Bodleian Malone 602 (1).

DEKKER, THOMAS. *The Dramatic Works of Thomas Dekker,* ed. F. T. Bowers, Vols. III and IV. Cambridge: Cambridge University Press, 1958 and 1961.

[DILKE, C. W., ed.] *Old English Plays,* Vols. IV and V. London: Whittingham and Rowland, 1815.

DOBRÉE, BONAMY. *Histriophone: A Dialogue on Dramatic Diction.* London: The Hogarth Press, 1925.

DUNKEL, W. D. *The Dramatic Technique of Thomas Middleton in His Comedies of London Life.* Chicago: University of Chicago Press, 1925.

ELLIS-FERMOR, U. M. *The Jacobean Drama.* London: Methuen and Co., (1936) 1958.

ELLIS-FERMOR, U. M. *Shakespeare the Dramatist,* ed. Kenneth Muir. London: Methuen and Co., 1961.

BIBLIOGRAPHY

EMPSON, WILLIAM. *Some Versions of Pastoral.* London: Chatto and Windus, (1935) 1950.

FLEAY, F. G. *A Biographical Chronicle of the English Drama, 1559–1642.* 2 vols., London: Reeves and Turner, 1891.

HENSLOWE, PHILIP. *Diary*, ed. W. W. Greg. 2 vols., London: A. H. Bullen, 1904–8.

HOLINSHED, RAPHAEL. *Holinshed's Chronicles of England, Scotland, and Ireland*, Vols. I and V. London: Richard Taylor and Co., 1807. (First edns. 1577, 1586.)

LAMB, CHARLES. *Specimens of English Dramatic Poets Who Lived about the Time of Shakespeare.* London: Longman, Hurst, Rees, and Orme, 1808.

LANGBAINE, GERARD. *An Account of the English Dramatick Poets*, Vol. II. Oxford, 1691. Bodleian Thorn-Drury f. 2.

LEECH, CLIFFORD. *John Ford and the Drama of his Time.* London: Chatto and Windus, 1957.

MIDDLETON, THOMAS.[1] *The Triumphs of Truth.* London, 1613. Bodleian London Gough 122 (5).

[MIDDLETON, THOMAS.] *The Peace-Maker.* London, 1618. Bodleian 4° L. 66. Art. (8).

MIDDLETON, THOMAS. *The Works of Thomas Middleton*, ed. Alexander Dyce. 5 vols., London: Edward Lumley, 1840.

MIDDLETON, THOMAS. *The Works of Thomas Middleton*, ed. A. H. Bullen. 8 vols., London: John C. Nimmo, 1885–6.

MIDDLETON, THOMAS. *The Ghost of Lucrece*, ed. J. Q. Adams. New York: Charles Scribner's Sons, 1937.

MIDDLETON, THOMAS. *A Game at Chesse*, ed. R. C. Bald. London: Cambridge University Press, 1929.

MIDDLETON, THOMAS. *The Witch*, ed. F. P. Wilson and W. W. Greg. Oxford: Oxford University Press, 1948 (1950).

MIDDLETON, THOMAS. *Hengist, King of Kent or The Mayor of Queenborough*, ed. R. C. Bald. New York: Charles Scribner's Sons, 1938.

MIDDLETON, THOMAS. *Women Beware Women*, ed. Margery Fisher. Oxford: unpublished thesis, 1954. Bodleian MS. B.Litt. d. 285.

MIDDLETON, THOMAS. *Women Beware Women*, ed. Roma Gill. London: Ernest Benn, 1968.

MIDDLETON, THOMAS. *A Chast Mayd in Cheape-side*, ed. Margery Fisher. Oxford: unpublished thesis, 1954. Bodleian MS. B.Litt. d. 286.

MIDDLETON, THOMAS, and WILLIAM ROWLEY. *The World tost at Tennis.* London, 1620. Bodleian Malone 246 (4).

---

[1] For the early printed editions of the plays of Middleton quoted from in the text see Appendix A.

MIDDLETON, THOMAS, and WILLIAM ROWLEY. *The Changeling*, ed. N. W. Bawcutt. London: Methuen and Co., 1958.

MIDDLETON, THOMAS, and WILLIAM ROWLEY. *The Spanish Gipsie and All's Lost by Lust*, ed. E. C. Morris. Boston, U.S.A.: D. C. Heath and Co., 1908.

MURRAY, J. T. *Elizabethan Dramatic Companies, 1558–1642*. 2 vols., London: Constable and Co., 1910.

O'DONOGHUE, E. G. *The Story of Bethlehem Hospital from its Foundation in 1247*. London: William Heinemann Ltd., 1923.

OLIVER, H. J. *The Problem of John Ford*. Carlton: Melbourne University Press, 1955.

PARROTT, T. M., and R. H. BALL. *A Short View of Elizabethan Drama*. New York: Charles Scribner's Sons, (1943) 1958.

REYNOLDS, JOHN. *The Triumphs of Gods Revenege [sic], Against the crying, and execrable Sinne of Murther.* . . . London, 1621. Bodleian Art 4° G. 29.

ROGERS, JOHN. *The Displaying of an horrible secte of grosse and wicked Heretiques naming themselves the Familie of Love.* . . . London, 1578. Bodleian Wood 795 (4).

ROGERS, JOHN. *An Answere unto a wicked & infamous Libel made by . . . one of the chiefe Elders of the . . . Family of Love.* . . . London, 1579. Bodleian Crynes 864.

ROWLEY, WILLIAM. *All's Lost by Lust*. London, 1633. Bodleian Malone 187 (2).

ROWLEY, WILLIAM. *A New Wonder, A Woman Never Vext*. London, 1632. Bodleian Malone 167 (4).

ROWLEY, WILLIAM. *A New Wonder: A Woman Never Vext* in *A Select Collection of Old English Plays (Originally Published by Robert Dodsley in the year 1744)*, ed. W. C. Hazlitt, Vol. XII. London: Reeves and Turner, 1875.

ROWLEY, WILLIAM. *William Rowley: His 'All's Lost by Lust', and 'A Shoemaker, a Gentleman'*, ed. C. W. Stork. Philadelphia: John C. Winston Co., 1910.

SARGEAUNT, M. J. *John Ford*. Oxford: Basil Blackwell, 1935.

SCHOENBAUM, SAMUEL. *Middleton's Tragedies*. New York: Columbia University Press, 1955.

SPINGARN, J. E., ed. *Critical Essays of the Seventeenth Century*, Vol. II. Oxford: Oxford University Press, 1908.

SYKES, H. D. *Sidelights on Elizabethan Drama*. Oxford: Oxford University Press, 1924.

TREVELYAN, G. M. *Illustrated History of England*. London: Longmans, Green and Co., 1956.

WARD, A. W. *A History of English Dramatic Literature to the Death of Queen Anne*, London: Macmillan and Co., 1875; 2nd edn., 1899.
WEBSTER, JOHN. *The Works of John Webster*, ed. F. L. Lucas, Vol. IV. London: Chatto and Windus, 1927.

ESSAYS AND ARTICLES

ANONYMOUS. 'A confession made by two of the *Familie of Love*' in John Roger's *The Displaying . . . of the Familie of Love* (see above, p. 229), sigs. Iiiii^v–Kiii^v.
ARROWSMITH, W. R. 'Note on Some Peculiarities in Mr. Dyce's Edition of Middleton's Works', *Notes and Queries*, XII (8 and 15 Dec. 1855), 443–5 and 464–6.
BALD, R. C. 'Middleton's Civic Employments', *Modern Philology*, XXXI (Aug. 1933), 65–78.
BALD, R. C. 'The Chronology of Middleton's Plays', *Modern Language Review*, XXXII (Jan. 1937), 33–43.
BALD, R. C. 'The Sources of Middleton's City Comedies', *Journal of English and Germanic Philology*, XXXIII (July 1934), 373–87.
BARBER, C. 'A Rare Use of the Word "Honour" as a Criterion of Middleton's Authorship', *English Studies*, XXXVIII (Aug. 1957), 161–8.
BUCKINGHAM, E. L. 'Campion's *Art of English Poesie* and Middleton's *Chaste Maid in Cheapside*', *PMLA*, XLIII (Sept. 1928), 784–92.
BULLOUGH, G. '"The Game at Chesse": How It Struck a Contemporary', *Modern Language Review*, XLIX (Apr. 1954), 156–63.
BYRNE, M. ST. C. 'Bibliographical Clues in Collaborate Plays', *The Library*, 4th Ser., XIII (June 1932), 21–48.
CHRISTIAN, M. G. 'Middleton's Residence at Oxford', *Modern Language Notes*, LXI (Feb. 1946), 90–1.
CHRISTIAN, M. G. 'An Autobiographical Note by Thomas Middleton', *Notes and Queries*, CLXXV (Oct. 1938), 259–60.
CHRISTIAN, M. G. 'A Side-light on the Family History of Thomas Middleton', *Studies in Philology*, XLIV (Feb. 1947), 490–6.
DOWLING, M. 'A Note on Moll Cutpurse—*The Roaring Girl*', *Review of English Studies*, X (Jan. 1934), 67–71.
DUNKEL, W. D. 'Did Not Rowley Merely Revise Middleton?', *PMLA* XLVIII (Sept. 1933), 799–805.
DUNKEL, W. D. 'The Authorship of *Anything for a Quiet Life*', *PMLA* XLIII (Sept. 1928), 793–9.
DUNLAP, RHODES. 'James I, Bacon, Middleton, and the Making of The Peace-Maker', in *Studies in the English Renaissance Drama*, ed. J. W. Bennett, O. Cargill, and V. Hall. New York: New York University Press, 1959; pp. 82–94.

Eccles, M. 'Middleton's Birth and Education', *Review of English Studies*, VII (Oct. 1931), 431–41.
Eccles, M. '"Thomas Middleton a Poett"', *Studies in Philology*, LIV (Oct. 1957), 516–36.
Engelberg, Edward. 'A Middleton–Rowley Dispute', *Notes and Queries*, CXCVIII (Aug. 1953), 330–2.
Fleay, F. G. 'On Metrical Tests as applied to Dramatic Poetry: Part I. Shakspere', and '... Part II. Beaumont, Fletcher, Massinger', *Transactions of the New Shakspere Society*, 1st Ser., Part I (1874), 1–15 and 51–72.
George, David. 'Weather-wise's Almanac and the Date of Middleton's "No Wit No Help Like a Woman's"', *Notes and Queries*, CCXI (Aug. 1966), 297–301.
George, David. 'The Problem of Middleton's "The Witch" and its Sources', *Notes and Queries*, CCXII (June 1967), 209–11.
Gordon, D. J. 'Middleton's *No Wit, No Help Like a Woman's* and della Porta's *La Sorella*', *Review of English Studies*, XVII (Oct. 1941), 400–14.
Hillebrand, H. N. 'Thomas Middleton's *The Viper's Brood*', *Modern Language Notes*, XLII (Jan. 1927), 35–8.
Hinman, Charlton. 'Cast-off Copy for the First Folio of Shakespeare', *Shakespeare Quarterly*, VI (Summer 1955), 259–73.
Levin, Richard. 'The Four Plots of *A Chaste Maid in Cheapside*', *Review of English Studies*, XVI (1965), 14–24.
Lloyd, Bertram. 'A Minor Source of "The Changeling"', *Modern Language Review*, XIX (Jan. 1924), 101–2.
Mathews, E. G. 'The Murdered Substitute Tale', *Modern Language Quarterly*, VI (June 1945), 187–95.
Olive, W. J. 'Imitation of Shakespeare in Middleton's *Family of Love*', *Philological Quarterly*, XXIX (Jan. 1950), 75–8.
Phialas, P. G. 'An Unpublished Letter About *A Game at Chess*', *Modern Language Notes*, LXIX (June 1954), 398–9.
Phialas, P. G. 'Middleton's Early Contact with the Law', *Studies in Philology*, LII (Apr. 1955), 186–94.
Price, G. R. 'The Latin Oration in *A Game at Chesse*', *Huntington Library Quarterly*, XXIII (Aug. 1960), 389–93.
Reed, R. 'A Factual Interpretation of *The Changeling*'s Madhouse Scenes', *Notes and Queries*, CXCV (June 1950), 247–8.
Ricks, Christopher. 'Word-Play in *Women Beware Women*', *Review of English Studies*, XII (Aug. 1961), 238–50.
Ricks, Christopher. 'The Moral and Poetical Structure of *The Changeling*', *Essays in Criticism*, X (July 1960), 290–306.

ROBB, D. M. 'The Canon of William Rowley's Plays', *Modern Language Review*, XLV (Apr. 1950), 129–41.

SOUTHALL, R. 'A Missing Source-Book for Middleton's "A Game at Chesse"', *Notes and Queries*, CCVII (Apr. 1962), 145–6. (See also R. Pineas's comments, ibid., CCX [Sept. 1965], 353–4.)

WIGGIN, P. G. 'An Inquiry into the Authorship of the Middleton–Rowley Plays', *Radcliffe College Monographs*, IX (1897).

WILSON, E. M., and O. TURNER. 'The Spanish Protest Against "A Game at Chesse"', *Modern Language Review*, LXIV (Oct. 1949), 476–82.

WRIGHT, L. B. 'Propaganda Against James I's "Appeasement" of Spain', *Huntington Library Quarterly*, VI (Feb. 1943), 149–72.

INDEX

Adams, J. Q., xvi (n. 8), 8 (n. 9)
Admiral's Men, xvii
All's Lost by Lust, 215, 217, 218 (n. 54)
Ant and the Nightingale, The, xvii, xviii, 7, 9 (n. 11), 24 (n. 1), 31 and n. 17
Anything for a Quiet Life, 43, 126 (n. 35), 153–60, 161, 162, 163, 167, 173, 175, 176, 177 (n. 48), 180 (n. 54), 181 (n. 61), 184, 187, 193, 196
Arrowsmith, W. R., 212 (n. 28)

Bald, R. C., vii, xvi, xviii (n. 17), 90 (n. 23), 130 (n. 1), 140 (n. 27), 153 (n. 2), 185, 187 and n. 9, 189 (n. 13), 193, 195, 197, 201 (n. 1), 202 (n. 4), 226 (n. 2)
Barber, C., 217
Barker, R. H., 16 (n. 13), 19 (n. 20), 101 (n. 4), 140 (nn. 27 and 28), 209 ff.
Bawcutt, N. W., 210–11
Bentley, G. E., 160 (n.), 161 (n. 1), 172 (n. 30), 185 (n. 3), 193, 214 (n. 37), 215
Birth of Merlin, The, 215
Black Book, The, xv, xviii, 7, 8 (n. 9), 9 (n. 11), 24 and n. 1, 27, 29, 40, 204
Blurt Master-Constable, viii, 10–23, 27, 33 (n. 20), 36, 41 (n. 10), 42, 44, 49, 51, 53, 54, 59, 60, 61, 64, 65, 70, 71, 92 (nn. 28 and 30), 74, 76 (n. 41), 77 (n. 45), 85 (n. 14), 88, 105, 118, 120, 121, 124, 129, 137, 139, 140, 143 and n. 36, 146, 164, 165, 166, 168, 171, 195, 196, 198, 214
Bowers, F. T., 17, 101 (n. 4)
Bradbrook, M. C., 16–17, 185, 194, 200
Buckingham, E. L., 90 (n. 23)
Bullen, A. H., vii, xvi, 3–4, 17–19, 71 (n. 29), 120 (n. 22), 154, 201, 220, 224 (n. 1)
Bush, D., 46
Byrne, M. St. C., 213 (n. 32)

Campion, T., 90 (n. 23)

Chambers, Sir E. K., 215 (nn. 39 and 44)
Changeling, The, viii, 20–1, 42, 113 (n. 1), 153, 159, 165 (n. 14), 172–84, 188, 189, 191, 193, 194, 195, 196, 198, 199, 200, 207, 208, 209, 210, 217, 219
Charge of Sir Francis Bacon Knight, The, 117 (n. 15), 197, 224–6.
Chaste Maid in Cheapside, A, xvii, 30–1 (n. 16), 59, 61, 78, 83 (n. 10), 90–8, 102, 103, 104, 115, 118, 155, 157, 171, 198, 222 (n. 1)
Chaucer, G., 18
Cheney, E. P., 31 (n. 18)
Children of Paul's, xviii, 195; of the Revels, ibid.
Christian, M. G., xvi (n. 7), xvii (nn. 11 and 12)
Crane, R., vii

Day, John, 214
Dekker, T., xviii, 16–17, 100, 109–10, 207, 214
Dilke, C. W., 71 (n. 29), 212 ff.
Discoverie of Witchcraft, 146
Dobrée, B., 213
Drayton, M., xviii
Dunkel, W. D., xv, 52, 118, 160 (n.), 207 ff.
Dunlap, R., 224
Dyce, A., vii, 4, 18, 20, 71 (n. 29), 154, 161 (n. 2), 197, 212, 222–3

Eccles, M., xvi (n. 6), xvii (nn. 9, 10, and 12), xix (n. 18)
Ellis-Fermor, U. M., xv, xvi, 9, 16–17, 50–1, 102, 163, 208, 220, 221
Empson, W., viii, 180–1, 182, 183
Engelberg, E., 207 ff.
Every Man out of his Humour, xv

Fair Quarrel, A, 29, 34, 42, and n. 14, 51, 52, 89, 98, 113–21, 122, 124 (n. 31), 125 (n. 33), 128, 129, 194, 195, 197, 198, 200, 207, 208, 209, 210, 213, 214, 215, 218, 219, 222–3, 224–6

INDEX

Family of Love, The, 20 (n. 22), 21 (n. 25), 29, 33 (n. 20), 36, 39 and n. 6, 42, 44, 47–8, 49, 50, 52–3, 54, 60, 62, 70, 74, 92 (n. 26), 93, 105, 107, 118–19, 120, 124, 139, 142, 164, 177, 187, 195, 196, 198, 199, 216, 218 (n. 56)
Farmer, J. S., vii
Fisher, M., 222 (n. 1)
Fleay, F. G., 101 (n. 4), 210 ff.
Fletcher, J., 140 (n. 28)
Florentine History, 146
Ford, J., 219, 220, 221
Forster, E. M., 51
Frith, M., 101–2, 110

Game at Chess, A, vii, xvii, xviii, 41 (n. 10), 52, 77 (n. 43), 153, 159, 160, 185–93, 196
George, D., 146 (n. 44), 202 (n. 2)
Ghost of Lucrece, The, xvi (n. 8), xvii, 7–8, 9, 20 (n. 24), 27, 28, 50, 66, 195, 196
Gill, R., 161 (n. 2)
Gordon, D. J., 89 (n. 20)
Greene, R., 32
Gregg, W. W., vii, 202 (n. 5)

Henslowe, P., xviii, 10, 214
Hillebrand, H. N., xviii (n. 51)
Hinman, C., 213
Holinshed's Chronicles, 131, 132, 135 (n. 14), 137, 139 (n. 24)
Honest Whore, The, xviii, 34, 214

Inner-Temple Masque, The, 215

James I, King, xviii, 24, 116, 117, 224
Jonson, B., xv, 43, 140 (n. 28)

King's Men, xviii, 215

Lady Elizabeth's company, xviii
Lamb, C., 18, 115
Langbaine, G., 215
Leech, C., 219
Levin, R., 93 (n. 28)
Lucas, F. L., 153 (n. 2)

Macbeth, 140 (n. 27), 193
Mad World, My Masters, A, 29, 30, 34, 36, 38, 39 and n. 6, 43, 45–6, 48, 49, 51, 54, 60, 66, 75 (n. 39), 79, 82, 92, 95, 97–8, 102, 103, 139, 141, 142, 162

Malcontent, The, 43
Marston, J., 43
Massinger, P., 113 (n. 1), 207 (n. 1)
Mayor of Queenborough, The, viii, 120 (n. 22), 130–40, 147, 164, 166, 168, 171 and n. 28, 184, 195, 199, 202 (n. 4)
Michaelmas Term, 24 (n. 1), 29–30 and n. 16, 31, 32–4, 36–7, 44, 48–9, 53–4, 55, 76, 85 (n. 14), 93, 126, 155, 162, 190, 196, 197, 200
Micro–cynicon, xvii, 5–7, 9, 40, 174 (n. 37), 194, 218
Milton, J., 46, 197
More Dissemblers Besides Women, 21 (n. 25), 59–77, 78, 79, 80 (n. 3), 82, 83 and n. 10, 84 (n. 11), 85 and n. 14, 88, 92, 95, 98, 103 (n. 12), 104, 105, 107, 110, 116, 117, 118, 122, 124, 133, 139, 141, 142, 148, 155, 157, 164, 171 (n. 28), 183 (n. 71), 187, 190 (n. 16), 196, 197, 198, 209, 215
Morris, E. C., 220
Moseley, H., 215
Muir, K., xv
Munday, A., xviii, 216
Murray, J. T., 215 (nn. 39 and 42)

New Wonder, a Woman Never Vext, A, xiii, 212, 213
Nicholas, H., 39 (n. 6)
No Wit, No Help Like a Woman's, 59, 61, 78, 84–9, 92, 94, 98, 99, 102, 103 (n. 10), 104, 105 (n. 17), 107, 110, 116, 118, 122, 125 (n. 33), 127, 129, 138, 139, 141, 155, 157, 166, 171, 196, 202 (n. 2)

O'Donoghue, E. G., 180 (n. 58)
Old Law, The, 29, 42, (n. 14), 113 and n. 1, 121–9, 139, 140, 143, 145, 155, 164, 168 (n. 19), 187, 192, 194, 196, 197, 198, 200, 207, 219
Oliphant, E. H. C., 16
Olive, W. J., 53 (n. 38)
Oliver, H. J., 219–20

Parrott, T. M., and R. H. Ball, 214
Peace-Maker, The, 117 (n. 15), 224–6
Phialas, P. G., xvii (nn. 9 and 14)
Phoenix, The, vii, 24–7, 28, 29, 30–1, 34, 35, 40–1, 42 and n. 14, 44, 46, 47,

INDEX

Phoenix, The—continued.
51–2, 54, 55, 66, 74, 76, 83 and n. 10, 93, 103, 105, 110, 113, 121, 123, 124, 126 (n. 36), 127, 128, 129, 147 (n. 47), 149, 169, 170, 192, 193, 194, 195, 196, 197, 198, 199
Prince Charles's company, xviii, 215

Queen's College, Oxford, xvii, 214

Reed, R., 180 (n. 58)
Reynolds, J., 172 (n. 30), 173 (n. 35), 174 (n. 37), 175, 184 (n. 73)
Ricks, C., 165 (n. 14), 168 (n. 19)
Roaring Girl, The, vii, xviii, 59, 99, 100–110, 157, 193, 195, 200, 207, 214
Robb, D. M., 210 (n. 17)
Rogers, J., 39 (n. 6)
Romeo and Juliet, 11, 13, 53, 66 (n. 19)
Rowley, W., viii, xviii, 49, 113 (n. 1), 189 (n. 13), 207–19, 220, 221

Sargeaunt, M. J., 219, 221
Schoenbaum, S., 140 (n. 27), 209 ff.
Sorella, La, 88, 89 (n. 20)
Spanish Gipsy, The, xvi, 113 (n. 1), 207, 208, 219–21
Spingarn, J. E., 89 (n. 20)
Stork, C. W., 210 (n. 17), 220
Sykes, H. D., 219

Travels of Three English Brothers, The, 214
Trevelyan, G. M., 117 (n. 14)

Trick to Catch the Old One, A, 45 (n. 19), 59, 61, 78, 79, 80–4, 85, 94, 99, 104, 105 (n. 18), 119, 121, 125 (n. 33), 127, 128, 133, 141–2, 198
Triumphs of Love and Antiquity, The, xvii (n. 12)
Triumphs of Truth, The, 216

Ward, A. W., 17–19, 64, 89 (n. 20), 100, 101, 153
Webster, J., xviii, 160 (n.)
Widow, The, 140–5, 146, 155, 157, 197, 198, 200
Wiggin, P. G., 49 and n. 26, 207 ff.
Wilkins, G., 214
Wilson, F. P., vii, 202 (n. 5)
Wisdom of Solomon Paraphrased, The, xvii, 3–5, 8, 9, 27, 29, 194, 196
Witch, The, vii, 145–50, 155, 157, 162, 165, 168, 169, 171, 172, 183 (n. 71), 184, 191, 192, 197, 199, 201 (n. 1)
Women Beware Women, 42, 77 (n. 43), 153, 159, 161–71, 172, 175, 176, 177, 178 (n. 50), 184, 187, 190, 196, 198, 209, 215, 222 (n. 1)
World Tost at Tennis, The, 30 (n. 15), 205–6, 207, 216, 218

Your Five Gallants, xiii, 24 (n. 1), 27–30, 30–1 (n. 16), 35, 36, 38, 40, 41, 42 and n. 14, 43, 45, 46, 54–6, 84, 87 (n. 18), 103, 110, 113, 121, 124, 127, 140, 153 (n. 3), 186, 193, 194, 196, 197, 204–5

Zola, E., 25